David Deschamps and Bennett Singer edited *Gay & Lesbian Stats*—the acclaimed first edition of this book—and, with Leslie D. Farrell, co-directed the award-winning PBS documentary *Electoral Dysfunction*, hosted by Mo Rocca, as well as four short videos on voting in America for the *New York Times* Op-Docs series. Deschamps has served as a researcher for numerous books, including John Nichols's *Jews for Buchanan* and William Martin's *With God on Our Side: The Rise of the Religious Right in America*.

Bennett Singer edited the books *Growing Up Gay/Growing Up Lesbian* (a Lambda Literary Award finalist) and *42 UP* (companion volume to Michael Apted's documentary series) and, with Nancy Kates, co-directed the film *Brother Outsider: The Life of Bayard Rustin*, which was broadcast nationally on PBS and Logo and won more than twenty international prizes, including the GLAAD Media Award. He is the former executive editor of *Time* magazine's education program. Singer and Deschamps are currently developing a television series on the history of same-sex love. They are married and live in Brooklyn.

Jennifer Finney Boylan is a writer, activist, and professor whose 2003 memoir, *She's Not There: A Life in Two Genders*, was the first bestselling work by a transgender American. She serves as national co-chair of the Board of Directors of GLAAD and on the Board of Trustees of the Kinsey Institute for Research in Sex, Gender, and Reproduction.

www.lgbtqstats.org

LGBTQ STATS

Lesbian, Gay, Bisexual, Transgender, and Queer People by the Numbers

DAVID DESCHAMPS AND BENNETT SINGER

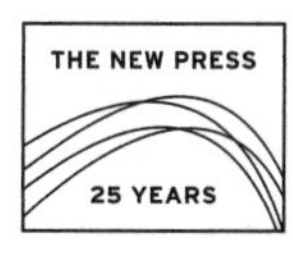

NEW YORK
LONDON

Published in the United States by The New Press, New York, 2017
Distributed by Perseus Distribution

ISBN 978-1-62097-244-1 (pb)
ISBN 978-1-62097-245-8 (e-book)
CIP data is available.

The New Press publishes books that promote and enrich public discussion and understanding of the issues vital to our democracy and to a more equitable world. These books are made possible by the enthusiasm of our readers; the support of a committed group of donors, large and small; the collaboration of our many partners in the independent media and the not-for-profit sector; booksellers, who often hand-sell New Press books; librarians; and above all by our authors.

www.thenewpress.com

Book design and composition by Bookbright Media
This book was set in Avenir and Jockey

Printed in the United States of America

10 9 8 7 6 5 4 3 2 1

We dedicate this book to the millions of people around the globe who have had the courage to come out. While their exact numbers are unknown, it is indisputable that their openness and honesty have sparked a revolution.

CONTENTS

We are perhaps in greater need of sound, factual information about ourselves than any other group of people in our society. . . . It is important to us to document the truth because we have paid such a heavy price for dishonesty—not only the lies of those who wish us ill, but also the fear that still compels so many of our sisters and brothers to lead lives of deception and concealment.

—Congressman Gerry Studds, the first openly gay member of the U.S. House of Representatives, in the introduction to Gay & Lesbian Stats: A Pocket Guide of Facts and Figures, *1994*

Back in 1993, when we set out to create the first edition of this book, finding statistics on lesbian, gay, and bisexual Americans was a daunting task. We spent months at various libraries poring through journals and databases and managed to produce an 80-page almanac that included a four-page chapter on family and relationships and a three-page chapter on public opinion. We noted that as of 1993, no president had ever appointed an openly lesbian or gay person to any of the nation's 1,000 federal judgeships; that 25 jurisdictions in the United States recognized some sort of domestic partnership for lesbians and gay men; and that 51 percent of college freshmen believed lesbians and gay men should try to be heterosexual.

Nearly 25 years later, creating the new edition of this book presented a different challenge: the explosion of information on lesbian, gay, bisexual, transgender, and queer issues meant that we had literally thousands of sources from which to draw data. Using statistics from government agencies (including the U.S. Census Bureau, the U.S. Department of Justice, and the Centers for Disease Control and Prevention), nonprofit organizations, think tanks, academic journals, and polls and surveys, we have sought to document the unprecedented social, legal, and cultural changes that have occurred over the past two decades. We have addressed a number of topics—including the rights of, and discrimination against, transgender Americans and milestones on the road to the Supreme Court's landmark 2015 decision on marriage equality—that were not covered in the book's first edition.

The statistics in this collection were current as of the summer of 2016. As such, this book represents a snapshot of an evolving community at a specific moment in time. Wherever possible, we have made an effort to situate facts and figures in historical context and to juxtapose the experiences of LGBTQ people with those of their straight peers. We hope that the portrait presented in this book provides an enlightening—and empowering—look at LGBTQ Americans on their ongoing quest for liberation, equality, and first-class citizenship.

David Deschamps and Bennett Singer
September 2016
Brooklyn, New York

ACKNOWLEDGMENTS

This book owes its existence to the researchers, pollsters, statisticians, economists, legal advocates, historians, journalists, authors, and activists whose surveys, studies, polls, reports, articles, monographs, and books are cited on the following pages. We are especially indebted to the Williams Institute for its groundbreaking research on an array of topics addressed throughout this compendium.

For reading and commenting on portions of the manuscript, or for contributing material for inclusion in the book, we extend our appreciation to Leslie Gabel-Brett, Tobin Grant, Loraine Hutchins, Joy Ladin, Abbe Land, Steve Mendelsohn, Shauna Shames, Maggie Wenig, and Clyde Wilcox. Thanks, too, to the following friends, family members, and colleagues who offered advice and support: Rosie Bruno, Elise Deschamps, Lawrence Eaton, Preston Fitzgerald, Rob Fox, Philip and Victorio Gallo, Kevin Jennings, David Kraiker, Lisa Linsky, Andra Miletta, Walter Naegle, Alison Oliver, Ellen Reeves, Jonathan Rosenbloom, Patrick Sammon, Paul and Chris Singer, Cedric Smith, Rachel Smith, Rachel and Jerry Sullivan, Robert Taylor, Lynne Tennenbaum, and Tristram Wyatt.

We appreciate the wise advice and unflagging good humor of our editor at The New Press, Julie Enszer, as well as the research that her students conducted for this project. We are also grateful to Emily Albarillo, the book's production editor, for her extraordinary dedication and meticulous attention to detail; to Sarah Scheffel for her skillful copyediting; to Jen Weers for her masterful indexing; to Cinque Hicks and his colleagues at Bookbright Media for designing the book with flair; and to New Press staffers Jed Bickman, Maury Botton, Julie McCarroll, Bev Rivero, and Ben Woodward for their insights and assistance. And finally, we would like to convey our deep gratitude to Diane Wachtell for commissioning the first edition of this book back in 1993 and for encouraging us to create this revised edition. Diane's visionary leadership is an inspiration to us, and we are honored to contribute to the growing collection of LGBTQ titles published by The New Press.

LGBTQ STATS

Sexual Orientation and Gender Identity: An LGBTQ Lexicon

New words and phrases are emerging to describe wide variations in sexual orientation and gender identity. A number of key terms that appear throughout this book are defined below; unless otherwise noted, these definitions are based on information from The Trevor Project (thetrevorproject.org), which works to empower and end suicide among LGBTQ youth, and are used with permission.

Ally: A straight and/or cisgender person (see definition below) who supports equal civil rights, gender equality, and LGBTQ social movements and challenges homophobia, biphobia, and transphobia.*

Asexual: A term describing individuals who do not experience sexual attraction or do not have interest in or desire for sex. Asexuality is different from **celibacy**, which means abstaining from sex. Asexuality is often viewed as a spectrum—meaning asexual individuals experience varying levels of emotional, spiritual, and romantic attraction and claim a range of identities to define them. The best way to refer to the asexual community is to use the umbrella term "ace," as in the "ace community," which acknowledges that spectrum.

Binary system: A binary system is something made up of two opposing parts. Gender (man/woman), sex (male/female), and sexual orientation (gay/straight) are examples of binary systems.

Biphobia: Aversion toward bisexuality and bisexual people as a social group or as individuals.†

Bisexual: A person who is attracted to both men and women, or to more than one gender identity.

---

* Source: GLSEN (glsen.org).

† Source: PFLAG (pflag.org).

Cisgender: Describes people who identify with the sex they were assigned at birth. For example, if you were told you were "male" at birth and still identify that way, you are cisgender.

Gay: In the past, only men who were attracted to men have used the word "gay." Now it is common for "gay" to be used by anyone who is attracted to people of the same sex or gender.

Gender: *Biological gender (sex)* includes physical attributes such as external genitalia, sex chromosomes, gonads, sex hormones, and internal reproductive structures. At birth, it is used to assign sex—that is, to identify individuals as male or female. *Gender,* on the other hand, is far more complicated. It is the complex interrelationship among an individual's sex **(gender biology)**, one's internal sense of self as male, female, both, or neither **(gender identity)**, as well as one's outward presentations and behaviors **(gender expression)** related to that perception, including one's gender role. Together, the intersection of these three dimensions produces an authentic sense of gender, both in how people experience their own gender as well as how others perceive it.*

Gender-fluid: A term that describes a person whose gender identity or gender expression is not fixed and shifts over time.†

Gender-nonconforming: A term describing people whose gender expression is, or appears to be, different from what we would expect from their assigned gender. Other terms include "gender-variant" or "gender-diverse."

Genderqueer: A term that describes someone whose gender identity is not just a man or a woman. This identity can mean different things to different people.

Homophobia: Hatred or fear of homosexuals—that is, lesbians and gay men—sometimes leading to acts of violence and expressions of hostility.

Intersex: A general term used for a variety of conditions in which a person is born with a reproductive or sexual anatomy that doesn't seem to fit the typical definitions of female or male. For example, a person might be born appearing to be female

---

* Source: Gender Spectrum (genderspectrum.org).

† Source: Dictionary.com.

on the outside but having mostly male-typical anatomy on the inside. Or a person may be born with genitals that seem to be between the usual male and female types—for example, a girl may be born with a noticeably large clitoris, or lacking a vaginal opening, or a boy may be born with a notably small penis or with a scrotum that is divided so that it has formed more like labia.*

Lesbian: A woman who is predominantly attracted to other women. Some women prefer the term "gay"; it's an individual choice.

LGBTQ: Acronym used to describe the lesbian, gay, bisexual, transgender, and queer or questioning community.

Nonbinary: Anything that falls outside the binary system (see definition above). Intersex, genderqueer, and bisexual identities are all examples of nonbinary identities.

Pansexual: Describes people who are capable of being attracted to multiple sexes or gender identities.

Queer: A broad term that is inclusive of people who are not straight and/or cisgender. In the past it was used as a discriminatory term. Today the word is often used in a positive way by folks who identify as queer as well as by allies of queer/LGBTQ people; however, some people still feel that the word carries negative weight.

Questioning: Describes people who may be processing or questioning their sexual orientation and/or gender identity.

Sexual orientation: A person's physical, romantic, emotional, and/or spiritual attraction to another person. Everyone has a sexual orientation.

Transgender (Trans*): An umbrella term used to describe people whose true gender identity does not "match" the sex or gender they were assigned at birth. Many identities fall under the transgender umbrella, which are often designated with an asterisk after the abbreviation "trans." However, not all genderqueer or nonbinary people identify as transgender—and some people who have transitioned to their true gender choose to identify as just a man or a woman instead of

* Source: Intersex Society of North America (isna.org).

transgender. It is respectful to address trans people by using their preferred identity, name, and pronouns.

Transitioning: The social, legal, and/or medical process that trans people may go through to make their gender identity fit their gender expression, presentation, or sex. This word means many different things to different people, and people don't have to experience all or any of these common transitioning elements to identify as their true gender.

Transphobia: Intense dislike of or prejudice against transgender people.*

Transsexual: An older term for people whose gender identity is different from their assigned sex at birth and who seek to transition from male to female or female to male. Many do not prefer this term because it is thought to sound overly clinical.†

Two-Spirit: A contemporary term that refers to First Nations people whose individual identities are a blend of male and female spirits. This term has been reclaimed by some in Native American LGBTQ communities to honor their heritage and provide an alternative to the Western labels of gay, lesbian, bisexual, or transgender.‡

---

* Source: Oxford English Dictionary (oxforddictionaries.com).

† Source: National Center for Transgender Equality (transequality.org).

‡ Ibid.

> We Are Everywhere.
>
> —*Gay Liberation slogan, first used in the early 1970s*[1]

> It doesn't take a degree in social science to figure out that LGBT people are likely to lie on official surveys . . . in fear of retaliation, losing their job or home, or any other number of consequences that could come from being outed. To many LGBT folks, the risks of checking that box far outweigh the contribution to accurate population estimates.
>
> —*Camille Beredjick, writer and activist, 2014*[2]

Quantifying the number of lesbian, gay, bisexual, transgender, and queer (LGBTQ) people in the United States is a task that has been and continues to be fraught with expectations, politics, and uncertainties. As we noted in the 1994 edition of *Gay & Lesbian Stats*, two challenges make this endeavor especially difficult. First, who counts as LGBTQ? Only people who self-identify? Or those who engage in same-sex behaviors but identify as straight? Do we count folks who are not sexually active but who have LGBTQ desires? What about asexual and pansexual people? Second, the ongoing stigma attached to being identified as LGBTQ makes the wording of survey questions and the process by which information is gathered significant factors in the responses that researchers elicit. A thought-provoking 2013 study by the National Bureau of Economic Research documented the role that stigma plays in the underestimation of the LGBTQ population; a summary of this study appears on page 10.

Nevertheless, recent surveys from the polling firm YouGov have shown that growing percentages of young people identify as "not 100 percent heterosexual":

31 percent of 18- to 29-year-olds in the United States and a whopping 49 percent of 18- to 24-year-olds in the United Kingdom describe themselves in this manner. As prejudice lessens, the percentage of LGBTQ people in population estimates may increase. The current consensus indicates that between 1.7 percent and 7.5 percent of American adults identify as LGB. Back in 1948, the precursor to all other prevalence studies, *The Kinsey Report*, found that roughly 10 percent of adult men are more or less exclusively homosexual, with 37 percent being bisexual. In the future, reduced stigma and refined research techniques may prove the Kinsey numbers accurate.

Curiously, when researchers ask Americans to estimate the size of the LGBTQ community, responses are greatly inflated: in a 2015 Gallup poll, for example, the average estimate among survey participants was that LGBT people account for 23.2 percent of the U.S. population.[3]

But why do accurate numbers matter? As Gary Gates of the Williams Institute at the UCLA School of Law has written, "Understanding the size of the LGBT population is a critical first step to informing a host of public policy and research topics." Gates cites a number of real-world issues—including the prevalence of anti-LGBTQ discrimination, the economic impact of marriage equality, and health disparities facing LGBTQ Americans. He goes on to point out that based on current estimates, the number of LGBTQ residents in the United States is roughly equivalent to the population of New Jersey, while the number of American adults who have engaged in same-sex sexual experiences approximates the population of Florida—a state with 20 million residents.[4]

Prior to 2016, when asked about the size of America's transgender population, researchers often cited studies that put the figure at approximately 0.3 percent of the population. This estimate came from a couple of regional surveys and underscored the need for national information about the number of transgender Americans. In June 2016, such information emerged with a new Williams Institute report that draws upon data from the Centers for Disease Control (CDC) to estimate the number of adults who identify as transgender nationally and in all 50 states. The 2016 report finds that 0.6 percent of U.S. adults, or 1.4 million Americans, identify as transgender—double the previous estimate.[5]

The table on pages 11–16 illustrates the range of findings across nearly 70 years of prevalence surveys. As noted in the comments column, the studies differ dramatically in methodology and response rates, and most are based on nonrandom samples. As a whole, these studies confirm that even as the United States makes great strides on many LGBTQ issues, the exact number of LGBTQ Americans remains an elusive—and highly charged—question.

The second half of this chapter focuses on demographics. In what regions of the country, and in what household configurations, do members of the LGBTQ population live? What is their average age and annual income, and how much education have they attained? To what racial and ethnic groups do they belong? These are among the vital questions that the demographic overview addresses.

HOW THE QUESTIONS ARE ASKED AFFECTS THE ANSWERS

A 2013 study of 2,516 Americans demonstrates how bias operates in surveys. On average, participants in this study were younger, more highly educated, and more liberal than the general population. Researchers believe that this profile is more likely to support LGBTQ people and issues, yet this survey still reveals bias among participants. Participants were randomly assigned to answer questions using one of two methods: a direct computer-based method that provided privacy and anonymity, or a veiled method that involved asking subjects to respond to a group of questions in an indirect manner, which has been shown to reduce the chances that a response will be biased toward social expectations. As the study authors put it, "Saying 'three items' might be easier to say than 'Yes, I cheat on my spouse.'"

The proportion of the sample that reported having had a sexual experience with a person of the same sex jumped from 17 percent via direct questioning to 27 percent via veiled questioning. Similarly, roughly 11 percent of the direct-questioning sample said they do not consider themselves heterosexual; with veiled questioning, this proportion rose to 19 percent. At the same time, the survey authors noted that veiled questioning "also increased the rates of anti-gay sentiment." Respondents were 71 percent more likely to say it is acceptable to discriminate against lesbian, gay, or bisexual individuals and 67 percent more likely to disapprove of an openly gay manager at work. The researchers concluded: "The results show non-heterosexuality and anti-gay sentiment are substantially underestimated in existing surveys, and the privacy afforded by current best practices is not always sufficient to eliminate bias."[6]

Table 1.1: What Is the Size of America's LGBTQ Population?

Study (year)	Percentage of sample that is LGB(TQ)	Comments
1. Kinsey et al. (1948)	10% of males reported being more or less exclusively homosexual for at least three years between the ages of 16 and 55; 37% of all males had some homosexual contact to orgasm.	Pioneering study of 5,300 white men, later criticized for using a nonrandom sample that included prisoners and students. These sampling flaws were addressed in a 1979 study by Gebhard et al. that yielded almost identical results of 9.9% and 34%, respectively.
2. Kinsey et al. (1953)	2%–6% of females reported being more or less exclusively homosexual between the ages of 20 and 35; 13% of females had some homosexual contact to orgasm.	Study of 5,940 white females.
3. *Psychology Today* (1970)	37% of males and 12% of females had some homosexual contact to orgasm.	Self-selected sampling of 20,000 readers.
4. Gagnon and Simon (1973)	5%–6% of males and 12% of females had substantial homosexual experiences; 30% of males had some homosexual contact to orgasm.	Reanalysis of Kinsey data focusing on the college population.
5. Hunt (1974)	7% of males and 3% of females had homosexual experiences during more than three years; 25% of males had some homosexual contact to orgasm.	Questionnaire survey of 2,036 people; not a representative sample.
6. Smith and Garner (1976)	40% of male athletes had sex to orgasm with another male at least twice within the prior two years.	Small sample (82 members of the National College Athletic Association) with a large margin of error.
7. Pietropinto and Simenauer (1977)	3.1% of men said they engage in sex with men and women.	Large-scale (nonrandom) survey of 4,066 respondents who completed a self-administered written questionnaire.

Study (year)	Percentage of sample that is LGB(TQ)	Comments
8. *Playboy* (1983)	35% of men and 22% of women reported some homosexual contact to orgasm during adolescence; 10% of men and 12% of women reported homosexual experience since adolescence.	Self-selected sampling of 100,000 male and female readers.
9. Cameron (1985)	5.8% of males identified themselves as gay; 3.1% of females identified themselves as lesbian.	Questions have been raised about bias in the survey; researcher has also misquoted his own findings in national publications.
10. Hatfield (1989)	6.2% of men and women identified themselves as homosexual.	Telephone survey by the *San Francisco Examiner.*
11. Fay et al. (1989)	20.3% of adult males had some homosexual contact to orgasm.	Analysis of data collected in national surveys between 1970 and 1988.
12. Harry (1990)	3.7% of males identified themselves as gay or bisexual.	National telephone survey of 663 males included one question on same-sex attraction.
13. Sell et al. (1990)	Males who report same-sex behavior since age 15: 11.6% (U.S.), 7.8% (U.K.), 11.6% (France).	Random survey of large number of men (5,700); used well-trained field staff to personally interview subjects.
14. Rogers and Turner (1991)	5%–7% of males experienced some same-sex contact as adults.	Results of five probability (i.e., random) samples from 1970–1990.
15. Smith (1991)	5%–6% of adults had some homosexual contact to orgasm since age 18; less than 1% of sample identified as exclusively gay.	Taken from National Opinion Research Center's General Social Surveys; criticized for not using professional sex researchers and lack of extensive interviews.
16. National Opinion Research Center (1989–1993)	2.8% of males identified as gay; 2.5% of females identified as lesbian.	Same as above.

Study (year)	Percentage of sample that is LGB(TQ)	Comments
17. Johnson and Spira (1992)	Subjects who had homosexual experience in the last five years—Britain: 6.1% of males; France: 4.1% of males and 2.6% of females.	Large representative samples of 18,000 respondents in Britain and 20,000 in France.
18. Janus and Janus (1993)	9% of males and 5% of females reported "ongoing" or "frequent" homosexual experiences; 4% of males and 2% of females identified as homosexual.	Cross-sectional nationwide survey of 2,765 men and women who answered a questionnaire; supplemented with some interviews.
19. Billy et al. (1993)	2% of sexually active males reported same-sex experience in last 10 years; 1% of males identified as exclusively homosexual during the same time period.	Batelle Human Affairs Research Center study of HIV risk in the sexual behavior of men ages 20–39; criticized for lack of professional sex researchers and lack of extensive interviews.
20. Taylor (1993)	4% of men ages 16–50 and 4% of women ages 16–50 reported a same-sex partner within the previous 5 years.	Data from a survey by Harris and Project Hope (an international health care organization) relating to AIDS from 1988; based on in-person interviews with 739 men and 409 women.
21. Laumann et al. (1994)	9% of men and 4% of women reported having at least one same-sex encounter since puberty; 2.8% of men and 1.4% of women had "some level of homosexual identity."	Random probability sample of 3,432 men and women from University of Chicago's National Health and Social Life Survey.
22. Binson et al. (1995)	Data derived from the GSS and NHSLS found 5.3% of men reported sexual activity with men since age 18 (see comments), while data from NABS showed 6.5% of men reported same-sex activity in the past 5 years; among "highly educated" white males, the figure was 10.4%.	Two national probability, in-person surveys of 4,300 men from the General Social Survey (GSS) and the National Health and Social Life Survey (NHSLS), along with data from the National AIDS Behavioral Studies (NABS).

Study (year)	Percentage of sample that is LGB(TQ)	Comments
23. Sell et al. (1995)	20.8%, 16.3%, and 18.5% of males and 17.8%, 18.6%, and 18.5% of females in the United States, the United Kingdom, and France, respectively, reported either homosexual behavior or homosexual attraction since age 15; 6.2%, 4.5%, and 10.7% of males and 3.6%, 2.1%, and 3.3% of females in the United States, the United Kingdom, and France, respectively, reported same-sex sexual contact or sexual contact with both sexes in the previous 5 years.	Reexamination of data from Taylor (1993), cited above.
24. Bagley et al. (1998)	15.3% of males 18–27 reported being homosexual to some degree.	Stratified random sample of 750 males in Calgary, Canada, using a computerized response format.
25. Mosher et al. (2005)	90% of women and men 18–44 identified as heterosexual; 2.3% of men and 1.3% of women identified as homosexual; 1.8% of men and 2.8% of women identified as bisexual; 3.9% of men and 3.8% of women identified as "something else."	The CDC's National Center for Health Statistics conducted in-person interviews with a nationally representative multistage area probability sample in 121 areas of the U.S.; 12,571 males and females were interviewed live; answers were entered into a laptop computer and were not told to the interviewer.
26. Pathela et al. (2006)	3.7% of men identified as homosexual, 1.2% as bisexual, 1.7% were not sure, 2.1% declined to answer, and 91.3% as heterosexual; 12.4% of men who answered the sexual orientation question reported having sex exclusively with men in the last 12 months.	Cross-sectional, random telephone survey of 4,193 men in New York City; researchers noted the discordance between sexual behavior and self-reported sexual identity.

Study (year)	Percentage of sample that is LGB(TQ)	Comments
27. Herbenick et al. (2010)	7% of 14- to 94-year-old women and 8% of 14- to 94-year-old men identified as LGB; the percentage of men and women who had some same-sex encounters during their lifetime was higher.	Nationally representative probability sample of 5,865 men and women using online survey.
28. Chandra et al. (2011)	2%–4% of 18- to 44-year-old men and 1%–2% of 18- to 44-year-old women identified as homosexual; 1%–3% of men and 2%–5% of women identified as bisexual; 4%–6% of men and 4%–12% of women had some same-sex contact.	Data from the CDC's 2006–2008 National Center for Health Statistics' in-person interviews with a nationally representative multistage area probability sample of 85 areas of the U.S.; 13,495 males and females were interviewed live, with answers entered into a laptop computer and not told to the interviewer.
29. Gates (2011)	3.5% of adults in the U.S. identified as LGB; 0.3% identified as transgender; 8.2% reported some same-sex behavior; and 11% acknowledged some same-sex attraction.	Review of existing data from five U.S and four international prevalence studies from 2004–2010; the author, a Williams Institute Scholar, makes estimates of the prevalence of LGBT populations and outlines the difficulties in measuring prevalence.
30. Gates and Newport (2012)	3.4% of the U.S. population aged 18 and over identified as LGBT; 4.4% refused to answer the question or didn't know. 6.4% of 18- to 29-year-olds identified as LGBT; 3.5% refused to answer or didn't know.	Gallup poll based on telephone interviews with 121,290 Americans—making it the largest-ever population-based survey asking about sexual orientation.

Study (year)	Percentage of sample that is LGB(TQ)	Comments
31. Ward et al. (2013)	1.6% of adults identified as homosexual; 0.7% identified as bisexual; 1.1% either refused to answer, identified as "something else," or "didn't know."	National Health Interview Survey data of 34,557 adults aged 18 and over collected in 2013 using sampling weights to produce estimates of the national civilian noninstitutionalized adult population.
32. Smith et al. (2015)	Roughly 5% of men and women identified as LGB; 3% refused to answer or didn't know.	Pew Research Center phone interviews (60% cell phone and 40% home phone) with a random, nationally representative group of 35,071 U.S. citizens; one demographic question in a study focusing on religion, not sexual behavior or orientation.

Sources: Studies 1, 2 4, 5, 7, 12, 14, 15, 18, 19, 20, 21, 22, 24, 25, and 28: The Kinsey Institute, "Historical Report: Diversity of Sexual Orientation," kinseyinstitute.org/research/publications/historical-report-diversity-of-sexual-orientation.php#other.

Studies 3, 6, 8, 9, 10, 11, 13, 16, and 17: Bennett L. Singer and David Deschamps, *Gay & Lesbian Stats: A Pocket Guide of Facts and Figures* (New York: The New Press, 1994).

Study 23: Randall L. Sell, James A. Wells and David Wypij, "The Prevalence of Homosexual Behavior and Attraction in the United States, the United Kingdom and France: Results of National Population-Based Samples," *Archives of Sexual Behavior* 24, no. 3 (1995): 235–48, img2.timg.co.il/forums/1_111838972.doc.

Study 26: Preeti Pathela et al., "Discordance Between Sexual Behavior and Self-Reported Sexual Identity," *Annals of Internal Medicine* 145, no. 6 (2006): 416–25, doi: 10.7326/0003-4819-145-6-200609190-00005.

Study 27: Debby Herbenick et al., "Sexual Behavior in the United States: Results from a National Probability Sample of Men and Women Ages 14–94," *Journal of Sexual Medicine*, supplement 5 (2010): 255–65, doi: 10.1111/j.1743-6109.2010.02012.x.

Study 29: Gary J. Gates, "How Many People Are Lesbian, Gay, Bisexual, and Transgender?" Williams Institute, April 2011, williamsinstitute.law.ucla.edu/wp-content/uploads/Gates-How-Many-People-LGBT-Apr-2011.pdf.

Study 30: Gary J. Gates and Frank Newport, "Special Report: 3.4% of U.S. Adults Identify as LGBT," Gallup, October 18, 2012, www.gallup.com/poll/158066/special-report-adults-identify-lgbt.aspx.

Study 31: Brian W. Ward et al., "Sexual Orientation and Health Among U.S. Adults: National Health Interview Survey, 2013," *National Health Statistics Report*, U.S. Department of Health and Human Services, July 15, 2014, www.cdc.gov/nchs/data/nhsr/nhsr077.pdf.

Study 32: Gregory Smith, "America's Changing Religious Landscape," Pew Research Center, May 12, 2015, www.pewforum.org/files/2015/05/RLS-08-26-full-report.pdf.

DEMOGRAPHICS

What do census data reveal about LGBTQ Americans?

The U.S. Census Bureau does not ask about sexual orientation in the questionnaire it sends to every U.S. household once per decade. But the decennial census of 2010 counted people of the same sex who live together and checked the boxes for "unmarried partner" or "husband and wife" when asked about the relationship between household residents. According to data gathered in response to this question, the top 10 cities with the highest number of same-sex couples per 1,000 people are:

1. Provincetown, MA
2. Wilton Manors, FL
3. Palm Springs, CA
4. Rehoboth Beach, DE
5. Guerneville, CA
6. West Hollywood, CA
7. Pleasant Ridge, MI
8. New Hope, PA
9. Rancho Mirage, CA
10. Oakland Park, FL[7]

The Census Bureau's American Community Survey (ACS) conducts an annual statistical survey that samples a small percentage of the population. According to ACS data:

- As of 2014, there were 783,100 same-sex couples in the United States—377,903 male couples and 405,197 female couples. (ACS does not distinguish between married and unmarried couples living in the same household.)
- In 59.5 percent of the same-sex couples, both partners were employed, compared to 47.8 percent of straight married couples and 59.4 percent of straight unmarried couples.
- 66.9 percent of the same-sex couples owned their own home, while 79.1 percent of the married straight

couples and 41.4 percent of the unmarried straight couples did, respectively.

- In 30.7 percent of the same-sex couples, both partners had at least a bachelor's degree. The figure was 23.7 percent for straight married couples and 12.5 percent for straight unmarried couples.
- The highest percentage of interracial partnerships was among male couples, at 17.3 percent. The figure was 12.4 percent for female couples, 6.8 percent for married straight couples, and 13.4 percent for unmarried straight couples, respectively.
- Lesbian couples were twice as likely to be raising children as gay male couples.[8]

AGE

What percentage of Americans in different age-groups identify as LGBTQ?

In the largest-ever population-based survey to ask about sexual orientation in the United States, conducted in 2012, 3.4 percent of the 121,290 respondents aged 18 and over identified as LGBT, while 4.4 percent of respondents refused to answer the question or said they didn't know.

- Among 18- to 29-year-old women who took part in this survey, 8.3 percent identified as LGBT. Results among other age-groups are presented in Table 1.2.

According to research published by the Williams Institute in 2014, LGBT individuals in all regions of the United States are significantly younger than their straight counterparts, as documented in Table 1.3.

Table 1.2: Self-Identification of LGBT Americans, by Age

Do you, personally, identify as lesbian, gay, bisexual, or transgender?

Age-group	Yes %	No %	Don't know/refused to answer %
Adults 18 to 29	6.4	90.1	3.5
Adults 30 to 49	3.2	93.6	3.2
Adults 50 to 64	2.6	93.1	4.3
Adults 65+	1.9	91.5	6.5
Women 18 to 29	8.3	88.0	3.8
Men 18 to 29	4.6	92.1	3.3

Source: Gary J. Gates and Frank Newport, "Special Report: 3.4% of U.S. Adults Identify as LGBT," Gallup, October 18, 2012, www.gallup.com/poll/158066/special-report-adults-identify-lgbt.aspx.

Table 1.3: Average Age of LGBT Americans, by Geographic Region

Region	LGBT individuals	Non-LGBT individuals
All individuals in the U.S.	40	47
Northeast	40	48
Midwest	40	48
South	40	47
Mountain	39	48
Pacific	39	46

Source: Amira Hasenbush et al., "The LGBT Divide: A Data Portrait of LGBT People in the Midwestern, Mountain & Southern States," Williams Institute, December 2014, williamsinstitute.law.ucla.edu/wp-content/uploads/LGBT-divide-Dec-2014.pdf.

GEOGRAPHY

Where does the LGBTQ population reside?

According to a 2014 report published by the Williams Institute and entitled "The LGBT Divide: A Data Portrait of LGBT People in the Midwestern, Mountain & Southern States":

- 63 percent of LGBT Americans live in the Midwest, Mountain, and Southern regions of the country.
    - 20 percent reside in the Midwest.
    - 8 percent live in the Mountain region.
    - 35 percent are based in the South.
- 19 percent live in the Northeast.
- 17 percent reside in the Pacific region.[9]

What are the most and least accepting regions of the country for LGB Americans?

According to the Williams Institute's LGB social climate index, which measures the social acceptance of lesbian, gay, and bisexual people based on approval levels for same-sex marriage, adoption rights for same-sex couples, laws that protect lesbians and gay men from employment discrimination, and the prevalence of the belief that homosexuality is a sin:

- The average score on the social climate index across the 50 states and the District of Columbia is 60 on a 100-point scale.
    - The index score for the Northeast is 71.
    - The Pacific region's score is 68.
    - The Midwest's score is 59.
    - The Mountain States' score is 56.
    - The South's score is 55.[10]

What states have the highest and lowest concentration of LGBTQ residents?

According to information gathered by Gallup in 2012, the U.S. states (including the District of Columbia) with the highest percentage of LGBT people are:

1. District of Columbia: 10 percent.
2. Hawaii: 5.1 percent.

3. Vermont: 4.9 percent.
4. Oregon: 4.9 percent.
5. Maine: 4.8 percent.[11]

The U.S. states with the lowest percentage of LGBTQ people in 2012 were:

5. Utah: 2.7 percent.
4. Tennessee: 2.6 percent.
3. Mississippi: 2.6 percent.
2. Montana: 2.6 percent.
1. North Dakota: 1.7 percent.[12]

What metropolitan areas have the highest and lowest percentage of LGBTQ adults?

Based on telephone interviews that Gallup conducted between 2012 and 2014 with a random sample of 374,325 employed adults, the U.S. metropolitan areas with the highest percentage of adults who identify as LGBT are:

1. San Francisco–Oakland–Hayward: 6.2 percent.
2. Portland–Vancouver–Hillsboro: 5.4 percent.
3. Austin–Round Rock: 5.3 percent.
4. New Orleans–Metairie: 5.1 percent.
5. Seattle–Tacoma–Bellevue: 4.8 percent.[13]

New York City–Newark–Jersey City ranked 23rd on the list, with the LGBT population estimated at 4 percent.[14]

In the same Gallup study, the U.S. metropolitan areas (of the 50 surveyed) with the lowest percentage of adults who identify as LGBT are:

5. Raleigh: 3.2 percent.
4. San Jose–Sunnyvale–Santa Clara: 3.2 percent.
3. Memphis: 3.1 percent.
2. Pittsburgh: 3.0 percent.
1. Birmingham–Hoover: 2.6 percent.[15]

How do concentrations of lesbians and gay men in residential areas affect housing prices?

According to sociology professor Amin Ghaziani, author of *There Goes the Gayborhood?*:

- In residential areas where female same-sex households comprise more than 1 percent of the population—a level three times the U.S. average—housing prices increase by approximately 16.5 percent.
- In residential areas with a comparable level of male same-sex households, housing prices increase by approximately 14 percent.
- Ghaziani notes that new clusters are forming within neighborhoods: "There are now more areas that have a distinct association with same-sex sexuality than we have ever seen before." He points to "clusters for LGBT people of color," adding that "New Yorkers talk about Chelsea on the one hand and 'Chocolate Chelsea' on the other hand, and they talk about 'Hell's Kitchen' on the one hand and an LGBT Latino 'Hell's Cocina' on the other."
- Ghaziani concludes: "In the U.S. at least, the gayer the block, the faster its values will rise."[16]

RACE AND ETHNICITY

What percentage of the LGBTQ population are people of color?

According to data from the Williams Institute, the LGBT population is more likely to be African American and Latino/a than the non-LGBT population. Table 1.4 provides national as well as regional data.

CHILDREN IN LGBTQ HOUSEHOLDS

What percentage of same-sex couples are raising children?

Twenty percent of same-sex couples are raising a child under 18 in their household, compared to 43 percent of different-sex married couples. The percentage by region of same-sex couples raising children is summarized at the top of page 24.

Table 1.4: Racial/Ethnic Distribution of LGBT Americans, by Employment Protection and Geographic Region

Individuals	White		African American		Latino/a		Asian/Pacific Islander	
	LGBT	Non-LGBT	LGBT	Non-LGBT	LGBT	Non-LGBT	LGBT	Non-LGBT
All individuals in the U.S.	63%	72%	15%	12%	18%	13%	2%	1%
21 state law states	61%	69%	12%	9%	23%	17%	3%	3%
29 non-state law states	65%	74%	18%	13%	14%	10%	1%	1%
Northeast	65%	74%	15%	11%	16%	12%	2%	2%
Midwest	74%	82%	13%	10%	10%	6%	1%	1%
South	59%	67%	22%	17%	16%	13%	1%	1%
Mountain	66%	77%	4%	3%	26%	17%	2%	1%
Pacific	55%	61%	7%	6%	30%	26%	4%	5%

Note: "State law states" are the 21 states that had statewide prohibitions against employment discrimination based on sexual orientation as of 2014; "non-state law states" are the 29 states without such protections in 2014.

Source: Hasenbush et al., "The LGBT Divide."

- 21 percent in the Midwest.
- 21 percent in the Mountain region.
- 20 percent in the South.
- 18 percent in the Pacific region.
- 17 percent in the Northeast.[17]

For more on children, see page 119 in the Marriage and Family chapter, as well as the Youth and Education chapter.

EDUCATION

What level of education have LGBTQ Americans attained?

Table 1.5 shows the breakdown of statistics on LGBT individuals and couples over age 25 with a college degree, including percentages in states that do and do not provide employment protections.

ECONOMICS

What is the average income for LGBTQ Americans?

- The average income for same-sex couple households throughout the United States is 12 percent higher than that of different-sex married couple households.
- The gap shrinks considerably, however, when one looks at same-sex couples in states that do not have protections for LGBT people. The picture further changes when one considers same-sex couples who are raising children and who face an income disadvantage compared to their straight peers. Average yearly household income for couples and parents is summarized in Tables 1.6 and 1.7 on pages 25 and 26, which were created by the Williams Institute in 2014.

Among individuals, more LGBT Americans report household incomes under $24,000 than their straight peers: 32 percent versus 24 percent, respectively. In addition, LGBT people are 60 percent more likely to report not having enough money for food than their straight peers, as shown in Table 1.8 on page 26.

Table 1.5: Percentage of Individuals and Couples with a College Degree

	LGBT individuals	Non-LGBT individuals
All individuals in the U.S.	34%	34%
21 state law states	39%	38%
29 non-state law states	31%	31%

	Same-sex couples	Different-sex married couples
All couples in the U.S.	48%	34%
21 state law states	53%	37%
29 non-state law states	43%	31%

Table 1.6: Average Household Income for Couples, by Employment Protections and Geographic Region

	Same-sex couples	Different-sex married couples	Difference
All couples	$109,369	$97,678	$11,691
21 state law states	$115,216	$101,211	$14,005
29 non-state law states	$88,551	$83,238	$5,313
Northeast	$119,697	$106,044	$13,653
Midwest	$87,869	$85,671	$2,198
South	$94,540	$85,526	$9,014
Mountain	$91,030	$83,305	$7,725
Pacific	$115,591	$98,251	$17,340

Note: "State law states" are the 21 states that had statewide prohibitions against employment discrimination based on sexual orientation as of 2014; "non-state law states" are the 29 states without such protections in 2014.

Source: Hasenbush et al., "The LGBT Divide."

Table 1.7: Average Household Income for Couples Raising Children Under 18, by Employment Protections and Geographic Region

	Same-sex parents	Different-sex married parents	Difference
All couples	$87,363	$94,945	-$7,582
21 state law states	$100,982	$105,315	-$4,333
29 non-state law states	$75,344	$86,604	-$11,260
Northeast	$110,542	$114,565	-$4,023
Midwest	$71,601	$91,527	-$19,926
South	$77,381	$88,256	-$10,875
Mountain	$87,776	$83,655	$4,121
Pacific	$102,724	$98,503	$4,221

Table 1.8: Percent of Individuals Reporting a Lack of Money for Food

	LGBT	Non-LGBT
All individuals	28%	18%
21 state law states	26%	16%
29 non-state law states	30%	19%
Northeast	26%	16%
Midwest	30%	16%
South	29%	20%
Mountain	31%	17%
Pacific	28%	18%

Note: "State law states" are the 21 states that had statewide prohibitions against employment discrimination based on sexual orientation as of 2014; "non-state law states" are the 29 states without such protections in 2014.

Source: Hasenbush et al., "The LGBT Divide."

> Never doubt that America will one day realize that her gay, bisexual, and transgender sons and daughters want nothing more—and deserve nothing less—than the rights accorded every other citizen. But we must make it so—by daring to dream of a world in which we are free. So if you dream of a world in which you can put your partner's picture on your desk, then put her picture on your desk—and you will live in such a world. And if you dream of a world in which you can walk down the street holding your partner's hand, then hold her hand—and you will live in such a world. And if you dream of a world in which there are more openly gay elected officials, then run for office—and you will live in such a world. And if you dream of a world in which you can take your partner to the office party, even if your office is the U.S. House of Representatives, then take her to the party. I do, and now I live in such a world. Remember, there are two things that keep us oppressed: them and us. We are half of the equation.
>
> *—Tammy Baldwin, who served from 1999 to 2013 as a U.S. Representative from Wisconsin and was elected in 2012 to the U.S. Senate, in a speech at the Millennium March for Equality on the National Mall, 2000*[1]

In 1980, there were five openly LGBTQ elected officials in the United States.[2] By 2012, LGBTQ political leaders had been elected to office in every one of the 50 states—and today more than 450 openly LGBTQ elected officials are serving across the nation.[3] This transformation in political visibility and power owes an immense amount to several generations of activists who have been fighting for LGBTQ rights and inclusion since the 1950s. As the statistics and turning points chronicled in this chapter demonstrate, progress toward equality has occurred at a pace that trailblazers like Mattachine Society co-founder Harry Hay and Audre Lorde—who described herself as a "Black feminist, lesbian, mother, warrior, poet"—might have found unimaginable. Such rapid change has led inevitably to backlash—but also to the widely shared belief that the movement for LGBTQ rights and freedoms has reached a tipping point. "When you achieve something that you thought was fanciful much quicker than you imagined was possible, that tells you you're on a really impressive arc," said Kate Kendell, executive director of the National Center for Lesbian Rights, in late 2015. "There's no doubt that we are clearly at a tipping point, but a tipping point is not a finish line."[4]

ACTIVISM

What are some of the first organizations that played a role in building the movement for LGBTQ equality and drawing attention to issues that affect the lives of LGBTQ Americans?

- The first "homosexual emancipation organization," the **Scientific-Humanitarian Committee**, was founded in Berlin by Dr. Magnus Hirschfeld on May 15, 1897.[5]
- The first formally organized LGBT movement group in the United States, the **Society for Human Rights**, was chartered by the State of Illinois in 1924. The organization's mission was "to promote and protect the interests of people who by reasons of mental and physical abnormalities are abused and hindered in the legal pursuit of happiness which is guaranteed them by the Declaration of Independence, and to combat the public prejudices against them." A few months after being chartered, the group ceased to exist in the wake of several members' arrests.[6]
- The **Mattachine Society**, founded in 1950 in Los Angeles by Harry Hay with co-founders Bob Hull and Chuck Rowland, and the Daughters of Bilitis, founded in 1955 in San Francisco by Del Martin and Phyllis Lyon,

were the first post–World War II civil rights organizations for gay men and lesbians, respectively.[7]

  - As legal scholar Nancy Knauer notes, during the late 1950s and 1960s, "simply attending a homophile conference would have been a dangerous proposition." When, for example, the Mattachine Society held a national convention in Denver in 1959, the organizers were arrested and one was jailed for 60 days. A year later, 84 gay men and lesbians attending a Mattachine meeting in suburban Philadelphia were arrested.[8]

- Prior to the Stonewall rebellion of 1969, there were an estimated 50 lesbian and gay organizations in the United States.[9] (For details on Stonewall, see pages 33–34.)
- In the aftermath of Stonewall, a new generation of activists founded organizations that openly claimed the word "gay," which had been avoided by earlier organizations that opted for cryptic, inoffensive names. The **Gay Liberation Front** (GLF) and the **Gay Activists Alliance** (GAA), both formed in 1969, were two of the most prominent new groups. Open to all persons in the New York metropolitan area regardless of sexual orientation, the GAA achieved recognition as a leader in the gay liberation movement and became a model for the creation of similar groups in other cities.[10]

What are some organizations—both large and small—that are currently working to advance LGBTQ rights?

As of 2016, there were at least 417 LGBTQ rights organizations throughout the United States.[11] Among them:

- The **National LGBTQ Task Force**, founded in 1973 as the National Gay Task Force and now the oldest national organization advocating for LGBTQ rights in America. In 2014, it utilized 844 volunteers, had a staff of 69, and operated on a budget of $8.5 million.[12] Since 1988, the National LGBTQ Task Force has hosted

Creating Change, the nation's largest annual gathering of LGBTQ activists and allies. Attendance at the conference has grown from 300 to more than 4,000 attendees in 2016.[13]

- **Lambda Legal**, the oldest and largest national legal organization dedicated to achieving full recognition of LGBTQ civil rights. It currently has a staff of 104 and an operating budget of $26 million.[14] Lambda's founder, William J. Thom, Esq., submitted incorporation papers for approval to the New York courts in 1971, but the application was denied on the grounds that the organization's proposed activities would be contrary to public policy. That decision was overturned in 1973 by the New York Court of Appeals, the highest court in New York State. In the landmark 2003 case *Lawrence v. Texas*, Lambda Legal persuaded the U.S. Supreme Court to overturn all remaining state sodomy laws. That ruling fundamentally transformed the legal landscape and stands as "the most important legal victory to date for LGBT equality," according to the organization.[15]
- The **National Center for Lesbian Rights** (NCLR), founded in San Francisco in 1977 by Donna Hitchens and originally called the Lesbian Rights Project. NCLR is a nonprofit, public-interest law firm committed to advancing the civil and human rights of lesbian, gay, bisexual, and transgender people and their families through litigation, legislation, policy, and public education. In 2013, NCLR's budget was $5 million, 85 percent of which was spent directly on legal programs and services.[16]
- The **Log Cabin Republicans**, founded in 1977 as an LGBT advocacy group that "support[s] equality under the law for all, free markets, individual liberty, limited government, and a strong national defense." One of the organization's first campaigns opposed the efforts of Republican California state senator John Briggs, who had ambitions to be governor and who in 1978 proposed a statewide ballot initiative to prevent gay and

lesbian teachers from working in public schools. The Briggs Initiative also permitted the firing of any educator who was determined to be "advocating, imposing, encouraging or promoting" homosexuality. Gay conservatives turned to former California governor Ronald Reagan, who went on record to declare that the initiative "is not needed to protect our children." Reagan's opposition helped defeat the initiative and motivated gay Republicans to educate and lobby members of the GOP on gay and lesbian issues at the local, state, and national levels. The organization now has 48 chapters nationwide, a full-time office in Washington, D.C., and federal and state political action committees.[17]

- The **Human Rights Campaign** (HRC), founded in 1980 and now the largest national LGBTQ political organization, with some 1.5 million members and supporters, 322 staff members, and a 2014 operating budget of $57 million. In 2014, HRC launched Project One America, an $8.5 million effort to advance equality for LGBT people across the deep South with campaigns in Mississippi, Alabama, and Arkansas, as well as HRC Global, a program to investigate and publicize the overseas activities of American anti-LGBT extremists.[18]
- **ACT UP**, the AIDS Coalition to Unleash Power, founded in New York City in 1987 by the playwright Larry Kramer and other activists. ACT UP is credited with accelerating the FDA's drug approval process, lowering the cost of drugs that treat HIV/AIDS, and forcing the U.S. government to address the AIDS crisis worldwide. ACT UP continues to engage in activism and is currently campaigning for a tax of 0.05 percent or less on Wall Street transactions and speculative trades in order to raise funds to end the global AIDS epidemic and provide universal health care in the United States.[19]
- The **National Black Justice Coalition** (NBJC), a civil rights organization founded in 2003 whose mission is to end racism and homophobia while empowering African American lesbian, gay, bisexual, and transgender

people. As America's leading national African American LGBT civil rights organization focused on federal public policy, NBJC leads African American families in bridging the gaps between the movements for racial justice and LGBT equality. An annual initiative, Out on the Hill, brings together hundreds of black LGBT activists, elected officials, faith leaders, elders, and young adults to D.C., where they participate in a week of organizing, action, and reflection on the role of the LGBTQ African American community within the movement for LGBTQ equality as well as within other justice movements, including Black Lives Matter.[20]

- The **National Center for Transgender Equality** (NCTE), founded in 2003 by Mara Keisling and other trans activists as a nonprofit organization dedicated to advancing the equality of transgender people by providing a voice for advocacy in Washington, D.C. In 2007, NCTE launched the Privacy and Documentation program as a centerpiece of its policy agenda; nearly half of all U.S. states have adopted NCTE's model legislation that allows transgender people to update driver's licenses and birth certificates to match their true gender identity. (For more details, see page 204 of the Transgender chapter.) In 2013, the organization had a staff of seven, 341,046 website and blog visitors, and a budget of $1.1 million.[21]
- **Freedom for All Americans**, established in 2015 by Quark founder Tim Gill and a bipartisan group of major donors to "bring together Republicans and Democrats, businesses large and small, people of faith, and allies from all walks of life to make the case for comprehensive nondiscrimination protections that ensure everyone is treated fairly and equally." According to *The Advocate*, "the organization is not intended to exist in perpetuity but rather to achieve its stated goal, and then fold. In many ways, this should help keep it focused on its goal rather than on continually growing a budget to meet multiple objectives that require the organiza-

tion to become more territorial even as it becomes less accountable."[22]

- The **Mattachine Society of Washington, DC** (MSDC), which is continuing the work of the organization co-founded in 1961 by Dr. Franklin E. Kameny and Jack Nichols, who led the first gay rights protests at the White House, the Pentagon, and the U.S. Civil Service Commission. MSDC, which reinstated the lapsed charter of the original organization, is currently engaged in "archive activism," which uncovers the hidden histories of LGBTQ Americans who faced persecution at the hands of the federal and state governments for more than 65 years. Based on Freedom of Information requests, MSDC has identified and published thousands of pages of previously undisclosed government documents that demonstrate the persistent culture of animus leveled against LGBT Americans by the federal government.[23]

What are some of the notable demonstrations, protests, meetings, and marches that have propelled LGBTQ activism?

- What is believed to be the first American gay rights demonstration—a protest against discrimination in the military—took place at the Whitehall Military Induction Center in New York City on September 19, 1963.[24]
- On April 17, 1965, members of the Mattachine Society and the Daughters of Bilitis gathered at the White House to protest discriminatory government policies that targeted lesbian and gay people for harassment and criminal prosecution.[25]
- In August 1966, transgender people rioted outside Compton's Cafeteria in San Francisco's Tenderloin district, protesting mistreatment and abuse by the police. Historian Susan Stryker calls this "the first known incident of collective militant queer resistance to police harassment in U.S. history."[26]
- On the night of June 27 to 28, 1969, New York City police raided the Stonewall Inn in Greenwich Village. It

was the sixth raid of a gay bar in New York City within three weeks. Police were surprised when trans people, lesbians, street people, and bar patrons fought back, hurling jeers and later stones and parking meters at the officers. This demonstration of collective resistance, known as the Stonewall Rebellion, was a watershed in the modern movement for LGBTQ rights and liberation.[27] In June 2016, President Barack Obama designated the Stonewall Inn as the first national monument to LGBT rights.[28]

- On March 26, 1977, for the first time ever, gay and lesbian activists were invited to the White House to meet with President Jimmy Carter's aides. Carter was the first U.S. president to support lesbian and gay rights.[29]
- In 1977, lesbian and gay residents of Dade County, Florida, mobilized to oppose Anita Bryant's Save Our Children campaign, an effort to repeal a county ordinance that banned discrimination in housing, employment, and public accommodations on the basis of sexual orientation. "As a mother," Bryant declared, "I know that homosexuals cannot biologically reproduce children; therefore, they must recruit our children." In June 1977, Bryant's campaign was successful and the ordinance was repealed by a margin of 69 to 31 percent.[30]
- Five national Marches on Washington have drawn LGBTQ citizens and their allies to the nation's capital to demand equal rights. The number of people attending has been a contentious topic, with widely varying figures provided by organizers, media sources, and government officials. Estimated attendance for each march is shown below:

    1. October 14, 1979—between 75,000 and 125,000 attendees.
    2. October 11, 1987—between 200,000 and 650,000 attendees.
    3. April 25, 1993—nearly 1 million attendees.

4. April 30, 2000—between 125,000 and 800,000 attendees.
5. October 11, 2009—200,000 attendees.[31]

These marches were modeled, in part, on the 1963 March on Washington for Jobs and Freedom, whose chief organizer, Bayard Rustin, received a posthumous Presidential Medal of Freedom in 2013. "As an openly gay African American, Mr. Rustin stood at the intersection of several of the fights for equal rights," said President Obama in presenting America's highest civilian honor to Rustin's surviving life partner, Walter Naegle.[32]

When and where have LGBTQ pride marches taken place?

- The first LGBTQ pride march took place in New York City on June 28, 1970, commemorating the Stonewall uprising of the previous year. More than 2,000 people participated.[33]
- On May 25, 1991, the District of Columbia's African American lesbian and gay community sponsored the first Black Lesbian and Gay Pride Day. Thirty other Black Pride celebrations now take place throughout the world.[34]
- In 2006, an estimated 3 million people attended the São Paulo pride parade—making it the world's largest-ever LGBT event.[35]
- More than 400 LGBTQ pride events took place worldwide in 2016, from Adelaide, Australia, to Zurich, Switzerland.[36]

For more on Pride events, see page 193 of the Sports and Leisure Activities chapter.

When is National Coming Out Day, and what is its purpose?

The first National Coming Out Day took place on October 11, 1988, the one-year anniversary of the Second National March on Washington for Lesbian and Gay Rights. This event was created by two Los Angeles activists: psychologist Rob Eichberg and Jean O'Leary, then head of National Gay Rights Advocates in Los Angeles. "Most people think they don't know anyone gay or lesbian," said Eichberg, "and in fact everybody does. It is imperative that we come out and let people know who we are and disabuse them of their fears and stereotypes."

- 18 states participated in the first National Coming Out Day. In 1990, 50 states and 7 foreign countries took part.
- Keith Haring donated a logo to the organization: his famous image of a person dancing out of a closet.
- Candace Gingrich, half-sister of then–House Speaker Newt Gingrich, became a National Coming Out Project spokesperson and full-time activist in 1995.
- The day continues to be observed annually as a celebration of coming out and an opportunity to promote LGBTQ visibility.[37]

Who are some notable Americans who never came out?

Despite new levels of openness among the LGBTQ community, it remains difficult for some people to come out; 20 or 30 years ago, it was considerably more traumatic. In 2014, *The Advocate* highlighted this reality in a feature entitled "They Died in the Closet." Among those on the *Advocate* list:

- J. Edgar Hoover (1895–1972)—director of the FBI from 1935 to 1972. The editors note that "Everyone from Ethel Merman to the Mattachine Society's Harry Hay has been quoted as saying Hoover was gay, even if he didn't himself acknowledge or accept it"—but no one disputes that Hoover was ruthless in his persecution of minorities, including gay men and lesbians.
- Ed Koch (1924–2013)—New York City mayor from 1978 to 1990 who was widely criticized for insufficient action on the AIDS epidemic.
- Rock Hudson (1925–1985)—actor and 1950s heartthrob who died of AIDS.
- Roy Cohn (1927–1986)—lawyer and persecutor of LGBTQ people who died of AIDS.

- Anthony Perkins (1932–1992)—actor and star of Alfred Hitchcock's *Psycho*.
- Barbara Jordan (1936–1996)—civil rights leader and Democratic congresswoman from Texas.
- Sally Ride (1951–2012)—the first American woman in space, whose long-term relationship with partner Tam O'Shaughnessy became public only in Ride's obituary. In 2013, O'Shaughnessy accepted a Presidential Medal of Freedom that Barack Obama bestowed posthumously on Ride.[38]

POLITICS AND ELECTED OFFICIALS

With what political parties do LGBTQ Americans identify?

In one of the largest-ever polls of LGBT Americans, conducted by Gallup in 2012:

- 44 percent of the 121,290 respondents said they were Democrats, compared with 32 percent of the general population.
- 43 percent described themselves as Independents, versus 39 percent of the general population.
- 13 percent identified as Republicans, in contrast to 30 percent of the general public.[39]

What are some political actions that individual lesbian and gay Americans have taken?

In a small, peer-reviewed 2013 study of 285 LG Americans:

- 83 percent had cast a vote in support of gay rights.
- 50 percent had written a letter in support of gay rights.
- 24 percent had signed a petition in support of gay rights.[40]

Who were America's first LGBTQ elected officials, and when and where did they serve?

- The first openly LGBT members to serve on a city council were Nancy Wechsler and Jerry DeGrieck. Both were elected as members of the Human Rights Party to the city council of Ann Arbor, Michigan, in 1972; both came out in 1973.

- The first out LGBT person elected to public office was Kathy Kozachenko, who won a seat on the city council of Ann Arbor, Michigan, in 1974.
- The first openly lesbian or gay candidate elected to a state legislature was Elaine Noble, an LGBT activist who served in the Massachusetts House of Representatives for two terms starting in January 1975.
- The first openly gay man who was a nonincumbent elected in the United States—and the first openly gay person elected to public office in California—was Harvey Milk, elected in 1977 to the San Francisco Board of Supervisors. Milk was assassinated in 1978 by Dan White, who also killed San Francisco Mayor George Moscone.
- The first openly gay mayor in the United States was Robert Gentry, who became mayor of Laguna Beach, California, in 1983 and served three terms.
- The first openly gay African American elected to public office in the United States was Keith St. John, elected to the common council of Albany, New York, in 1989.
- The first openly gay Latino elected to public office in the United States was Ricardo Gonzalez, elected alderman in Madison, Wisconsin, in 1989.
- The first openly transgender member of a city council was Joanne Conte, a trans woman who served on the city council of Arvada, Colorado, from 1991 to 1995.
- The first openly lesbian African American elected official was Sherry Harris, elected to the Seattle, Washington, city council in 1991.
- The first openly gay mayor of a U.S. state capital was David Cicilline, who became mayor of Providence, Rhode Island, in 2002.
- The first openly gay governor was Jim McGreevey, Democratic governor of New Jersey, who came out in 2004 during the same speech in which he announced his resignation as governor.

- The first openly lesbian city council speaker was Christine Quinn, elected speaker of the New York City Council in 2006.
- The first trans mayor was Stu Rasmussen of Silverton, Oregon, elected in 2008.
- The largest U.S. city to have a lesbian mayor is Houston, Texas, which was governed by Annise Parker from 2010 to 2016.
- The first openly bisexual member of a city council was Marlene Pray, who joined the city council of Doylestown, Pennsylvania, in 2012 and was also the first openly bisexual officeholder in Pennsylvania.
- The largest U.S. city with a gay male mayor is Seattle, Washington, where Ed Murray was elected to a four-year term beginning in 2014.
- The first openly bisexual governor and first governor to be openly LGBT at the time of taking office was Kate Brown, Democratic governor of Oregon, who became governor in 2015 after her predeccesor resigned.[41]

Who were the first LGBTQ members of Congress?

- The first out U.S. representative to serve in the House of Representatives was Democrat Gerry Studds of Massachusetts, who served from 1973 to 1997 and was outed in 1983 when the House Ethics Committee found that Studds had engaged in an affair with a 17-year-old male congressional page in 1973.[42]
- The first U.S. representative to come out voluntarily was Democrat Barney Frank of Massachusetts, who served from 1980 to 2013 and came out in 1987.[43]
- The first out Republican to serve as a U.S. representative was Steve Gunderson of Wisconsin, who served from 1981 to 1997 and was outed in 1994 on the House floor by Representative Bob Dornan (R–California) during a debate over federal funding for gay-friendly curricula.[44]
- The first Republican representative to come out

voluntarily was Jim Kolbe of Arizona, who served from 1985 to 2007 and came out in 1996.[45]

- The first U.S. representative who was out at the time of her first election was Tammy Baldwin, a Wisconsin Democrat who served from 1999 to 2013.[46]
- The first openly LGBT U.S. senator who was out at the time of her election was Tammy Baldwin, elected in 2012 to represent Wisconsin.[47]
- In 2016, there was not one openly LGBT Republican serving in Congress; however, the 2016 election cycle saw four openly gay Republicans running for the House and one running for the Senate.[48]

As of the 2010 census, there were approximately 511,000 elected officials in the United States.

- If the percentage of the population that is LGBT were to be proportionally represented, there would be 15,300 LGBT elected officials.[49]
- There are currently an estimated 450 openly LGBT elected officials in the United States.[50]

Who were the first LGBTQ judges to serve in the United States?

- The first openly gay judge in the United States was Stephen M. Lachs, appointed by California governor Jerry Brown to the Los Angeles County Superior Court in 1979. Before leaving office in 1981, Brown appointed three more lesbian and gay judges to the California courts, including the nation's first openly lesbian judge, Mary Morgan, who served on the San Francisco municipal court.[51]
- Deborah A. Batts was the nation's first openly LGBT federal judge. Batts, an African American lesbian, was appointed by President Bill Clinton to the U.S. District Court for the Southern District of New York and confirmed by the Senate in a 1994 voice vote.[52]
- The first openly LGBT justice of a state supreme court was Rives Kistler, appointed to the Oregon Supreme

Court in 2003 and retained by voters the following year.[53]

- President Barack Obama has appointed eleven openly gay or lesbian federal judges and the first openly LGBT judge of a federal court of appeals, Todd M. Hughes of the U.S. Court of Appeals for the Federal Circuit.[54]
- Victoria Kolakowski, the first openly transgender person to serve as a trial judge in the country, was elected to California's Alameda County Superior Court in November 2010. She serves as president of the International Association of LGBT Judges.[55]

What are some milestones in the appointment of openly LGBTQ Americans to key government positions?

- James Hormel, an American philanthropist, was the first openly LGBTQ person to serve as a U.S. ambassador. Hormel was ambassador to Luxembourg from 1999 to 2001.[56]
- Attorney and law professor Chai Feldblum became the first openly lesbian commissioner on the U.S. Equal Employment Opportunity Commission when she was appointed in 2010. President Obama nominated her to serve a second term ending in 2018; the Senate confirmed her in 2013.[57]
- The Obama administration has appointed more than 250 openly LGBT professionals to full-time and advisory positions in the executive branch—more than all known LGBT appointments of other presidential administrations combined.[58]

How do Americans feel about electing an LGBTQ president?

- No openly LGBTQ person has ever been elected president or vice president, named to the Supreme Court, or appointed to a cabinet position.[59]
- In 2015 Gallup asked 1,527 Americans if they would vote for a presidential candidate who was gay or lesbian. 74 percent answered yes.[60]

LOBBYING AND GRANTMAKING

What organizations have funded lobbying on behalf of LGBTQ causes?

Open Secrets: The Center for Responsive Politics reported that in 2015, $3,564,864 was spent to cover the work of 32 lobbyists working to promote LGBTQ rights. These organizations spent the following amounts:

- American Unity Fund—$1,950,000.
- HRC Foundation—$1,180,000.
- Freedom to Marry Action—$233,854.
- Gay, Lesbian & Straight Education Network—$141,000.
- Family Equality Council—$60,000.[61]

How much did foundations and corporations invest in LGBTQ issues in 2014?

Funders for LGBTQ Issues reported that in 2014, the total investment in LGBTQ issues by foundations and corporations was $153,248,693. The top five grantmakers—whose collective donations totaled $52 million—were:

- Arcus Foundation—$17 million.
- Ford Foundation—$15.4 million.
- Gill Foundation—$7.0 million.
- Open Society Foundations—$6.5 million.
- Gilead Sciences—$6.1 million.

Of the 100 largest foundations in the United States, 62 provided no grants that focused specifically on LGBTQ communities.[62]

LAW

What is the history of sodomy laws in the United States?

- Until 1961, every state had a law proscribing sodomy—generally defined as oral or anal sex between homosexuals and, in most cases, between heterosexuals.[63]
- In 1948, Alfred Kinsey estimated that 95 percent of American men were committing criminal sexual acts.[64]

- In 1950, all but two states classified sodomy as a felony, with only murder, kidnapping, and rape commanding heavier sentences.[65]
- The first state to decriminalize sodomy was Illinois, in 1961.[66]
- In November 2015, at a campaign event in Iowa, former Arkansas governor and then–Republican presidential candidate Mike Huckabee said, "Sodomy is against the law, on the books, this very day, and the Supreme Court has issued a decree and we have states' rights here. They have no jurisdiction over Iowa." Huckabee's remarks contradicted the fact that the U.S. Supreme Court struck down all sodomy laws in 2003.[67]
- In 2016, Michigan updated its laws regarding bestiality but failed to eliminate the state's prohibition on same-sex relations, which is part of the same statute.[68]
- 11 states still have sodomy laws on their books.[69]

For more on the history of sodomy laws in a global context, see page 92 of the International chapter.

How has the U.S. government treated LGBTQ people seeking to visit or immigrate to the U.S.?

- Until 1990, when Congress amended U.S. immigration policy, the United States was the only country in the world with an explicit policy that excluded visitors and potential immigrants because of their sexual orientation.
- Explains Shannon Minter, legal director of the National Center for Lesbian Rights: "Although the word 'homosexual' has never appeared in U.S. immigration law, from 1952 to 1990 most U.S. courts interpreted the provision excluding persons 'afflicted with a psychopathic personality' to require the exclusion of any person identified as homosexual or who engaged in homosexual acts. Countless individuals have been excluded at the border, deported, or denied naturalization under this provision."[70]

What major Supreme Court decisions have addressed LGBTQ issues?

One, Inc. v. Olesen (1958)

One: The Homosexual Magazine was labeled as obscene by the U.S. Postal Service, which refused to deliver it. The publishers sued and lost; their appeal went to the Supreme Court, which reversed the ruling. This was the first U.S. Supreme Court ruling to deal affirmatively with homosexuality, and the first to address free speech rights with respect to LGBT issues.

Boutilier v. Immigration and Naturalization Service (1967)

The Supreme Court affirmed that the Immigration and Naturalization Service could legally exclude homosexuals from entering the United States.

Doe v. Commonwealth's Attorney (1976)

The Supreme Court voted 6–3 not to hear the appeal in this case, thereby upholding a Virginia court's ruling that there is no constitutional right to engage in private homosexual activity.

Enslin v. North Carolina (1976)

The Supreme Court upheld the conviction of a Jacksonville, North Carolina, man who had been sentenced to one year in prison for having oral sex with a consenting male partner in the privacy of his home.

Bowers v. Hardwick (1986)

The Supreme Court upheld a Georgia law by ruling that consenting adults do not have a constitutional right to engage in homosexual acts in private.

Romer v. Evans (1996)

In a 6–3 decision, the Supreme Court struck down Colorado's Amendment 2, which denied gay men, lesbians, and bisexuals protections against discrimination.

Boy Scouts of America v. Dale (2000)

The Supreme Court ruled that the Boy Scouts of America have a constitutional right to ban gay members and leaders because the organization's opposition to homosexuality is part of its "expressive message."

Lawrence v. Texas (2003)

The Supreme Court struck down a Texas sodomy law and overturned the 1986 *Bowers v. Hardwick* decision, declaring for the first time that lesbians and gay men have a fundamental right to engage in private sexual activity with another adult.

United States v. Windsor (2013)

The Supreme Court ruled that the 1996 Defense of Marriage Act (DOMA) violated the rights of gay men and lesbians and was unconstitutional.

Hollingsworth v. Perry (2013)

The Supreme Court ruled that same-sex marriage opponents in California did not have legal standing to appeal a lower court ruling that overturned the state's ban on same-sex marriage, known as Proposition 8.

Obergefell v. Hodges (2015)

The Supreme Court ruled that the fundamental right to marry is guaranteed to same-sex couples by both the Due Process Clause and the Equal Protection Clause of the 14th Amendment to the U.S. Constitution.[71]

Where in the U.S. were the first laws enacted to protect gay men and lesbians from discrimination?

- The first city to ban discrimination against gay men and lesbians was East Lansing, Michigan, in 1972.[72]
- The first county to prohibit job discrimination against gay men and lesbians was California's Santa Cruz County in 1975.[73]
- The first law protecting gay and lesbian rights in a

North American state or province was passed in 1977 by Quebec.[74]

- The first U.S. state to pass a civil rights law protecting gay men and lesbians was Wisconsin in 1982.[75]

What state and federal laws protect LGBT people from discrimination in housing?

- According to HRC, as of 2016 20 states—California, Colorado, Connecticut, Delaware, Hawaii, Illinois, Iowa, Maine, Maryland, Massachusetts, Minnesota, Nevada, New Jersey, New Mexico, New York, Oregon, Rhode Island, Utah, Vermont, and Washington—and the District of Columbia protect LGBT people from housing discrimination. Two states—Wisconsin and New Hampshire—protect LGB people.[76]
- Beyond this, the U.S. Department of Housing and Urban Development prohibits inquiries regarding the sexual orientation or gender identity of a prospective tenant or applicant for assisted housing in every state.[77]

What states protect LGBT people from discrimination in public accommodations?

- As of 2016, 19 states and the District of Columbia protect LGBT people from discrimination in public accommodations, while two protect LGB people. These are the same states that protect against housing discrimination, minus Utah, which permits discrimination. "Public accommodations" refers both to governmental entities and private businesses that provide services to the general public, including restaurants, movie theaters, retail establishments, and libraries.[78]

For statistics on nondiscrimination laws relating to employment, see pages 240 to 244 in the Workplace chapter.

> Ending the AIDS epidemic as a public health threat by 2030 is ambitious, but realistic, as the history of the past 15 years has shown . . .
>
> —*Ban Ki-moon, United Nations Secretary General, in* How AIDS Changed Everything, *2015*[1]

In the 1994 edition of *Gay & Lesbian Stats*, we included the Harvard AIDS Institute's projection that there would be 100 million HIV infections worldwide by the year 2000. In fact, there were roughly 34 million cases at the turn of the century. By 2016, approximately 37 million people worldwide were living with HIV, the virus that causes AIDS, and close to 35 million had died from AIDS-related causes, according to the World Health Organization. With the advent of effective antiretroviral therapy in the mid-1990s and the FDA's 2012 approval of Truvada—the first drug that reduces the risk of HIV infection—Secretary General Ban Ki-moon's hope of ending the AIDS epidemic by 2030 doesn't seem like a utopian dream. AIDS prevention and treatment have become the most highly funded response to a disease in the history of the world, thanks in large measure to innovative and highly effective activism waged by ACT UP, whose slogan—"Silence = Death"—sparked action and reform.[2] Much has changed since 1981, when the Reagan administration greeted the first cases of AIDS in the United States with silence, followed by ridicule and indifference.[3]

AIDS IN THE UNITED STATES

How many people are living with HIV in the United States?

- More than 1.2 million people in the United States are living with human immunodeficiency virus (HIV), which if left untreated can cause Acquired Immune Deficiency Syndrome (AIDS). More than

1 in 8 people with HIV—12.8 percent—are unaware of their infection.[4]

- 57 percent of those living with HIV in the United States are gay and bisexual men.[5]
- 65 percent of Americans living with HIV are untreated.[6]
- Gay and bisexual men represented an estimated 85.7 percent of new HIV diagnoses among men over 13 in the United States in 2014.[7]
- Of the gay and bisexual men diagnosed with HIV in 2014, 38 percent were African American.[8]

How have attitudes toward HIV changed?

- When asked about AIDS at a 1982 press conference, White House Press Secretary Larry Speakes responded: "What's AIDS?" He added: "I don't have it. Do you? There has been no personal experience here." Reporters at the briefing erupted in laughter.[9]
- President Ronald Reagan did not mention AIDS until 1985.[10] That same year, 51 percent of Americans wanted people with AIDS quarantined, while 15 percent favored tattoos.[11]
- Among Americans surveyed in 1987, 68 percent considered AIDS "the most urgent heath problem facing the U.S." In 2011, 7 percent viewed HIV/AIDS as the country's most pressing health concern. Topping the 2011 list were cancer (25 percent), obesity (20 percent), and the problem of the uninsured (15 percent).[12]
- 40 percent of African Americans who took part in a 2011 study were "very concerned" that they might become infected with HIV. The figure was 11 percent for white respondents.[13]
- 87 percent of the U.S. population surveyed in 2011 believed it was possible for people with AIDS to live a healthy, productive life.[14]
- 16 percent of participants in a 2011 survey said contracting HIV is punishment for declining moral standards, down from 47 percent in a 1987 survey. Nearly a third of respondents in the 2011 study believed it was

"a person's own fault" if he or she became infected with HIV.[15]

- The number of people who know someone with AIDS increased from 2 percent in 1993 to 41 percent in 2011. Among African Americans, 57 percent know someone with AIDS.[16]
- Only about half the respondents in the 2011 survey said they would feel "very comfortable" working with someone with HIV.[17]
- In a 2014 study of gay and bisexual men, 51 percent said that AIDS was "not too significant" or "not a significant issue" for them.[18]
- In the same study, gay and bisexual men of color were more likely than white men to say HIV/AIDS is a significant issue for them personally (64 percent versus 42 percent) and that they are personally concerned about becoming infected (53 percent versus 28 percent).[19]
- 30 percent of gay and bisexual participants in the same study who did not self-identify as HIV-positive said they had been tested for HIV within the last year.[20]

How have laws relating to HIV changed?

- In 1983, the Food and Drug Administration (FDA) banned gay and bisexual men who have sex with men from ever giving blood. The FDA revised this policy in 2015 by recommending that men who have sex with men remain celibate for 12 months before donating blood. In response, Kelsey Louie, the CEO of Gay Men's Health Crisis, said: "The United States government has to stop reacting to HIV like it is the early 1980s. It is time for the FDA to implement a policy that is truly based on science, not blanket bans on certain groups of people."[21]
- Beginning in 1987, the U.S. banned HIV-positive people from traveling or immigrating to the United States. Strengthened in 1993 by Congress, this policy led to separations within families and discouraged some from

learning their HIV status or seeking treatment. President Barack Obama lifted this restriction in October 2009, stating that it was "rooted in fear rather than fact."[22]

What is the incidence of HIV?

- Roughly 50,000 people become infected with HIV in the United States every year. This figure remains stable. Analysis by the Centers for Disease Control and Prevention (CDC) shows that new infections peaked in the mid-1980s at approximately 130,000 per year and reached a low of about 50,000 in the early 1990s.[23]
- According to CDC data, the U.S. states with the highest estimated number of new diagnoses of HIV infections in 2014 were:
    1. California—5,551 new diagnoses.
    2. Florida—5,347.
    3. Texas—4,833.
    4. New York—3,825.
    5. Georgia—2,253.[24]
- The U.S. metropolitan areas with the highest estimated percentage of the population diagnosed with HIV infections in 2014 were:
    1. Baton Rouge, LA
    2. Miami–Fort Lauderdale–West Palm Beach, FL
    3. New Orleans–Metairie, LA
    4. Jackson, MS
    5. Orlando–Kissimmee–Sanford, FL[25]
- An estimated 493,543 gay and bisexual men were living with diagnosed HIV infection in the United States at the end of 2013. Of these, more than 50 percent were African American or Hispanic/Latino.[26]
- African American men, women, and children represent approximately 13.2 percent of the U.S. population but accounted for an estimated 38 percent of new HIV infections in 2014. African American men, women, and children also accounted for 31 percent of people living with HIV in 2013.[27]

What trends have been identified concerning new diagnoses of HIV infection?

- In 2010, young gay and bisexual men aged 13 to 24 accounted for 72 percent of new HIV infections among all persons in this age-group, and for 30 percent of new infections among all gay and bisexual men.[28]
- Among young African American gay and bisexual men, the rate of HIV infection increased by 20 percent from 2008 to 2010.[29]
- San Francisco, ground zero for the AIDS epidemic, had 2,332 new cases of HIV at the epidemic's height in 1992—more than any other U.S. city. In 2014, there were 302 new HIV diagnoses in San Francisco.[30]
- Although only 28 percent of the U.S. population lives in the South—Alabama, Florida, Georgia, Louisiana, Mississippi, North Carolina, South Carolina, Tennessee, and Texas—these nine states account for 38 percent of HIV diagnoses in the United States.[31]
- 54.2 percent of people with HIV infection in the South are African American.[32]
- More than 2 million people are incarcerated in the United States. Incarcerated people are five times more likely to have HIV.[33]

What percentage of people living with HIV are women?

- 25 percent of people living with HIV in the United States are women. Only 45 percent of these women are getting the care they need.[34]
- In 2013, African Americans accounted for 63 percent of HIV infections among women.[35]
- One of the first cases of lesbian transmission of HIV in which the women had no history of sex with men or intravenous drug use occurred in the United States in 2012.[36]

How are transgender people affected by HIV?

- According to a 2009 NIH study:

- Nearly a third of transgender Americans are HIV-positive.
- 56 percent of African American trans women are HIV-positive.
- 16 percent of Latina trans women in the United States are HIV-positive.[37]

- Among the 3.3 million people in the U.S. who were tested for HIV in 2013, the highest percentage of new infections was among trans persons.[38]
- Although prevalence of HIV among trans men is relatively low—between 0 and 3 percent—a 2011 study found that transgender men who have sex with men are at "substantial risk" for acquiring HIV.[39]

What percentage of gay and bisexual male teens have been tested for HIV?

A 2015 study of young men between the ages of 14 and 18 who identify as gay or bisexual found:

- Only 1 in 5 had been tested for HIV.
- About one-third didn't believe they were at risk for HIV.
- About one-third cited stigma—including not wanting others to know they were being tested—to explain why they chose not to be screened for HIV.
- 57 percent didn't know of a place to get tested.[40]

How many states have laws that criminalize the transmission of HIV from person to person?

As of May 2016:

- 34 U.S. states and territories have criminal statutes that allow prosecutions for allegations of nondisclosure of, exposure to, and/or transmission of the HIV virus.
- Prosecutions have occurred in at least 39 states under HIV-specific criminal laws or general criminal laws.
- Most of these laws treat HIV exposure as a felony.
- People convicted under these laws are serving sentences as long as 30 years or more.
- 13 of the 34 states have laws against HIV-positive peo-

ple spitting on or biting someone, neither of which has ever been proven to transmit HIV.[41]

How many people with AIDS have died in the United States?

- Between 1981 and 2015, 658,507 people with AIDS died in the United States.
- Nearly half of those who have died of AIDS in the United States were gay or bisexual men.[42]

What are some notable cultural responses to AIDS?

- The first major film to deal with HIV and AIDS was *An Early Frost*, a made-for-TV movie that aired on NBC in 1985.[43]
- *The Normal Heart*, a largely autobiographical play by Larry Kramer that tells the story of the HIV crisis in New York City from 1981 through 1984, had a successful run at New York's Public Theater in 1985. It was made into a film and broadcast on HBO in 2014.[44]
- In November 1986, the *New Yorker* published Susan Sontag's short story "The Way We Live Now." Told through a series of conversational fragments, the story chronicles an unnamed man's struggle with AIDS and reactions among his circle of friends.[45]
- "That's What Friends Are For," *Billboard*'s number-one single of 1986, was sung by Dionne Warwick and other artists, including Stevie Wonder and Elton John. Released as a charity single, the song raised $3 million for the American Foundation for AIDS Research.[46]
- In 2003, HBO adapted Tony Kushner's Pulitzer Prize–winning two-part play *Angels in America: A Gay Fantasia on National Themes* into a miniseries starring Meryl Streep, Al Pacino, Emma Thompson, and Jeffrey Wright, who won a Tony Award in 1994 for his performance in the Broadway version. A complex and metaphorical meditation on homosexuality and AIDS in America, the play was adapted into an opera in 2004 with music by Hungarian composer Péter Eötvös.[47]

- The AIDS Memorial Quilt, first unveiled at the Second National March on Washington for Lesbian and Gay Rights on October 11, 1987, is composed of more than 48,000 panels—each a tribute to someone who has died of an AIDS-related illness. The largest piece of folk art in the world, the quilt covers 1.3 million square feet (or about 50 miles), weighs more than 54 tons, and has been viewed by more than 14 million people at thousands of displays worldwide. It was nominated for the Nobel Peace Prize in 1989.[48]

WORLD STATS: AN OVERVIEW OF AIDS AROUND THE GLOBE

- Worldwide, 36.7 million people were living with HIV at the end of 2015.[49]
- Globally, new HIV infections per year have decreased from 3.1 million in 2000 to roughly 2 million in 2014.[50]
- Every day about 5,753 people contract HIV—more than 240 per hour.[51]
- More than half the people with HIV worldwide are unaware of their infection.[52]
- Women represent approximately 51 percent of all adults living with HIV worldwide. HIV is the leading cause of death among women of reproductive age.[53]
- HIV is the leading cause of death in Africa. Roughly 70 percent of the world's new cases of HIV infection are found in sub-Saharan Africa.[54]
- As a result of homophobic laws, lack of sex education, and the absence of needle-exchange programs, the size of Russia's HIV-infected population has nearly doubled between 2010 (when it stood at 500,000) and 2015 (when it reached 930,000).[55]
- It is estimated that legalizing sex work would reduce female sex workers' risk of contracting HIV by up to 46 percent over the next decade.[56]

Worldwide, what is the impact of HIV on gay and bisexual men?

- The United Nations estimates the prevalence of HIV among men who have sex with men (MSM) to be between 1 and 57 percent, depending on the region in which they live.[57]
- As of 2014, gay and bisexual men worldwide were 19 times more likely to be living with HIV than the heterosexual adult population.[58]
- In Indonesia, new HIV infections have risen by 48 percent since 2005. It is estimated that 20 percent of gay and bisexual men in Jakarta and Bali are infected.[59]

Worldwide, what is the impact of HIV on trans women, and how are governments responding?

- An estimated 19 percent of trans women around the globe are living with HIV.[60]
- Trans women are 49 times more likely to have HIV than other adults of reproductive age.[61]
- As of 2014, 39 percent of countries reported that their AIDS prevention strategies included trans people.[62]

How many people worldwide have died from AIDS-related complications?

- 35 million people worldwide have died from AIDS. The disease is expected to become the largest global pandemic since the Black Death, which killed an estimated 40 million people between 1348 and 1351.[63]
- In 2015, tuberculosis was the leading cause of death among people with HIV worldwide.[64]
- Global deaths from AIDS peaked at around 2 million a year between 2003 and 2006. In 2015, 1.1 million people worldwide died of AIDS-related causes.[65]
- It is estimated that if Thabo Mbeki—who served as South Africa's president from 1999 to 2008—had not questioned the scientific consensus that HIV causes AIDS, 380,000 deaths could have been prevented and 180,000 new infections avoided.[66]

HIV / AIDS TREATMENT

What is antiretroviral therapy (ART) and how common is its use worldwide?

ART involves the use of medications that treat HIV. The drugs do not kill or cure the virus, but when taken in combination they can prevent its growth. When the virus is slowed down, so is HIV disease.

- The combination ART treatment known as the "AIDS cocktail" was introduced in 1995.
- In 2000, fewer than 1 percent of people living with HIV in low- and middle-income countries had access to ART.
- In 2011, UNAIDS set a goal of having 15 million people receive ART by 2015. At the end of 2015, 17 million people were on ART.[67]
- In 2015, 2 million people worldwide enrolled in ART, the largest yearly increase ever.[68]
- Of the roughly 37 million people worldwide who are estimated to have HIV, 20 million are not receiving ART.[69]
- In 2014, UNAIDS launched an ambitious worldwide program to end AIDS as we know it. The program has three primary goals:

    1. By 2030, 95 percent of people with AIDS will know their status;
    2. 95 percent of these people will receive sustained ART; and
    3. 95 percent of this population will have an undetectable HIV viral load.[70]

How effective and widespread is ART in the United States?

- In 1987 there was one FDA-approved drug to treat HIV in the United States. According to the National Institutes of Health, 39 drugs are now available to treat HIV.[71]
- In the United States in 2000, antiretroviral therapy required up to eight pills a day and cost roughly

$10,000 a year. In 2015, it can consist of one pill a day and cost $100 per year.[72]

- 39 percent of all HIV-infected Americans have seen an HIV doctor, while only 30 percent were taking medication consistently enough to be "virally suppressed," meaning they were not infectious. In San Francisco, 82 percent of residents with HIV were receiving care, while 72 percent were virally suppressed as of 2015.[73]
- In 2014, New York governor Andrew Cuomo proposed an ambitious plan to eliminate AIDS in the state by 2020. The proposal estimates that it would cost $375 million to get all HIV-infected New Yorkers on ART—and that successful implementation of the plan would result in Medicaid savings of between $6 and $8 billion.[74]
- A 2015 study published in the *New England Journal of Medicine* found that starting ART early in HIV-infected people reduced serious AIDS-defining illnesses by 72 percent and serious non-AIDS illnesses by 39 percent.[75]
- The first at-home HIV test in the United States was released in 2012. The U.K.'s first home test went on sale in April 2015.[76]

According to research reported by the CDC in 2014, the average life expectancy in the United States is:

- 32 years for a person with HIV diagnosed at age 20 and not taking current HIV medications.
- 71 years for a person with HIV diagnosed at age 20 taking current HIV medications.
- 79 years for a person without HIV.[77]

What is Truvada and how common is its use?

- Truvada, commonly referred to as PrEP, is a fixed-dose combination of two antiretroviral drugs that are used for the treatment of HIV. In conjunction with safer sex practices, Truvada is recommended for pre-exposure prophylaxis (PrEP) to reduce the risk of sexually acquired HIV infection.[78]

- The FDA approved Truvada for preventative use on July 16, 2012. The drug is recommended for uninfected people who are at high risk of contracting HIV through sex, including sex workers and people whose partners are HIV-positive or who engage in high-risk behaviors.[79]
- It is estimated that Truvada is between 90 and 99 percent effective in preventing HIV infection when taken as directed.[80]
- In a 2014 study, only 26 percent of gay men surveyed knew about Truvada and its potential to prevent HIV infection.[81]
- In 2015, the CDC issued a report recommending that 1 in 4 sexually active gay and bisexual men take Truvada. According to the CDC, only 21,000 people—less than 1 percent—who could benefit from Truvada were taking the drug in 2015.[82]
- While most public-health experts note that Truvada is intended to be used in addition to condoms—not instead of them—some have criticized it. Michael Weinstein, president of AIDS Healthcare Foundation, called Truvada "a party drug" and charged that its use would lead to irresponsible sexual practices.[83]
- According to the CDC, 34 percent of primary care physicians and nurses were not aware of Truvada as of 2015.[84]

> Bisexuality means I am free and I am as likely to want to love a woman as I am likely to want to love a man, and what about that? Isn't that what freedom implies?
>
> —*June Jordan, poet and activist*[1]

Although the term "bisexual" was first used in an 1892 translation of *Psychopathia Sexualis* by the German sexologist Richard von Krafft-Ebing, there is a "long history of research suggestive of the prevalence of bisexual practices in most human cultures," writes Steven Angelides in *A History of Bisexuality*.[2] In recent years, as the statistics presented below demonstrate, bisexual activists have achieved breakthroughs on a number of fronts, ranging from a 2013 White House roundtable on bisexual issues to the swearing in of America's first openly bisexual governor, Kate Brown of Oregon, in 2015. Record numbers of Americans are describing themselves as "other than 100% heterosexual," suggesting that the practice of bisexuality—if not actual identification as bisexual—is surging.

At the same time, violence against bisexual women and men persists at alarming rates. According to a national report published in 2013, "bisexual women experienced significantly higher lifetime prevalence of rape, physical violence, and/or stalking by an intimate partner when compared to lesbian and heterosexual women."[3] And while bisexual people comprise the largest segment within the LGBTQ community, they remain among the most invisible. Notes Ellyn Ruthstrom, former president of the Bisexual Resource Center: "The fear of being stereotyped manifests itself in a real way: bisexual people are six times more likely than gay men and lesbians to be closeted. This impacts the emotional well-being of many bisexual people and is a contributing factor to the community's higher rates of poor physical and mental health."[4]

IDENTITY AND BEHAVIOR

What percentage of adults identify as bisexual?

Of the more than 9 million LGB people in the United States, more than half identify as bisexual. According to the Williams Institute, the breakdown is as follows:

Figure 4.1: What Percentage of LGB Americans Are Bisexual?

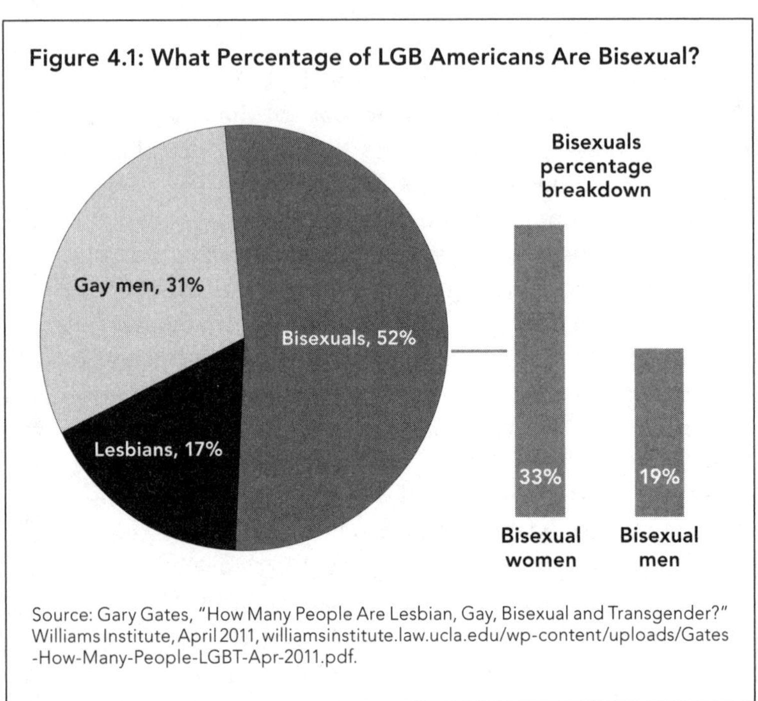

Source: Gary Gates, "How Many People Are Lesbian, Gay, Bisexual and Transgender?" Williams Institute, April 2011, williamsinstitute.law.ucla.edu/wp-content/uploads/Gates-How-Many-People-LGBT-Apr-2011.pdf.

In a large study of sexual activity and attraction conducted by the Centers for Disease Control and based on data gathered between 2011 and 2013 through in-person interviews with 9,000 18- to 44-year-olds in the United States:

- 5.5 percent of women identified as bisexual, up from 3.9 percent based on data collected between 2006 and 2010.
- 2 percent of men identified as bisexual, up from 1.2 percent based on data collected between 2006 and 2010.[5]

How many adults engage in bisexual activity?

Among the 9,000 participants in the CDC survey:

- 17.4 percent of women and 6.2 percent of men reported having sexual contact with members of their own sex.
- 11.2 percent of Hispanic women, 19.4 percent of African American women, and 19.6 percent of white women reported same-sex sexual contact.[6]

In a 2015 poll of the U.S. population by YouGov—which describes itself as "the world's largest opinion database"—16 percent of American adults placed themselves somewhere on the scale of bisexuality. (The margin of error was ±4.2 percent.) The findings varied considerably among age-groups:

- 31 percent of 18- to 29-year-olds were not completely heterosexual.
- 24 percent of 30- to 44-year-olds were not completely heterosexual.
- 8 percent of 45- to 64-year-olds were not completely heterosexual.
- 7 percent of those 65 and older were not completely heterosexual.
- 12 percent of self-identified heterosexuals—15 percent of women and 8 percent of men—reported having had some same-sex experiences.[7]

In a 2015 online poll of the British public, 49 percent of 18- to 24-year-olds surveyed by YouGov categorized themselves as something other than 100 percent heterosexual.[8]

A 2012 peer-reviewed study of 26,042 bisexual men recruited from an Internet site for men who have sex with men found that of the men who categorized themselves as bisexual daters:

- 83 percent had multiple sex partners.
- 94 percent had engaged in sexual activity with women in the past year.
- 99 percent had engaged in sexual activity with men in the past year.[9]

What percentage of LGBTQ youth identify as bisexual?

In 2012, Human Rights Campaign surveyed 10,000 LGBT American youth ages 13 to 17 and found:

- Almost 40 percent of youth surveyed identified as bisexual.
- 50 percent of the female respondents identified as bisexual, while 20 percent of the male respondents did.
- 25 percent of transgender youth identified as bisexual.
- Almost 29 percent of bisexual youth said they had been "frequently or often" harassed or called names at school.
- 44 percent of bisexual youth said they had an adult family member to whom they could turn for support.
- 56 percent of bisexual youth reported experimenting with alcohol and drugs, compared with 50 percent of lesbian and gay youth and 22 percent of straight youth.[10]

MYTHS, STEREOTYPES, AND BIPHOBIA

What are some common misperceptions about bisexuals?

At the 1999 BECAUSE conference in Minneapolis, William Burleson, the author of *Bi America: Myths, Truths and Struggles of an Invisible Community*, invited a workshop audience to create a list of the most "tiresome, irritating, angering, irksome stereotypes, myths, and other falsehoods heaped on bisexuals." The top responses:

1. Bisexuals are easy.
2. All bisexuals are swingers.
3. Bisexuals have the best of both worlds and are twice as likely to get a date.
4. Bisexuals are unable to commit to either gender.
5. Bisexual women are all wives just trying to please their husbands, and bisexual men are all married guys cheating on their wives.
6. Bisexuality is just a phase on the way to being lesbian or gay.[11]

The decision by British Olympic diver Tom Daley to come out as bisexual at the end of 2013 sparked a controversy as to whether he was "bridging" to being gay. In response, the *New York Times* published an article on the "fraught conversation within the L.G.B.T. community, having to do with its third letter." The article describes "the knowing disdain that many gay men show toward their bisexual counterparts"; mentions one of the sexual arousal studies cited later in this chapter (see page 67); and features a discussion of biphobia that includes these noted bisexuals:

- Singer Katy Perry
- Actress Maria Bello
- Actor Alan Cumming
- Actress Cynthia Nixon
- Writer Chirlane McCray, the wife of New York City mayor Bill de Blasio[12]

The controversial pop star Miley Cyrus, who as of June 2016 had the 20th-most-popular Instagram account with 45,996,751 followers, confirmed in an *Elle UK* interview that she identifies as "pansexual."[13] Pansexuals are attracted to others regardless of their gender identity or biological sex; the term describes those who are capable of falling in love with all genders, including those who identify as transgender, androgynous, and gender-fluid.

OPENNESS AND VISIBILITY

How open are bisexual Americans about their identity?

In a 2013 Pew Research Survey of 1,200 LGBT people:

- 28 percent of those who identified as bisexual said they were open about it.
- In contrast, 77 percent of gay men and 71 percent of lesbians were open about their identity.[14]

According to a 2015 HRC report on bisexual visibility in the workplace:

- 59 percent of bisexuals said they would report their sexual identity in an anonymous, confidential human resources survey.
- 43 percent of LGBT workers reported hearing jokes about bisexuals.
- Bisexuals are less likely to have someone at work acknowledge their orientation in a positive way. Only 7 percent say this happens frequently, compared to 27 percent of gay men and 31 percent of lesbians.[15]

In 2013, using in-depth interviews and self-administered questionnaires, a study of 150 Latino bisexual men aged 18 to 60 found that although all engaged in sexual behavior with men as well as women:

- Men aged 26 to 60 were characterized "by their unwillingness to label their sexual identity."
- Men in the 18–25 age-group "overwhelmingly identified as bisexual."[16]

What are some bisexual firsts in American politics and culture?

- Kyrsten Sinema became the first openly bisexual member of Congress when she was sworn in on January 3, 2013, as the representative from Arizona's Ninth Congressional District.[17]
- On January 20, 2015, President Barack Obama became the first U.S. president to use the word "bisexual" in a State of the Union address.[18]
- On February 18, 2015, Kate Brown became the first openly bisexual governor in American history. Brown was sworn in as Oregon's governor following the resignation of her predecessor.[19]
- The first bisexual lead character on a TV series was Clarke Griffin (played by Eliza Taylor) on the science fiction show *The 100*, which premiered in 2014 on the CW network.[20]
- In 2002, Lena Kundera became the first recurring bisexual character on a daytime soap opera, *All My Children*.[21]

- The character C.J. Lamb on *L.A. Law* (which aired from 1986 to 1994) became the first recurring bisexual character on prime-time television in 1990. She was also involved in the first kiss between two women shown on prime-time TV.[22]
- The first film with "arguably bisexual characters" is *The Florida Enchantment*, a silent film from 1914 starring, directed by, and produced by Sidney Drew.[23]
- The first bisexual character in a modern novel was Fanny Hill in British author John Cleland's novel *Fanny Hill*, published in 1748.[24]
- The first novel with black male bisexuality as its primary theme was E. Lynn Harris's *Invisible Life*, published in 1991.[25]

What organizations have worked or are working to advocate for bisexual rights and visibility?

- The National Bisexual Liberation Group, the first bisexual-specific group, was founded in New York City by psychologist Don Fass in 1972.[26]
- In 1972, at a workshop organized by activist Stephen Donaldson at the annual Friends (Quaker) General Conference, some 130 Quakers drafted the Ithaca Statement on Bisexuality, which is thought to be the first public declaration of a bisexual movement. This groundbreaking statement was later published in *The Advocate*.[27]
- Founded in 1983, the Boston Bisexual Women's Network is the oldest still-existing bisexual women's advocacy group in the United States.[28]
- The Bisexual Resource Center, founded in 1985 and based in Boston, is America's oldest still-existing bisexual advocacy group for both men and women.[29]
- The first national bisexuality conference in the United States took place in 1990 in San Francisco and marked the inception of America's oldest bisexual network, BiNet.[30]
- The first national march to include bisexuals in its

name was the March on Washington for Lesbian, Gay, and Bi Equal Rights and Liberation, which took place in Washington, D.C., on April 25, 1993. According to Brett Genny Beemyn in the *glbtq Encyclopedia*, the March's steering committee voted to add "bi" instead of "bisexual" to the event name, "fearing that the word 'bisexual' would overly sexualize the event." Attempts to add the word "transgender" to the march title failed, although the rights of transgender people were included in the list of demands.[31]

- The American Institute of Bisexuality (AIB) was founded in 1998 by psychiatrist Fritz Klein and has an endowment of nearly $17 million.[32] AIB's mission is to educate the public on bisexuality and the concerns of bi people, fund research on bisexuality, and organize conferences and other activities that increase understanding about bisexuality.[33]
- Three bisexual advocates—Wendy Curry, Michael Page, and Gigi Raven Wilbur—launched Celebrate Bisexuality Day in 1999 as an annual event that takes place on September 23 as a way to combat bisexual invisibility.[34]
    - On Celebrate Bisexuality Day 2013, a roundtable with leaders of the bisexual community took place for the first time at the White House.[35]

FAMOUS BISEXUALS, PAST AND PRESENT

In 2016, *SheWired* published a list of "historical bisexual women artists you should know." The top five artists were:

1. Violette Leduc, acclaimed French author (April 7, 1907–May 28, 1972).
2. Tamara de Lempicka, Polish Art Deco painter (May 16, 1898–March 18, 1980).
3. Dolores del Río, film star (August 3, 1904–April 11, 1983).
4. Colette, French novelist, mime, actress, and journalist (January 28, 1873–August 3, 1954).
5. Dusty Springfield, British pop and soul singer (April 16, 1939–March 2, 1999).[36]

In 2010, *Flavorwire* published a list of "Famous Male Bisexuals Who Aren't David Bowie." The list included:

- Nicholas Ray, mid-century filmmaker responsible for such masterpieces as *Rebel Without a Cause* and *In a Lonely Place.*
- Malcolm X, civil rights activist. (Malcolm X's bisexuality was discussed in *Malcolm X: A Life of Reinvention*, a 2011 biography by the late Columbia University professor Manning Marable.[37])
- Michael Chabon, author whose books include *The Mysteries of Pittsburgh* and *The Amazing Adventures of Kavalier & Clay*, which won a Pulitzer Prize.
- Billie Joe Armstrong, Green Day front man.
- Leonard Bernstein, composer, conductor, and pianist.
- Cary Grant, iconic leading man in dozens of feature films, including *The Philadelphia Story* and *North by Northwest.*[38]

RESEARCH AND FUNDING

What trends have been identified regarding researchers' approaches to bisexuality?

A 2012 review of 348 articles on bisexual health listed in PubMed, a free database that includes 25 million citations of biomedical literature, found that:

- 16.6 percent of the articles framed bisexuality as a legitimate identity.
- Fewer than 20 percent of the articles analyzed data for bisexuals separately from data for homosexuals.
- More than 90 percent of the medical research on bisexuality was atheoretical, meaning it made no attempt to put forward a theory regarding the causes of bisexuality.[39]

What has research shown about arousal patterns related to bisexuality?

- A 2015 British study that tested sexual responses among 345 women found that 74 percent of the women who self-identified as straight responded sexually to both men and women.[40]

- In a 2015 study that compared 50 self-identified bisexual men and 34 self-identified bisexual women to 52 self-identified gay men and 47 self-identified lesbians, the authors looked at how participants viewed sexually provocative pictures depicting people of both sexes. The researchers found that:
  - Bisexuals looked at the opposite-sex photos longer than gay men and lesbians did.
  - Bisexuals also rated pictures of the opposite sex as sexually more appealing than gay men and lesbians did.[41]
- A 2011 study of arousal patterns among 35 bisexual men, 31 gay men, and 35 straight men using three-minute videos (two neutral, two with a pair of women having sex, and two with a pair of men having sex) found that the bisexual men exhibited both subjective and genital arousal to both genders. The study also showed that some men demonstrated more arousal toward one gender and that this preference can change over time.[42]

How much funding has been allocated to research on bisexuality?

Although bisexuals represent more than 50 percent of the LGBTQ population, Funders for LGBTQ Issues reports that of total funding awarded by foundations for research on the LGBTQ community in the United States, the percentage of grants made for bi-specific studies was:

- 2014: Under 1 percent ($292,955).
- 2013: Under 1 percent ($474,650).
- 2012: Under 1 percent ($452,251).
- 2011: Under 1 percent (1 grant for $5,000).
- 2010: 0 percent.
- 2009: 0 percent.[43]

HEALTH CONCERNS

What are some physical and mental health issues facing bisexuals?

In a 2015 study of 2,500 LGB people that examined stress and anxiety levels among bisexual men, bisexual women, lesbians, and gay men:

- Bisexual women reported the highest levels of stress, depression, and anxiety.
- Bisexual men reported higher levels of anxiety than lesbians and gay men.
- Bisexuals were less comfortable discussing their sexual identity with health care providers.[44]

A 2014 review of the literature pertaining to suicide among bisexuals found that bisexuals had an increased risk of suicide attempts compared to their homosexual and heterosexual peers. Bisexuals also reported higher rates of mental illness and substance abuse.[45]

VIOLENCE AND POVERTY

How many members of the bisexual community have experienced rape or other forms of physical violence?

As of 2010, based on information from the Centers for Disease Control (CDC):

- 46 percent of bisexual women have experienced rape. The figures are 13 percent for lesbians and 17 percent for straight women, respectively.
- 61 percent of bisexual women and 37.3 percent of bisexual men have experienced rape, physical violence, and/or stalking by an intimate partner. The figures are 43 percent for lesbians and 26 percent for gay men, respectively.
- 47 percent of bisexual men report experiencing sexual violence other than rape in their lifetime.[46]

What percentage of bisexuals live in poverty?

U.S. government information from 2006 to 2010 revealed that bisexuals face a high rate of poverty:

Figure 4.2: Percent of Poor Bisexual, Lesbian, Gay, and Heterosexual Men and Women

% of people at or below 100% of the federal poverty level
(From 2006–2010 National Survey of Family Growth)

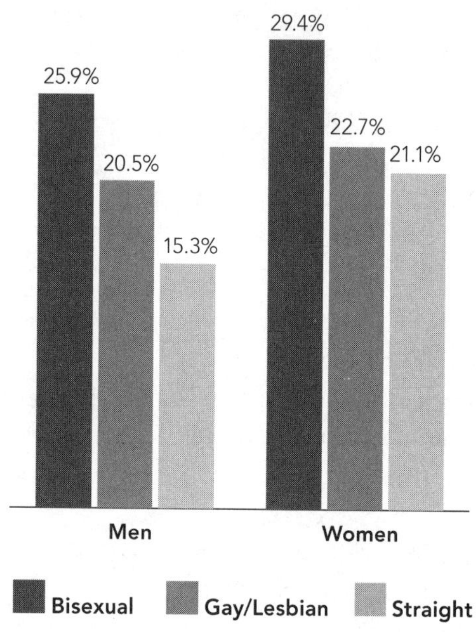

Source: M.V. Lee Badgett, Laura E. Curso, and Alyssa Schneebaum, "New Patterns of Poverty in the Lesbian, Gay, and Bisexual Community," Williams Institute, June 2013, williamsinstitute.law.ucla.edu/wp-content/uploads/LGB-Poverty-Update-Jun-2013.pdf.

PUTTING THE *B* IN LGBTQ

How effectively do national LGBTQ organizations address bisexual issues?

To determine the extent to which national LGBTQ groups have worked proactively to "embrace, support, and develop the bisexual component within their own organizations' inner structure," author and activist Ron Suresha sent an eight-question survey to the nation's leading LGBTQ organizations in 2013. Based on the results of this survey, he then issued the following "report card":

- National Gay and Lesbian Task Force (the Task Force*): A–
- Point Foundation: B+
- Gay and Lesbian Victory Fund: B
- Marriage Equality USA: B–
- Gay and Lesbian Medical Association (GLMA): B–
- Log Cabin Republicans: D+

Suresha pointed out: "Given the overwhelming evidence in the past few years showing that bisexual persons exist in greater numbers than the combined gay male, lesbian and transgender populations, we must ask whether some of the national queer organizations that send out donation requests demanding that we 'demand equality for everyone' are themselves paying attention to the particular needs of bisexual folks, not merely as lip service, not just as an afterthought, but in any sort of tangible way."[47]

* In 2014, the Task Force changed its name to the National LGBTQ Task Force and issued a press release stating that "the new, more inclusive name adds bisexual, transgender and queer to lesbian and gay in the form of LGBTQ."

> While L, G, B, and T are usually tied together as an acronym that suggests homogeneity, each letter represents a wide range of people of different races, ethnicities, ages, socioeconomic status, and identities. What binds them together . . . with respect to health care [are] a long history of discrimination and lack of awareness of health needs by health professionals. As a result, LGBT people face a common set of challenges in accessing culturally competent health services and achieving the highest possible level of health.
>
> —*Kevin L. Ard, MD, and Harvey J. Makadon, MD, in* Improving the Health Care of Lesbian, Gay, Bisexual and Transgender People: Understanding and Eliminating Health Disparities, *2012*[1]

For decades, LGBTQ people were considered sick and in need of a cure. When the American Psychiatric Association (APA) published the first edition of its *Diagnostic and Statistical Manual of Mental Disorders (DSM)* in 1952, homosexuality was classified as a "sociopathic personality disturbance," meaning that all gay men and lesbians—no matter how well-adjusted—were considered mentally ill.[2] In 1973, following intense protests and an internal review process, the APA's board voted to remove homosexuality from the organization's manual of mental disorders. The following year, the APA held a referendum in which its entire membership was invited to vote on the board's decision. While 37 percent of the 10,091 referendum participants voted to reclassify homosexuality as a disease, they were outnumbered by the 58 percent of APA voters who supported the deletion of homosexuality from the *DSM*.[3]

Now that science has come to the consensus that being

gay, lesbian, bisexual, transgender, and heterosexual are all natural variations of human experience,[4] advocates are seeking to reduce the inequities that continue to affect the physical and psychological health of LGBTQ people. For older LGBTQ Americans, disparities related to health care—and to an array of other issues related to aging, including housing and economic security—are especially striking. At present, between 1 and 3 million LGB Americans are 65 or older; by 2030, between 2 and 6 million LGB Americans will be part of this demographic.[5] A 2015 report by Services & Advocacy for GLBT Elders (SAGE) provides one example of the challenges that face LGBT elders: When inquiring about housing in a senior living facility, 48 percent of same-sex couples experienced "profound discrimination."[6] "No LGBT older adult should need to reside in a home that feels unsafe or deal with a provider who unfairly denies them housing," writes Robert Espinoza, author of the SAGE report, adding that more research and data are needed on the challenges that face LGBT people as they age—especially LGBT elders of color and transgender elders.[7]

MEDICINE AND HEALTH CARE

How has the medical establishment's view of LGBTQ people evolved?

- In 1981, the American Medical Association (AMA) issued a report that encouraged the development of programs "to acquaint [homosexuals] with . . . sex-preference reversal in selected cases."[8]
- In 1993, the AMA expanded its nondiscrimination policy to include sexual orientation, thereby banning discrimination against LGB doctors.[9]
- In 1994, the organization released a policy statement that encouraged "the physician's nonjudgmental recognition of sexual orientation and behavior" and stated that aversion therapy—intended to make patients give up specific behaviors by causing them to associate these behaviors with an unpleasant effect—"is no longer recommended."[10]

- In 2013, the American Psychiatric Association appointed an openly gay man, Dr. Saul Levin, as its CEO and medical director.[11]
- In 2013, the World Medical Association issued a statement declaring that "homosexuality does not represent a disease, but rather a natural variation within the range of human sexuality. The WMA condemns all forms of stigmatisation, criminalisation and discrimination of people based on their sexual orientation." The statement went on to condemn "so-called 'conversion' or 'reparative' methods. These constitute violations of human rights and are unjustifiable practices . . ."[12]
- In 2016, the District of Columbia became the first jurisdiction in America to require LGBTQ cultural-competency training for health care providers. The measure requires all licensed medical professionals in the city to take two credits of cultural-competency training related to LGBTQ patients.[13] "During the hearing on this bill, we heard truly heartbreaking stories from LGBTQ residents about mistreatment they experienced at the hands of medical providers," said council member David Grosso, who initiated the bill.[14]

How frequently do LGBTQ people disclose their sexual orientation to health care providers?

In a 2015 peer-reviewed study of 632 LGBT Floridians in the Tampa Bay region:

- 67 percent of respondents always or often reported their sexual orientation/identity to health care providers.
- 16.4 percent always, often, or sometimes feared a negative reaction from a health care provider.
- 12 percent experienced a negative reaction from a health care provider.
- 88 percent had health insurance.[15]

A 2013 study of 396 LGB New York City residents found that the following percentage of respondents did not report their sexual orientation to their health care providers:

- 39.3 percent of bisexual men.
- 32.6 percent of bisexual women.
- 12.9 percent of lesbians.
- 10 percent of gay men.[16]

What forms of discrimination do LGBTQ Americans experience in health care?

In 2009, Lambda Legal conducted a landmark study focusing on discrimination against LGBT people and people living with HIV. Although the sample of 4,016 LGBT Americans was not random, researchers believe that the study provides significant data because it represents a diverse cross section of the LGBT community with respect to geography, sexual orientation, gender identity, HIV status, race, age, and ethnicity. Compared to the LGBT population as a whole, participants in this study had higher household incomes, better health insurance coverage, and a higher proportion of advanced degrees. Because of the improved health care access associated with these factors, the researchers cautioned that the report most likely "understates the barriers to health care experienced by all LGBT people and those living with HIV." The study found that:

- 50 percent of LGB patients, 63 percent of respondents with HIV, and 70 percent of transgender patients experienced some type of discrimination in health care.
- 8 percent of LGB patients, 19 percent of respondents with HIV, and 27 percent of transgender and gender-nonconforming patients reported being denied care altogether.
- Just over 10 percent of LGB patients reported that health care professionals (HCP) used harsh language toward them.
- 11 percent of LGB patients reported that HCP refused to touch them or used excessive caution; 12 percent reported being blamed for their health status.

- Almost 36 percent of HIV-positive respondents had HCP refuse to touch them or use excessive caution, and 26 percent were blamed for their health status.
- Nearly 21 percent of transgender and gender-nonconforming patients reported being subjected to harsh or abusive language, and almost 8 percent reported physically rough or abusive treatment from HCP. Over 20 percent reported being blamed for their own health conditions.[17]

What sort of obstacles do transgender people encounter when seeking medical care?

Of the 6,456 respondents who took part in the 2011 National Transgender Discrimination Survey:

- 50 percent had to teach their physician how to care for them.
- 28 percent experienced verbal harassment in a medical setting.
- 19 percent had been refused medical care.
- 2 percent had been physically assaulted in a physician's office.[18]

How many health care facilities provide equitable treatment to LGBTQ patients?

Since 2007, the Human Rights Campaign Foundation has released an annual report, the Healthcare Equality Index (HEI), that "evaluates healthcare facilities' policies and practices related to the equity and inclusion of their LGBT patients, visitors and employees." For the 2016 HEI, 568 health care facilities actively participated, compared to 122 in 2012, and the total number of facilities evaluated was 2,060.

- 496 facilities received the highest ranking in 2016, indicating that they met the following four criteria:
    - An LGBT-inclusive patient nondiscrimination policy.
    - An LGBT-inclusive visitation policy.
    - An LGBT-inclusive employment nondiscrimination policy.
    - Staff training in LGBT-patient-centered care.[19]

CONVERSION THERAPY

What is conversion therapy and how does it affect those who undergo it?

Also known as "reparative therapy," conversion therapy claims to be able to change a person's sexual orientation or gender identity or expression. A 2013 survey of 400 self-selected men and women who had undergone conversion therapy found that:

- Nine in ten respondents said the experience harmed them.
- More than three-quarters of respondents terminated the therapy because it did not make them straight.
- Twenty percent said they quit because they had a nervous breakdown.[20]

What organizations have issued warnings about the dangers of conversion therapy?

The following organizations have all stated publicly that homosexuality is not a mental disorder and thus not something that needs to or can be "cured": the American Academy of Pediatrics, the American Counseling Association, the American Psychiatric Association, the American Psychological Association, the American School Counselor Association, the National Association of School Psychologists, the National Association of Social Workers, and the World Medical Association.[21]

How have leaders of conversion therapy organizations responded to critics?

- In 2013, Alan Chambers, president of Exodus International, America's largest ex-gay Christian ministry, apologized to the LGBT community and shuttered his organization. He was quoted as saying: "99.9 percent of people I met through Exodus' ministries had not experienced a change in orientation."[22]
- The following year, nine former leaders of the ex-gay movement denounced conversion therapy in an open letter and advocated a ban of the practice. "We now stand united in our conviction that conversion therapy is

not 'therapy,' but is instead both ineffective and harmful," they stated.[23]

- Despite these statements, some conservative religious organizations and therapists continue to offer conversion therapy.[24] 76 percent of LGBTQ Americans live in states with no laws banning conversion therapy for minors.[25]

What steps have been taken to ban conversion therapy?

- California, Illinois, New Jersey, Oregon, Vermont, and the District of Columbia have passed laws to prevent licensed mental health providers from offering conversion therapy to minors; these laws do not apply to adults. More than 20 states have introduced similar legislation.[26]
- In 2016, New York governor Andrew Cuomo announced regulations banning insurers from covering conversion therapy for minors.[27]
- In 2016, Senators Cory Booker and Patty Murray, of New Jersey and Washington State, respectively, introduced the Therapeutic Fraud Prevention Act, which would classify all efforts to change the sexual orientation or gender identity of a minor or adult as an "unfair or deceptive act or practice." If this measure becomes law, the Federal Trade Commission would be responsible for enforcing a nationwide ban on conversion therapy.[28]

HEALTH ISSUES

How does the health of LGBTQ Americans compare to that of straight Americans?

In 2013, for the first time in its history, the CDC's National Health Survey included a question on sexual orientation. The survey had a large sample size of 33,557 adults between the ages of 18 and 64 and included face-to-face interviews as well as follow-up telephone queries. Key comparisons between LGBTQ and straight Americans are shown in Figure 5.1.

Figure 5.1: Health Statistics for Gay, Lesbian, and Straight Americans: A Comparison

Current cigarette smoker

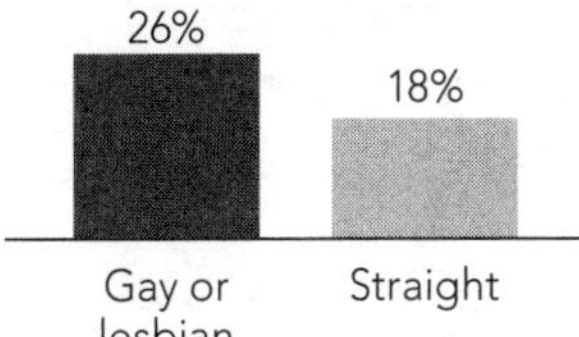

Five or more alcoholic drinks in 1 day at least once in past year

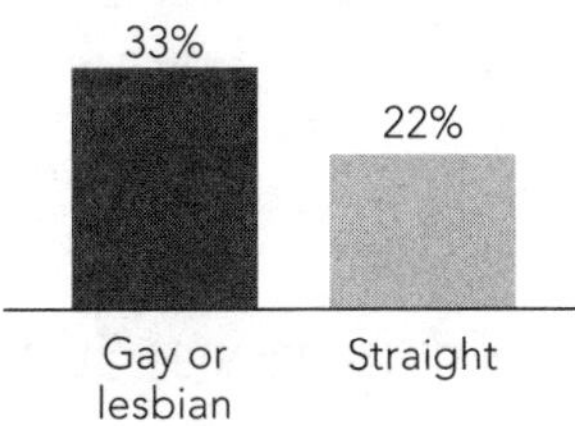

Met federal guidelines for aerobic physical activity

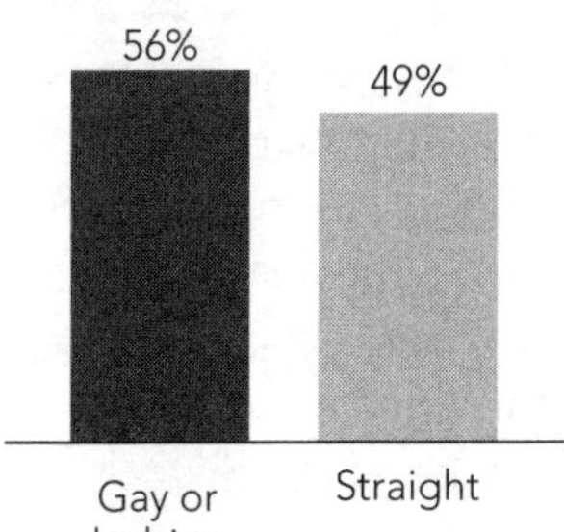

Ever been tested for HIV

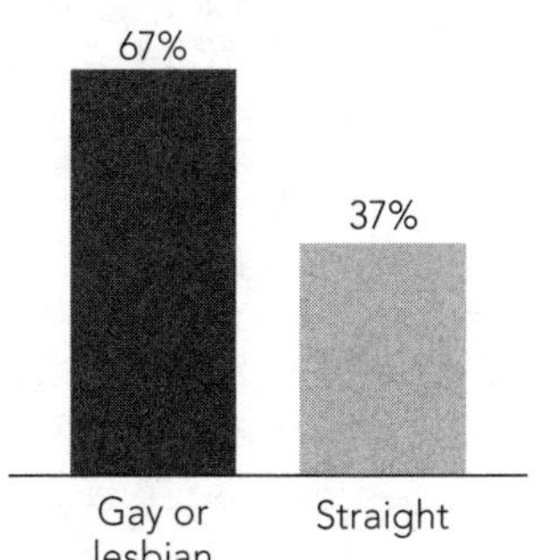

Received influenza vaccine during the past year

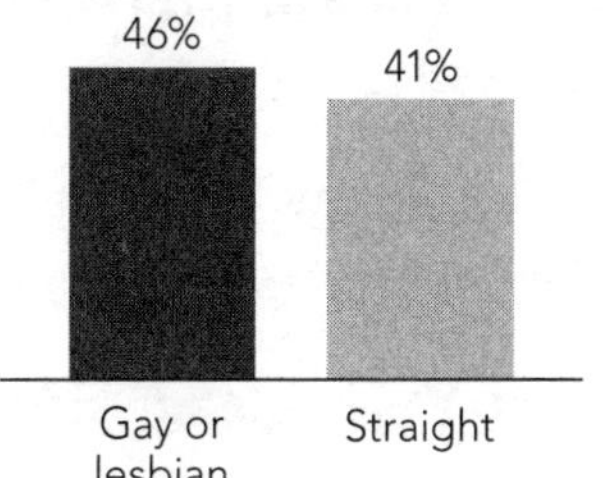

Source: CDC, "National Health Statistics Report," July 15, 2014, www.cdc.gov/nchs/data/nhsr/nhsr077.pdf.

In a 2012 study that looked at 18 years of data (spanning 1993 to 2010) from the CDC's U.S. Behavioral Risk Factor Surveillance System:

- 28.7 percent of men in same-sex couples reported being in excellent health.
- The figures for men in married heterosexual couples and in unmarried heterosexual couples were 23.2 percent and 20.4 percent, respectively.[29]

According to Community Marketing's 2012 LGBT Community Survey:

- 69 percent of the LGBT community uses vitamins, compared to the national average of 54 percent.
- 38 percent of the LGBT community has a gym membership, compared to the national average of 24 percent.
- 9 percent of the LGBT community takes yoga classes outside a gym, compared to the national average of 7 percent.[30]

What have researchers learned about alcohol use among LGBTQ Americans?

In a 2012 review of the literature on gay men and drinking, the researcher cited conflicting results in the available studies:

- In two studies from 2008, one showed alarmingly high rates of binge drinking among young men who have sex with men, while the other study found that "gay men increased their alcohol use at greater rates than heterosexual men during their initial transition to the college and university setting." The first study was a sampling of 526 men between the ages of 18 and 24 in Los Angeles, while the sample for the second study comprised 64 gay or bisexual men.
- Another study from 2005 found that drinking patterns among gay men did not differ from those of straight men, but the population it studied was small: 60 men who have sex with men.

- In one of the most comprehensive examinations of the relationship between alcohol use and internalized homophobia and heterosexism, an analysis of studies conducted between 1988 and 2008 found:
  - Four studies showed a statistically significant relationship between internalized homophobia and alcohol and/or substance abuse.
  - Seven studies indicated partial support for this relationship.
  - Five studies failed to show support for this relationship.[31]

Do LGBTQ people smoke more than straight people?

- The National LGBT Tobacco Control Network, which is affiliated with the Fenway Health Institute of Boston, reports that members of the LGBT community are 50 percent to 200 percent more likely to be addicted to smoking than non-LGBT Americans.
- The American Cancer Society estimates that more than 30,000 LGBT people die each year of tobacco-related diseases.[32]

How many GBQ men experience antifat bias?

In a 2016 study of 215 GBQ men ages 18 to 78, more than 33 percent had experienced antifat bias—even though many of them were not overweight using common body-mass index guidelines.[33]

How many LBTQ women have been vaccinated against HPV?

A 2015 review of data on 3,253 women aged 15 to 25 from the 2006–2010 National Survey of Family Growth found:

- 84.4 percent of women and girls who took part in the survey had heard of the human papillomavirus (HPV) vaccine, which protects against certain types of HPV—the virus responsible for nearly all cases of cervical cancer.
- 8.5 percent of the lesbians, 28.4 percent of the straight

women and girls, and 33.2 percent of the bisexual women and girls had started the vaccine process.[34]

How do health outcomes differ for LGBTQ people in rural versus urban settings?

In a 2014 study of 770 LGBT Nebraskans that compared health outcomes for rural versus urban residents:

- Rural and urban participants were equal in their perceived general health.
- 29.3 percent of the rural sample smoked, compared to 25.1 percent of the urban sample.
- 72 percent of the rural sample had health insurance, compared to 83.8 percent of the urban sample.
- The researchers concluded: "Results of this study suggest that regional culture may be more salient to health for lesbian, gay, bisexual, and transgender persons living in the Midwest than rural or urban residence."[35]

How do health outcomes differ for transgender Americans in rural versus nonrural settings?

In a 2014 study of transgender Americans—including 214 rural transwomen,* 478 nonrural transwomen, 130 rural transmen, and 393 nonrural transmen—a comparison of rural and nonrural health outcomes revealed:

- 6 percent of the rural and 7 percent of the nonrural transwomen reported heavy alcohol use.
- 25 percent of the rural and 27 percent of the nonrural transwomen reported a previous suicide attempt.
- 38 percent of the rural and 41 percent of nonrural transmen reported a previous suicide attempt. There were "significant differences in mental health between rural and nonrural transmen," with rural transmen reporting lower self-esteem and higher levels of anxiety than their nonrural counterparts.

---

* This section uses terminology that appears in the study, including "transmen" and "transwomen."

- 7 percent of the rural and 12 percent of the nonrural transmen reported heavy alcohol use.
- There was little difference between rural and nonrural incidences of sexual risk behavior among both transwomen and transmen.[36]

INTERSEX

What steps are intersex activists taking to assert their rights?

"Intersex" is an umbrella term used to describe a wide variety of body variations of gender. Intersex people are born with sex characteristics including genitals, gonads, and chromosome patterns that do not fit typical binary notions of male or female bodies.

- Free & Equal, a United Nations campaign for LGBT equality, estimates the number of intersex people at between 0.05 percent and 1.7 percent of the world population.[37]
- According to the Intersex Society of North America, an advocacy group that works to "end shame, secrecy, and unwanted genital surgeries," there is virtually no evidence that growing up intersex without corrective surgery causes any psychological damage.[38]
- On February 1, 2013, in its report on torture, the Special Rapporteur to the U.N. Human Rights Council released a statement condemning nonconsensual treatment of intersexuality.[39]
- In 2011, Christiane Völling, a citizen of Germany, became the first intersex person to sue successfully for damages in a case brought for nonconsensual surgical intervention. A surgeon was ordered to pay 100,000 euros to compensate Völling for removing her ovaries without her consent in 1977, when she was 18.[40]
- In 2013, Australia enacted the first law to add intersex status to existing antidiscrimination statutes.[41]
- In 2015, Malta became the first country to outlaw nonconsensual surgery to modify sex anatomy.[42]
- Later in 2015, Chile's government released

recommendations urging doctors to stop performing surgical procedures to "normalize" intersex children.[43]

MEDICAL LITERATURE

How are LGBTQ Americans portrayed in medical literature?

An analysis of 21,728 articles on LGBT Americans that were published in the medical literature between 1950 and 2007 found:

- 25.2 percent of the articles dealt with HIV, AIDS, or AIDS-related opportunistic infections.
- 9.7 percent addressed adolescent health.
- 6.6 percent were about sexually transmitted infections other than HIV, AIDS, and opportunistic infections.
- 6.4 percent covered tobacco, alcohol, and substance use, abuse, or addiction.
- 5.4 percent focused on race and ethnicity.
- 5.3 percent characterized homosexuality as a deviant, immoral behavior or psychiatric illness.
- 4.6 percent focused on diagnosing homosexuality or otherwise linking it to biological factors, genetics, or size or proportions of the human body.
- 4.6 percent addressed "risk behaviors."
- 3.3 percent examined health care provider interactions with LGBT patients.
- 3.2 percent looked at the legal rights and privileges of patients.[44]

A 2014 review of research projects funded by the National Institutes of Health (NIH) between 1998 and 2011 found that NIH funded 628 studies related to LGBT health. Excluding studies on HIV/AIDS and sexual health, 113 studies—representing 0.1 percent of all NIH studies conducted during this period—dealt with topics concerning LGBT health. Among the 628 LGBT-related projects funded by NIH:

- 86.1 percent studied sexual-minority men.
- 13.5 percent studied sexual-minority women.

- 6.8 percent studied transgender populations.
- 79.1 percent focused on HIV/AIDS.
- 30.9 percent addressed illicit drug use; 23.2 percent focused on mental health; and 12.9 percent examined alcohol use.
- The study's authors concluded: "The lack of NIH-funded research about LGBT health contributes to the perpetuation of health inequities."[45]

An analysis of the Psychiatric Residency-in-Training Exam, a two-day test given to residents in psychiatry training programs, showed that out of a total of 1,500 questions used between 2009 and 2013, three question or answer choices addressed LGBT content.[46]

HEALTH INSURANCE

What percentage of LGBTQ Americans have health insurance?

According to the Center for American Progress:

- In 2013, 66 percent of LGBT adults with incomes of $44,000 or below had health insurance.
- After the Affordable Care Act (ACA) went into effect in 2014, 74 percent of LGBT adults in this income bracket had health insurance.[47]

In 2014, Gallup reported that:

- LGBT Americans are more likely to be uninsured than their heterosexual peers.[48]
- The percentage of LGBT Americans without insurance dropped due to the ACA, from 22 percent at the end of 2013 to 17.6 percent during the second quarter of 2014.[49]
- 25 percent of LGBT Americans (21 percent of men and 29 percent of women) reported not having enough money for health care needs at least once in the past year, compared to 17 percent of their straight peers (15 percent of men and 19 percent of women).[50]

- 29 percent of LGBT Americans reported not having their own personal doctor, versus 21 percent of their straight peers.[51]

LOOKING TO THE FUTURE

What are the top health objectives for the LGBTQ population?

For the first time, LGBT Americans were included in the 2000 edition of the U.S. Department of Health and Human Services' Healthy People initiative, a 10-year national set of objectives that was launched in 1979 with the goal of improving the health of all Americans. In "Healthy People 2020," released in 2010, the initiative identified a variety of objectives for LGBT Americans, ranging from reductions in youth bullying, obesity, and suicide to increases in HIV testing, condom usage, and screenings for breast and cervical cancer. [52]

AGING

What are the key concerns about aging among LGBTQ elders?

Founded in 1978, Services & Advocacy for GLBT Elders (SAGE) is America's oldest and largest organization dedicated to improving the lives of older LGBT adults. In 2014, SAGE surveyed a nationally representative sample of 1,857 LGBT elders and 519 straight elders ages 45 to 75 and found that:

- 51 percent of the LGBT sample were very or extremely concerned about having enough money to live on, compared to 36 percent of the straight sample.
- 65 percent of transgender respondents felt they will have limited access to health care as they get older.
- 34 percent of Hispanic LGBT respondents, 22 percent of African American LGBT respondents, and 18 percent of white LGBT respondents were concerned about losing their attractiveness as they get older.
- 34 percent of the LGBT elders who were surveyed live alone, compared to 21 percent of non-LGBT elders.
- 78 percent of LGBT respondents were at least some-

what interested in living in LGBT-friendly affordable housing.[53]

How do financial factors affect the quality of life for older LGBTQ Americans?

According to a comprehensive 2010 report co-authored by Movement Advancement Project and SAGE:

- Financial problems are a big concern for 42 percent of all LGBT Americans over 65.
- 47 percent reported having less than $10,000 in savings and other assets.
- 30 percent are concerned about meeting their housing needs.
- Older lesbian couples are 72 percent to 84 percent more likely to qualify for public assistance than heterosexual couples.
- A San Francisco study showed that 90 percent of straight seniors have children to rely on, compared to 29 percent of LGBT seniors.[54]

To what extent do LGBTQ Americans experience discrimination based on age?

- 75 percent of LGB Americans ages 60 to 91 reported being victimized because of their sexual orientation, according to a 2001 study with 416 participants.[55]
- A 2008 study of 383 African American and white gay men found that the African American men experienced "significantly higher" levels of ageism (that is, prejudice or discrimination on the basis of age) than the white men.[56]
- A 2015 peer-reviewed study of 312 gay men between ages 48 and 78, of whom 61 percent were HIV-negative, found that internalized negative feelings about growing and being old were prominent among study participants.[57]
- A small 1999 study of lesbians ages 54 to 75 found that 80 percent had not experienced discrimination, and all were "very pleased" with their current health care.[58]

What is the status of LGBTQ elders' physical health?

In a 2014 peer-reviewed study of 113 LGB Americans ages 60 to 88:

- 71 percent reported that their physical health was good to excellent.
- 25 percent described their physical health as fair.
- 4 percent said they are in poor health.
- 50 percent reported doing regular exercise; 30 percent reported sometimes exercising; 20 percent said they exercise seldom or never.[59]

What is the status of LGBTQ elders' mental health?

- In a 2014 study of LGB Americans who are 60 and older, 80 percent of participants reported their mental and emotional health as excellent.[60]
- In a 2001 study of 416 LGB people ages 60 to 91, most respondents reported their self-esteem as "fairly high," though 10 percent had considered suicide.[61]

What sources of social support do LGBTQ Americans have as they age?

- In a 2008 study of 220 LGB Americans ages 50 to 79, respondents on average had 2.5 people in their social network.
- Support from friends rather than family members was the best indicator of higher mental quality of life and of lower levels of depression and internalized homophobia.[62]

What trends have emerged regarding interactions between LGBTQ elders and caregivers?

- In a 2014 study of LGB elders, 91 percent of respondents who reported having caregivers said they were open about their sexual identity when interacting with those who provided their care.[63]
- 22.1 percent of respondents in the same study reported experiencing some type of harm from their caregivers,

including physical, emotional, verbal, sexual, and financial abuse and neglect.[64]

- A 1999 study of 1,466 LG Americans ages 17 to 81 found that 32 percent were providing some kind of caregiving assistance.[65]
- A 2007 study of 199 LGB people ages 40 to 85 found that 75 percent were willing to provide care to others in the future.[66]

> We should all be outraged when people suffer discrimination, assault or even murder simply because they are lesbian, gay, bisexual or transgender. We should all speak out when someone is arrested and imprisoned because of who they love or how they look. This is one of the great neglected human rights challenges of our time. . . . Some may oppose change. They may invoke culture, tradition or religion to defend the status quo. Such arguments have been used to try to justify slavery, child marriage, rape in marriage and female genital mutilation. I respect culture, tradition and religion, but they can never justify the denial of basic rights. My promise to the lesbian, homosexual, bisexual and transgender members of the human family is this: I'm with you. I promise that as Secretary-General of the United Nations, I will denounce attacks against you and I will keep pressing leaders for progress.
>
> —*United Nations Secretary-General Ban Ki-moon, addressing the 2013 International Conference on Human Rights, Sexual Orientation and Gender Identity*[1]

Secretary-General Ban Ki-moon's promise to "keep pressing leaders for progress" comes at an urgent moment: worldwide, more than 2.7 billion people live in countries where being LGBTQ is punishable by imprisonment, violence, or even death.[2] Indeed, according to the International Lesbian, Gay, Bisexual, Trans and Intersex Association (ILGA), there is no country on earth in which LGBTQ citizens enjoy the same legal rights that their heterosexual counterparts take for granted.

In August 2015, the U.N. Security Council held its first meeting dedicated to addressing the persecution of

LGBTQ people.[3] Security Council members discussed LGBT rights in the Middle East and anti-LGBTQ attacks by the Islamic State of Iraq and the Levant (ISIL), which has taken responsibility for executing at least 30 people accused of sodomy through stonings, beheadings, firing squads, and pushing people from tall buildings.[4] In response, the U.S. ambassador to the United Nations, Samantha Power, told reporters: "It's about time, 70 years after the creation of the UN, that the fate of LGBT persons who fear for their lives around the world is taking center stage."[5]

THE GLOBAL STRUGGLE FOR LGBTQ RIGHTS

How many countries have pro-LGBTQ laws?

- According to ILGA, sexual activity between consenting adults of the same gender is legal in 118 countries, including 19 nations in Africa. This constitutes 61 percent of countries that belong to the United Nations.
- 69 countries and 85 entities have some form of antidiscrimination laws that protect people on the basis of sexual orientation and/or gender identity.
- 34 countries and 65 entities recognize same-sex unions.
- 17 countries and 28 entities recognize adoptions by same-sex parents.[6]

Do legal protections for LGBTQ citizens have an economic impact?

A 2014 Williams Institute study on the economic impact of LGBT rights in 39 countries around the globe, including 29 emerging economies, found that:

- Exclusion of LGBT people causes economic harm. Such harm stems from diminished productivity, lost labor time, underinvestment in human capital, and the inefficient allocation of human resources through discrimination in hiring practices and education.
- Expansion of rights for LGBT people is correlated with higher per capita income and higher levels of well-being. This finding prompted the study's authors

to conclude that LGBT equality should be incorporated into development programs and policies.[7]

How many countries imprison or put to death those accused of homosexual acts?

- As of 2016, in 13 countries the maximum penalty for engaging in same-sex acts is death. The map on the facing page delineates these countries.[8]
- According to human rights activists, between 4,000 and 6,000 gay men and lesbians have been put to death in Iran since 1979. Some executions have taken the form of public stonings and of men being pushed off rooftops.[9]
- Afghanistan, Mauritania, Pakistan, Qatar, and the United Arab Emirates have laws on the books stating that the punishment for homosexual acts is death, but the death penalty is not currently enforced.[10]
- 73 countries and 5 entities imprison consenting adults for homosexual acts. In 45 of these nations, the law is applied to women as well as men. In 14 countries, including Uganda and India, the potential penalty for engaging in same-sex activity is life in prison.[11]

What are the origins of sodomy laws?

The word "sodomy" is derived from the story of Sodom and Gomorrah, which appears in Genesis, the first book of the Bible.

- Early interpretations of this story—including the commentary in Ezekiel 16:19—described the sins of Sodom as "pride, gluttony, and laziness, while the poor and needy suffered outside her door."[12]
- The first person to link "the sin of Sodom" to homosexuality was Philo of Alexandria (20 BC–50 CE), a Jewish thinker and writer who, in the words of historian Louis Crompton, thought "effeminate men should not be allowed to live 'for a day or even an hour' and in effect urge[d] his co-religionists in Alexandria to attack and kill them on sight."[13]
- Around the time that Philo was writing, early Christians

Figure 6.1: LGBTQ Rights: Where Homosexuality Is Punishable by Death

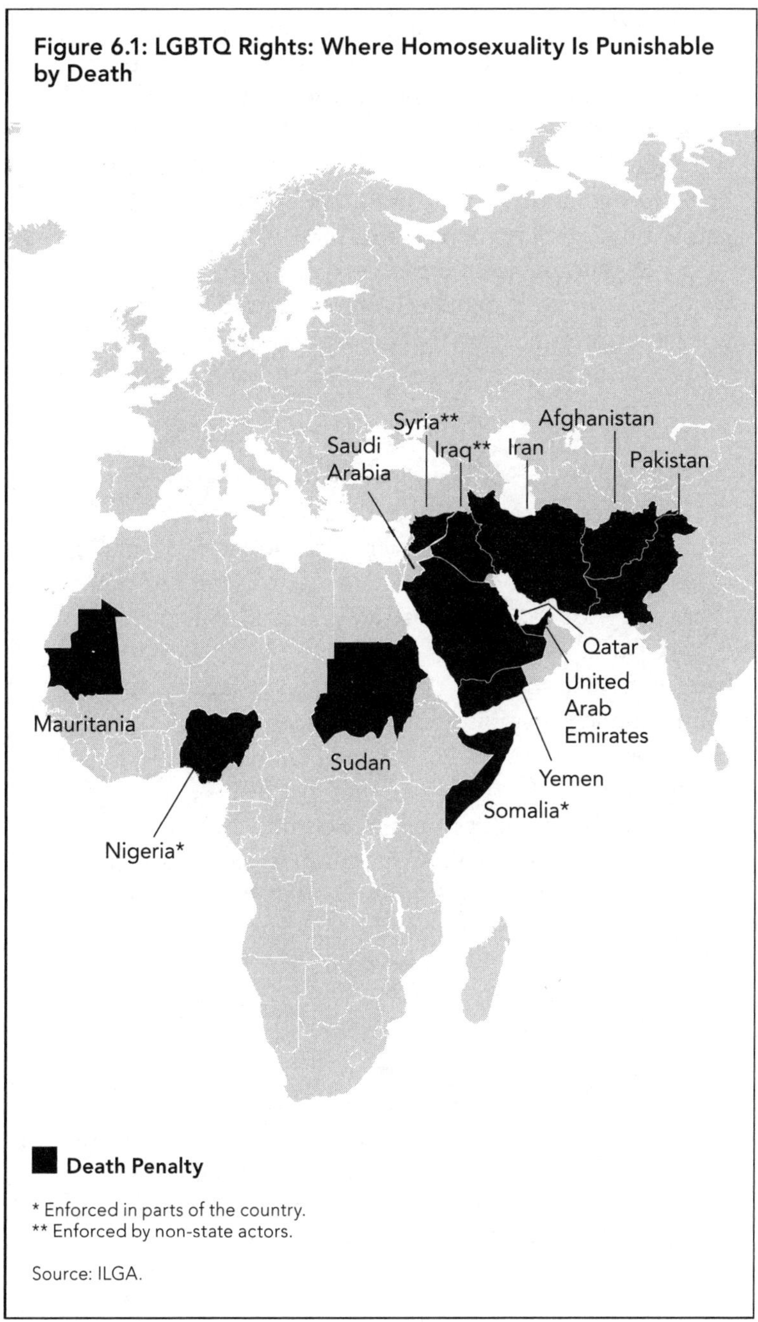

* Enforced in parts of the country.
** Enforced by non-state actors.

Source: ILGA.

took up anti-homosexual tenets, in part because they sought to differentiate their new religion from paganism, which they associated with same-sex behavior and effeminacy in men.[14]

- In 342 CE, Constantius and Constans, co-emperors of the Roman Empire, enacted a law stating that any man found guilty of homosexual acts would "be subjected to exquisite punishment."[15]
- Justinian I, the Byzantine emperor from 527 to 565, enacted a legal code that incorporated the laws of Constans and Constantius and added the death penalty for sodomy.[16]
- The definition of sodomy broadened during the early medieval period to include most non-procreative sex acts, which were defined as "crimes against nature." Under some statutes, sodomy was defined to include heresy, and sodomy laws sometimes applied to oral or anal sex between heterosexuals as well as to same-sex acts.[17]
- Beginning in the 12th century, sodomy laws were enacted in most European states; penalties included beheading, burning at the stake, castration, and imprisonment.[18]
- The number of people put to death for sodomy between the 10th and 13th centuries is unknown, in part because trial records were often burned along with the sodomite, reflecting the belief that this crime was "so hideous it could not be named."[19]
- In Florence between 1432 and 1502, 15,000 men and boys were tried on charges of sodomy; 2,000 were convicted.[20]
- In 1533, England passed its first Buggery Act, outlawing sodomy between men. Sodomy laws were subsequently imposed on all colonies over which Britain took control, including those in America, where sodomy was generally punishable by death.[21]

What countries have repealed sodomy statutes?

- In 1791, France became the first European country to decriminalize same-sex activity between consenting adults of the same gender.[22] The following countries repealed sodomy laws in the years indicated:
    - Brazil in 1830.
    - Mexico in 1871.
    - Russia in 1917 (recriminalized in 1933 and decriminalized in 1993).
    - Poland in 1932.
    - Switzerland in 1942.
    - Spain in 1979.
    - All of Australia in 1997.
    - All of the U.S. in 2003.[23]

What is the legal status of same-sex acts in the United Kingdom?

On July 27, 1967, an act of Parliament in Great Britain, the Sexual Offenses Act, decriminalized private homosexual acts between two men in England and Wales. The age of consent was set at 21, compared to 16 for heterosexual acts.[24]

- Scotland decriminalized homosexual acts in 1980.[25]
- In 1981, the European Court of Human Rights case *Dudgeon v. the United Kingdom* held that Section 11 of the Criminal Law Amendment Act 1885, which criminalized male homosexual acts in Northern Ireland, violated the European Convention on Human Rights. As a result, Northern Ireland decriminalized homosexual acts in 1982.[26]
- In 2013, Alan Turing—a gay British mathematician whose code-breaking during World War II is credited with saving thousands of lives and helping to change the course of the war—received a royal pardon from Queen Elizabeth II nearly 60 years after he was convicted of "gross indecency" for engaging in homosexual activity. Turing committed suicide in 1954 after being subjected to chemical castration—"a sentence we would now consider unjust and discriminatory and

which has now been repealed," said British Justice Secretary Chris Grayling.[27]

- In the aftermath of Turing's pardon, advocates called on the British government to pardon the 49,000 other men convicted under Britain's antisodomy statute, of whom an estimated 15,000 are believed to be alive. A petition signed by more than half a million people and delivered to Prime Minister David Cameron in 2015 stated: "[T]his intolerant law brought not only unwarranted shame, but horrific physical and mental damage and lost years of wrongful imprisonment."[28]
- As of 2015, homosexuality remained a crime in 40 of the 53 nations that make up the British Commonwealth.[29]

What is Paragraph 175, and when did Germany decriminalize same-sex activity?

On August 29, 1867, Karl Heinrich Ulrichs became the first self-proclaimed homosexual to speak out publicly for homosexual rights when he urged the Congress of German Jurists in Munich to support a resolution that would repeal anti-homosexual laws. He was shouted down at the congressional meeting.[30]

- Four years later, in 1871, Germany added Paragraph 175 to its penal code, establishing "unnatural lewdness" as a criminal offense.[31]
- Magnus Hirschfeld founded the Scientific Humanitarian Committee on May 14, 1897, to organize for homosexual rights and to advocate for the repeal of Paragraph 175.[32]

According to official records, between 50,000 and 63,000 men, including 4,000 juveniles, were accused of violating Paragraph 175 and convicted of homosexuality in Germany between 1933 and 1944.[33]

- The estimated number of gay men exterminated during the Third Reich ranges from 10,000 to 1,000,000; 220,000 is one of the most frequently cited numbers.[34]
- Under the Nazis, homosexuals were required to wear a pink triangle, pointing downward. Activists have

reclaimed this symbol and inverted it; the upward-facing pink triangle has become an international symbol of LGBT pride, while the black triangle—which the Nazis used to identify "asocial prisoners"—has become a symbol of lesbian pride.[35]

- Paragraph 175 remained part of German law into the 1960s. Unlike Jews, political prisoners, and other groups of survivors of the concentration camps, none of the gay inmates who survived Nazi camps was granted any compensation. Some men were rearrested and imprisoned based on evidence collected during the Nazi years. It was not until 2002 that the German government apologized to the gay community.[36]

Homosexual acts were decriminalized in East and West Germany in 1968 and 1969, respectively. A memorial to homosexuals persecuted under Nazism opened in Berlin in 2008.[37]

What is the history and status of sodomy laws in Asia?

- There have never been Western-style sodomy-related laws in Taiwan, North Korea, South Korea, or Vietnam.[38]
- Japan holds the distinction of having one of the shortest-lived sodomy laws in the world: the statute was in place from 1873 to 1883. The law was repealed in part because of strong resistance from samurai warriors, who had a long tradition of same-sex relations.[39]

On June 29, 2016, the Supreme Court of India refused to hear a challenge to Section 377, a colonial-era law that criminalizes sex between consenting lesbian, gay, bisexual, and transgender partners. The statute had been ruled unconstitutional in 2009 but was reenacted in 2013 by India's Supreme Court.

- Since 2013, hundreds have been arrested under the law. In 2014 alone, at least 587 people were arrested under Section 377 of the Indian Penal Code, which makes "carnal intercourse against the order of nature" a crime without distinguishing between consensual sex and rape.[40]

When did South Africa abolish sodomy laws?

South Africa's post-apartheid constitution of 1996 was the first in the world to prohibit discrimination on the basis of sexual orientation.

- In 1998, in response to lawsuits brought by LGBTQ organizations, South Africa's highest court overturned sodomy laws, which had been instituted by the apartheid-era government and remained on the books after the new constitution went into effect.
- In announcing his decision, Judge Jonathan Heher of the Johannesburg High Court stated: "Constitutionally, we have reached a stage of maturity in which recognition of the dignity and innate worth of every member of society is not a matter of reluctant concession, but is one of easy acceptance."[41]

When did Russia enact its ban on LGBT "propaganda," and what effect has this measure had?

In 2013, Russia's parliament voted 436–0 in favor of a federal law banning the spreading of "propaganda of non-traditional sexual relations" among minors. President Vladimir Putin signed the measure into law in June 2013, months before Russia hosted the 2014 Winter Olympics. The Russian government's stated purpose for the law was to protect children from being exposed to content recognizing homosexuality as a norm in society.[42]

- In one example of the law's enforcement, Elena Klimova—the founder of Deti-404.com, an online community for LGBT teens in Russia—was fined 50,000 rubles ($750 U.S.) in 2015 after a court found her guilty of distributing propaganda promoting nontraditional sexual relations among minors. Klimova appealed the ruling and stated: "The law against gay propaganda legitimized violence against LGBT people, and they now are banning street actions under it. People are afraid because they understand that gay propaganda is banned, and even mentioning LGBT relations is essentially forbidden."[43]

- Algeria and Nigeria have followed Russia's lead and enacted anti-LGBT propaganda laws.[44]

What levels of discrimination do LGBTQ people face in Europe?

A large 2013 study conducted by the European Union Agency for Fundamental Rights using data acquired in 2012 from 93,079 LGBT Europeans found that:

- 47 percent of respondents said they were harassed or discriminated against in the last 12 months.
- 91 percent said they had heard negative comments or seen negative conduct because a schoolmate was perceived to be LGBT during his or her schooling before the age of 18.
- 6 percent said they had been attacked or threatened with violence in the last 12 months partly or completely because they were perceived to be LGBT.
- Of the transgender respondents who had been attacked or threatened with violence in the last 12 months, 28 percent reported that the attacks or threats occurred more than three times.
- 3 percent of respondents said same-sex couples holding hands in public is "very widespread"; the percentage for straight couples was 75 percent.[45]

In how many countries can LGBTQ people serve in the military?

- LGB people can serve openly in the military in 49 countries, including Albania, Germany, Israel, Japan, and Thailand. Two additional countries, Mexico and South Korea, don't ban LGB people from serving in the military, but they are often harassed and/or discharged.[46]
- Transgender people can serve in the military in 19 countries, including Australia, Canada, Sweden, the United Kingdom, and the United States.[47]

What are some other examples of recent progress on global LGBTQ issues?

- In September 2015, lawmakers in Nepal approved a new constitution that specifically protects "sexual minorities."
- Two months later, members of Vietnam's National Assembly passed a measure that legalizes gender-reassignment surgery and allows trans people who have undergone the procedure to change their gender marker on official documents.
- Botswana's highest court ruled in 2016 that an LGBT advocacy group can register with the country's government.
- Argentina in 2016 became the third Latin American country to join the Global Equality Fund, a U.S. initiative that seeks to promote LGBT rights around the world.[48]

ELECTED OFFICIALS

In what countries have openly LGBTQ politicians been elected to high public office?

Jóhanna Sigurðardóttir became Iceland's first female prime minister—and the world's first openly lesbian head of government—on February 1, 2009. She served until 2013. There have been two other openly LGBT heads of state:

- Elio Di Rupo, prime minister of Belgium from 2011 to 2014.
- Xavier Bettel, prime minister of Luxembourg from 2013 to the present.[49]

According to a *Washington Post* analysis published in December 2015:

- Since 1977, 139 transgender candidates have run for more than 200 races in 31 countries.
- 52 transgender candidates were elected.
- Nearly 90 percent of these candidates were trans women.

- As of December 2015, 20 transgender elected officials were in office.[50]

UNITED NATIONS

What is the first international LGBTQ organization to be recognized by the United Nations?

Founded in 1978, the International Lesbian, Gay, Bisexual, Trans and Intersex Association (ILGA) is an umbrella organization that brings together more than 1,200 LGBTQ and intersex groups from around the world. Acting as "a global voice for the rights of those who face discrimination on the grounds of sexual orientation, gender identity and/or gender expression and sex (intersex)," ILGA in 1993 became the first LGBTI organization to be recognized by the United Nations.[51]

What has the U.N. done to document and combat anti-LGBTQ violence?

In 2011, the U.N. released its first-ever report on the human rights of LGBTQ people around the world. Four years later, the U.N. released an updated report, which pointed out that "Due to poor data collection and a fear of reporting the crimes to authorities, many violent and discriminatory acts against LGBT people go undocumented." The report confirmed the following crimes and patterns:

- Between 2008 and 2014, there were 1,612 murders, across 62 countries, of transgender persons—equivalent to one killing every two days.
- The Inter-American Commission on Human Rights documented 594 hate-related killings of LGBT persons in the 25 member nations of the Organization of American States between January 2013 and March 2014.
- In 2012, Brazil saw 310 murders in which homophobia or transphobia was a motive. According to the campaign group Grupo Gay da Bahia, 44 percent of the world's anti-LGBT violence occurs in Brazil. In 2013, the nation's lawmakers rejected a bill that would have prohibited

discrimination or the incitement of violence on the basis of sexual orientation or gender identity.[52]

THE U.S. ROLE IN GLOBAL LGBTQ ISSUES

What role has the U.S. government played in advancing LGBTQ rights and in providing asylum to LGBTQ refugees?

Since 2012, the American government has spent more than $41 million to promote LGBT rights globally and has supported LGBTQ causes and communities with a portion of $700 million earmarked for marginalized groups.[53]

- In 2015, Randy Berry became America's first special envoy for the human rights of LGBT persons. In his first 12 months on the job, Berry—a career foreign service officer who is openly gay and who speaks Spanish and Arabic in addition to English—traveled to 42 countries, including Honduras, Bosnia and Herzegovina, and Indonesia, to promote LGBT rights. "We live in a world where many governments use LGBTI issues as a political wedge to bolster their own positions," Berry told reporters at a 2016 briefing.[54]

In 2011, President Obama released a memorandum stating that "the Departments of State and Homeland Security shall enhance their ongoing efforts to ensure that LGBT refugees and asylum seekers have equal access to protection and assistance, particularly in countries of first asylum."

- Of the 70,000 refugees that the United States took in during 2014, fewer than 100 were LGBT, according to U.S. Ambassador to the U.N. Samantha Power.[55]

What role have American evangelicals played in fomenting anti-LGBTQ violence and legislation?

In 2009, after three American evangelicals held an anti-LGBT conference in Uganda, the country's parliament passed a bill that, among other things:

- Criminalized touching another person anywhere with the intention of committing the "act of homosexuality."

- Affirmed Uganda's lifetime imprisonment for those convicted of homosexuality.
- Criminalized the act of obtaining a same-sex marriage abroad by making it punishable with lifetime imprisonment.
- Required friends or family members to report LGBT persons to police within 24 hours of learning about that individual's homosexuality or face fines or imprisonment for up to three years.
- Created a new category of "aggravated homosexuality" that carried the death penalty.

The bill was signed into law by Uganda's president, Yoweri Museveni, in February 2014, but overturned on technical grounds by Uganda's Supreme Court in August 2014. There are plans to reintroduce it.[56]

- A 2015 public opinion survey by Afrobarometer found that 92 percent of Ugandans believe homosexuality is inconsistent with Ugandan culture and religion, and that LGBT people do not deserve the same constitutional protection as other Ugandans.[57]

In 2012, the U.S.-based Center for Constitutional Rights filed a lawsuit known as *SMUG v. Lively* on behalf of Sexual Minorities Uganda (SMUG), a nonprofit umbrella organization for LGBT groups in Uganda. The lawsuit charges Scott Lively, a Massachusetts-based pastor and one of the three evangelicals who held the 2009 anti-gay conference in Uganda, with violating international law by persecuting Ugandan homosexuals and seeking to deprive LGBT Ugandans of human rights.

- Oral arguments in the case are expected to be heard in November 2016.
- The case has been brought under the Alien Tort Statute, which allows non-U.S. citizens to sue Americans in U.S. federal courts for violations of international law.
- While the Alien Tort Statute is regularly used in cases of torture, war crimes, and violence against women, *SMUG v. Lively* is the first case to address human

rights violations based on sexual orientation or gender identity.[58]

LGBTQ PEOPLE AND GLOBAL HAPPINESS

In what parts of the world are gay people the most and least happy?

In a 2015 study of 115,000 of its members, Planet Romeo—an international social network for GBT men—created a "gay happiness index" based on three criteria:

- How do gay men feel about society's view of homosexuality?
- How do gay men experience the way they are treated by other people?
- How satisfied are gay men with their lives, and do they accept themselves?

Based on these criteria, of the 127 countries rated, the top nations in the gay happiness index were:

1. Iceland
2. Norway
3. Denmark
4. Sweden
5. Uruguay
6. Canada
7. Israel
8. Netherlands

(The United States ranked 26th.)[59]

The lowest-ranked nations (in descending order) were:

8. Cameroon
7. Iran
6. Nigeria
5. Iraq
4. Kyrgystan
3. Ethiopia
2. Sudan
1. Uganda[60]

GLOBAL PUBLIC OPINION

What countries are most and least supportive of homosexuality?

In 2013, the Pew Research Center surveyed 37,653 respondents in 39 countries around the globe regarding societal acceptance of homosexuality. Results are summarized in Figure 6.2.

Figure 6.2: Should Society Accept Homosexuality?

	No %	Yes %
North America		
Canada	14	80
U.S.	33	60
Europe		
Spain	11	88
Germany	11	87
Czech Republic	16	80
France	22	77
Britain	18	76
Italy	18	74
Greece	40	53
Poland	46	42
Russia	74	16
Middle East		
Israel	47	40
Lebanon	80	18
Turkey	78	9
Palestinian Ter.	93	4
Egypt	95	3
Jordan	97	3
Tunisia	94	2
Asia/Pacific		
Australia	18	79
Philippines	26	73
Japan	36	54
South Korea	59	39
China	57	21
Malaysia	86	9
Indonesia	93	3
Pakistan	87	2
Latin America		
Argentina	21	74
Chile	24	68
Mexico	30	61
Brazil	36	60
Venezuela	42	51
Bolivia	49	43
El Salvador	62	34
Africa		
South Africa	61	32
Kenya	90	8
Uganda	96	4
Ghana	96	3
Senegal	96	3
Nigeria	98	1

Source: Pew Research Center, "The Global Divide on Homosexuality: Greater Acceptance in More Secular and Affluent Countries," June 4, 2013, www.pewglobal.org/2013/06/04/the-global-divide-on-homosexuality.

Table 6.1: Cross-National Differences on LGBTQ Rights

Study/measure	Highest approval		Lowest approval	
Intercontinental:				
WVS (2005–2008)				
Homosexuality always justifiable	Andorra	60.0%	Georgia	0.1%
Not object to gay neigbors	Sweden	96.4%	Jordan	4.9%
ISSP (2008)				
Same-gender sex not wrong at all	Netherlands	69.6%	Turkey	2.1%
Pew (2013)				
Society should accept homosexuality	Spain	88.0%	Nigeria	1.0%
Ipsos (2013)				
For gay marriage	Sweden	81%	Poland	21%
Regional:				
LB (2009/2010)				
Homosexuality always justifiable	Uruguay	33.6%	Ecuador	1.6%
Supports gay marriage	Uruguay	57.3%	Guatemala	12.0%
EB (2006/2012)				
Has gay friends/ acquaintances	Netherlands	78.9%	Romania	2.1%
Comfortable with gay government leaders	Denmark	80.8%	Slovakia	6.8%
For gay marriage in Europe (2006)	Netherlands	81.5%	Romania	10.7%
For gay adoption in Europe (2006)	Netherlands	68.7%	Malta	6.8%
ESS (2010)				
Gays free to live own lives	Netherlands	92.6%	Russia	25.4%
EVS (2008/2010)				
Homosexuality always justifiable	Iceland	60.5%	Armenia	0.1%
Not object to gay neighbors	Iceland	86.6%	Azerbaijan	8.8%

Source: Tom Smith, Jaesok Son, and Jibum Kim, "Public Attitudes Towards Homosexuality and Gay Rights Across Time and Countries," NORC and Williams Institute, November 2014, williamsinstitute.law.ucla.edu/wp-content/uploads/public-attitudes-nov-2014.pdf.

What countries are most and least supportive of homosexuality and LGBTQ rights?

A 2014 joint study by the National Opinion Research Center at the University of Chicago and the Williams Institute analyzed 2,000 data points in dozens of cross-national surveys of global public opinion and found dramatic differences in attitudes toward LGBTQ rights and homosexuality. Table 6.1 summarizes highest and lowest levels of approval.

In commenting on their findings, the study's authors wrote: "There has been a general shift in a majority of countries towards greater acceptance of homosexuality and gay rights. But the trends are far from universal and mostly moderate in magnitude. Change has been slower and more sporadic in ex-Communist states, and the available evidence on trends from many geocultural regions such as Moslem countries and Africa are too incomplete to establish certain patterns. Overall, on average there is still considerable room for support for homosexuality and gay rights to increase."

No union is more profound than marriage, for it embodies the highest ideals of love, fidelity, devotion, sacrifice, and family. In forming a marital union, two people become something greater than once they were. As some of the petitioners in these cases demonstrate, marriage embodies a love that may endure even past death. It would misunderstand these men and women to say they disrespect the idea of marriage. Their plea is that they do respect it, respect it so deeply that they seek to find its fulfillment for themselves. Their hope is not to be condemned to live in loneliness, excluded from one of civilization's oldest institutions. They ask for equal dignity in the eyes of the law. The Constitution grants them that right.

—Supreme Court Justice Anthony Kennedy, in the majority opinion in Obergefell v. Hodges, *2015*

During the 2000 election campaign, Republican George W. Bush and his Democratic opponent, Al Gore, disagreed on an array of issues. But they found common ground on one topic: both voiced strong and unequivocal opposition to same-sex marriage. At the time, every state in the country prohibited marriage between two men or two women. Four years earlier, Democratic president Bill Clinton had signed into law the Defense of Marriage Act, defining—and "defending"—marriage for federal purposes as the union of one man and one woman. Even in Massachusetts, which became the first state to legalize same-sex marriage in 2003, a 2004 poll found that voters disapproved of marriage between two men or two women by a margin of 53 to 35.[1] In 2004, President Bush called for a constitutional amendment that would restrict marriage to one man and one woman. "Marriage cannot be severed from its cultural, religious and natural roots without weakening the good influence of society," Bush asserted, adding: "After more than two centuries of American jurisprudence and millennia of human experience, a few judges and local authorities are presuming to change the most fundamental institution of civilization."

One short decade later, the Supreme Court issued a watershed ruling that did indeed change "the most fundamental institution of civilization" by declaring that America's same-sex couples are entitled to the same marriage rights as straight couples. How and why did this profound transformation occur? What are its political, psychological, and economic ramifications? This chapter probes these questions while examining related data on LGBTQ parenting, families, and children.

SAME-SEX MARRIAGE

Milestones on the Road to Marriage Equality

1970	Jack Baker and Michael McConnell apply for a marriage license in Minnesota. Their case goes to the U.S. Supreme Court, which dismisses it "for want of substantial federal question."[2]
1971	The Gay Activists Alliance takes over the New York City Marriage License Bureau and throws an engagement party for two same-sex couples.[3]
1973	A year after ratifying the Equal Rights Amendment, Maryland becomes the first state to pass a law that declares: "Only a marriage between a man and a woman is valid in this State."[4]

1973–74	Two other court cases regarding same-sex marriage go to trial: the Kentucky Court of Appeals dismisses one case, involving two lesbians, in 1973, and the Supreme Court of Washington State rejects a case brought by a gay couple in 1974.[5]
1975	In January, Maricopa County, Arizona, issues the first marriage license to a same-sex couple in the United States; the license is later revoked.[6]
	Clela Rorex, a county clerk in Boulder, Colorado, issues marriage licenses to six same-sex couples, based on a legal opinion from the assistant district attorney in Boulder. Her actions make headlines across the country. Colorado's attorney general calls Rorex's act "useless and an official act of no validity," but Rorex contends that the licenses are valid. One of the couples stays married for 37 years.[7]
1984	Berkeley, California, becomes the first jurisdiction in America to pass a domestic-partnership ordinance covering municipal employees with same-sex partners as well as those with opposite-sex partners.[8]
1993	Hawaii's Supreme Court, with one dissenting vote, rules that barring same-sex couples from marrying violates the state constitution's ban on gender-based discrimination and sends the case back to a lower court for a trial on Hawaii's justification for restricting marriage to heterosex-

uals. In 1996, the lower court declares the heterosexual-only definition of marriage unconstitutional and orders that marriage licenses be issued to same-sex couples. The state legislature then passes a constitutional amendment barring same-sex marriage. Voters ratify this amendment and the state's Supreme Court upholds it in 1999.[9]

1995	Utah bans same-sex unions and also announces it will not recognize same-sex marriages performed in other states.[10]
1996	The Defense of Marriage Act (DOMA) passes both houses of Congress by veto-proof majorities; President Bill Clinton signs it into law in September 1996. This measure defines marriage for federal purposes as the union of one man and one woman, and allows states to refuse to recognize same-sex marriages granted under the laws of other states.[11]
1998	A Superior Court judge in Alaska rules that the right to privacy under the state's constitution protects same-sex marriage. The Alaska Supreme Court upholds the decision; the legislature passes a state constitutional ban on same-sex marriage. Voters approve this ban in November 1998.[12]
2000	Howard Dean, then governor of Vermont, signs into law a civil-union bill granting to same-sex partners all the legal rights and obligations of marriage. This entitles same-sex couples in the state to roughly

	25 percent of the 1,138 rights, benefits, and privileges associated with marriage.[13] The bill also defines "marriage" as a union between one man and one woman.[14]
	70 percent of Nebraska voters approve a measure to ban same-sex marriage.[15]
2002	For the second time, Nevada voters approve a constitutional ban on same-sex marriage. State law requires voter approval in two consecutive elections for a state constitutional amendment to take effect.[16]
2003	The Massachusetts Supreme Judicial Court rules that "barring an individual from the protections, benefits, and obligations of civil marriage solely because that person would marry a person of the same sex violates the Massachusetts Constitution." The first legal same-sex marriage in the United States takes place on May 17, 2004—50 years to the day after the Supreme Court struck down "separate but equal" public schools in its *Brown v. Board of Education* decision.[17]
2004	President George W. Bush announces support for a federal constitutional amendment banning same-sex marriage.[18]
2004–2006	23 states approve constitutional amendments banning same-sex marriage.[19]
2006	Arizona voters reject a constitutional amendment banning same-sex

	marriage—making it the first state in the country to do so.[20]
2008	California's Supreme Court holds that the state's ban on same-sex marriage violates the state's constitution.[21]
	The Connecticut Supreme Court rules that same-sex couples can marry.[22]
	California voters approve Proposition 8, a referendum seeking to ban same-sex marriage in the state; as a result, the legal status of approximately 17,000 same-sex marriages performed in California comes into question. Florida and Arizona also approve constitutional bans on gay marriage.[23]
2009	The Iowa Supreme Court, the Vermont and New Hampshire legislatures, the governor of Maine, and the District of Columbia legalize same-sex marriage.[24]
	Maine's voters repeal the law legalizing same-sex marriage.[25]
2010	Joseph Tauro, U.S. District Court judge for the District of Massachusetts, becomes the first justice to rule that a key section of the Defense of Marriage Act is unconstitutional.[26]
	A U.S. District Court judge in California rules that the ban on same-sex marriage enacted under Proposition 8 is unconstitutional.[27]
2011	President Barack Obama declares DOMA unconstitutional and directs the

	Department of Justice to stop defending the law.[28]
	New York governor Andrew Cuomo signs a bill making same-sex marriage legal.[29]
2012	The U.S. Ninth Circuit Court of Appeals upholds the District Court's ruling that California's Proposition 8 is unconstitutional.[30]
	Barack Obama becomes the first sitting U.S. president to announce his support for same-sex marriage.[31]
	Voters for the first time approve the legalization of same-sex marriage at the ballot box in Maryland, Washington, and Maine. Minnesota voters reject a proposal to amend the state constitution to define marriage as between one man and one woman.[32]
	The Supreme Court agrees to hear challenges to the Defense of Marriage Act and the ruling against California's Proposition 8.[33]
2013	Rhode Island, Delaware, Minnesota, New Jersey, Hawaii, Illinois, and New Mexico legalize same-sex marriage.[34]
	The Supreme Court strikes down a key section of DOMA and dismisses the challenge to the Proposition 8 ruling, once again making same-sex marriage legal in California.[35]
	U.S. District Judge Robert Shelby strikes down Utah's gay-marriage ban; more than

	1,000 same-sex couples marry over the next two weeks. With Utah appealing, the Supreme Court on January 6, 2014, halts further marriages from taking place.[36]
2014	Multiple U.S. district and appeals courts reject state bans on same-sex marriage as unconstitutional. On October 6, 2014, the U.S. Supreme Court refuses to hear state appeals from Utah, Oklahoma, Virginia, Indiana, and Wisconsin, paving the way for same-sex marriage in six other states that fall within those federal circuits: Colorado, Kansas, North Carolina, South Carolina, West Virginia, and Wyoming.[37]
2015	The Supreme Court agrees to hear six consolidated cases from four states with bans on same-sex marriage; the outcome could decide whether all 50 states must allow gay and lesbian couples to marry.[38]
	37 states throughout the United States permit same-sex marriage.[39] Public approval for same-sex marriage stands at 60 percent as of May, according to Gallup.[40]
	On June 26, the Supreme Court issues a 5–4 ruling in the case of *Obergefell v. Hodges*, legalizing same-sex marriage across the United States.[41]

How many same-sex couples are married?

According to the Williams Institute, 491,000 lesbian and gay couples—49 percent of all same-sex couples in the United States—were married as of June 2016.[42]

What is the economic impact of same-sex marriage?

- A 2016 Williams Institute study reported that 123,000 same-sex weddings took place in the 12 months following the *Obergefell* decision. These events generated an estimated $1.58 billion, including $1.35 billion in spending by the couples and $228 million in spending by out-of-state guests. In addition, $102 million in state and local sales tax revenue resulted from the weddings.[43]

How does being married affect partners in a same-sex relationship?

- In a 2011 study of the first same-sex partnerships to be legally recognized in the United States, researchers looked at 452 couples who had entered civil unions in Vermont in 2000. Members of these couples considered the civil union to be "highly significant" and pointed to:
    - increased psychological benefits;
    - tangible benefits;
    - legitimacy by family of origin; and
    - legitimacy by religious organizations.[44]
- In a 2013 study in the *American Journal of Public Health* using data from the California Health Interview Survey, researchers found that same-sex married LGB Californians were "significantly less distressed" than LGB persons not in a legally recognized relationship.[45]
- In a 2015 peer-reviewed online study of 526 individuals in same-sex couples, 90 percent perceived marriage as important. 91 percent of respondents cited the desire for legal benefits and financial protections for the couple, including parental/child legal rights if children are part of the relationship.[46]

How does support for marriage equality vary according to age and political affiliation?

Figure 7.1 documents support for same-sex marriage among Democrats and Republicans:

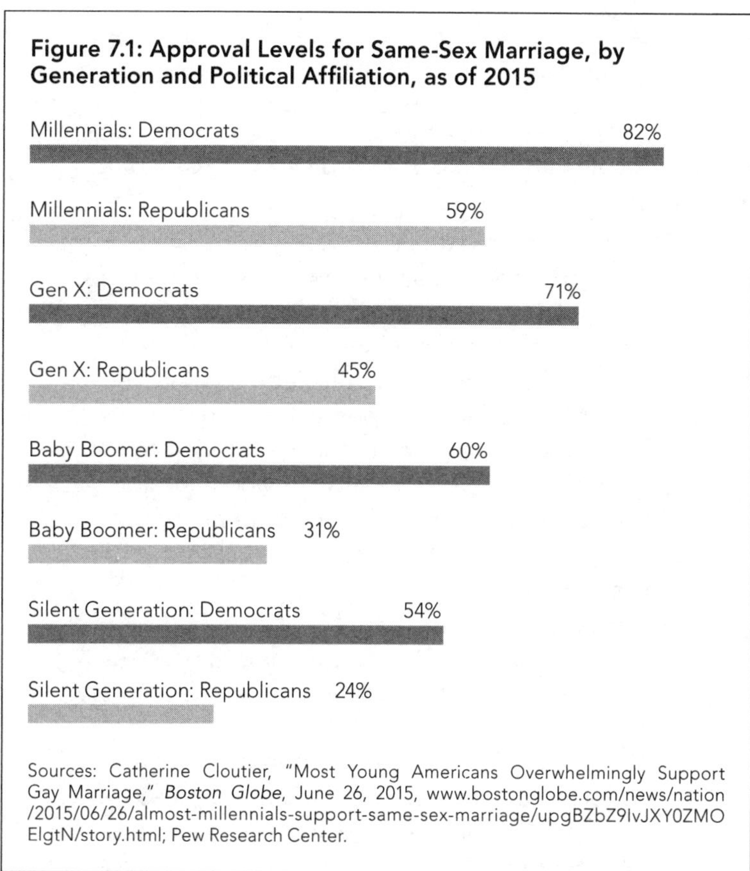

How have activists responded to the Supreme Court's marriage ruling?

Freedom to Marry, a nonprofit organization that worked to legalize same-sex marriage, disbanded after the Supreme Court decision legalizing same-sex marriage.

- Founded in 2001 by Evan Wolfson, one of the earliest proponents of same-sex marriage and the organization's president from 2003 to 2015, Freedom to Marry raised and invested close to $60 million for its successful campaign.

- Between January 2010 and August 2015, the organization secured more than $3 million in online donations from more than 18,000 supporters.[47]

How have opponents of same-sex marriage reacted to its legalization?

- A 2015 Williams Institute study found that in states that legalized marriage equality between November 2012 and July 2013, 47 percent of residents who were initially opposed have changed their minds.[48]
- In a December 2015 report, the Center for American Progress reported that 0.1 percent of LGBT couples nationally lived in counties that were refusing to implement the *Obergefell* ruling and denying marriage licenses to same-sex couples. The strongest opposition was occurring in Alabama, as well as in counties in Texas and Kentucky.[49]
    - On January 6, 2016, the chief justice of the Alabama Supreme Court, Roy S. Moore, ordered probate judges in the state not to issue marriage licenses to same-sex couples.[50]
    - On January 7, 2016, the *Montgomery Advertiser* reported that at least 13 Alabama counties were refusing to issue marriage licenses to all couples.[51]
- The ACLU reported that state legislators introduced 61 bills between January and June 2016 seeking to create exemptions for religious beliefs regarding marriage.[52]

What effect does same-sex marriage have on opposite-sex marriage?

In a peer-reviewed study of the effect of same-sex marriage as a "perceived assault" on opposite-sex marriage, researchers looked at marriage records from all 50 states and the District of Columbia from 1989 to 2009. They found that allowing same-sex couples to wed had no effect on the rate of straight marriages in the short or long term.[53]

What is the rate of same-sex divorce?

According to a 2014 Williams Institute report, the average divorce rate for same-sex couples was 1.1 percent annually, compared to an annual average divorce rate of 2 percent for heterosexual couples.[54]

Beyond the United States, what countries have legalized same-sex marriage?

Of the 196 countries in the world, same-sex marriage has been legalized in 24 countries, including the Netherlands (which in 2000 became the first nation to legalize the practice), as well as South Africa (2006), Brazil (2013), Uruguay (2013), Ireland (2015), and Colombia (2016).[55]

FAMILY AND CHILDREN

How many LGBTQ Americans are parents?

A 2013 Williams Institute report on LGBT parenting in the United States estimated that 37 percent of LGBT adults have had a child at some time in their lives.[56] Additional findings are shown in Figure 7.2 on page 120.

How many LGBTQ Americans are currently raising children?

More than 125,000 same-sex households (19 percent) include more than 220,000 children.

- 48 percent of LBT women under 50 are raising a child under the age of 18.
- 20 percent of GBT men under 50 are raising a child under the age of 18.
- 39 percent of individuals in same-sex couples who have children under 18 in their home are people of color.
- 50 percent of children under 18 living with same-sex couples are nonwhite. The figure for straight couples is 41 percent.
- Same-sex couples raising children are four times more

Figure 7.2: LGBT Parenting in the United States

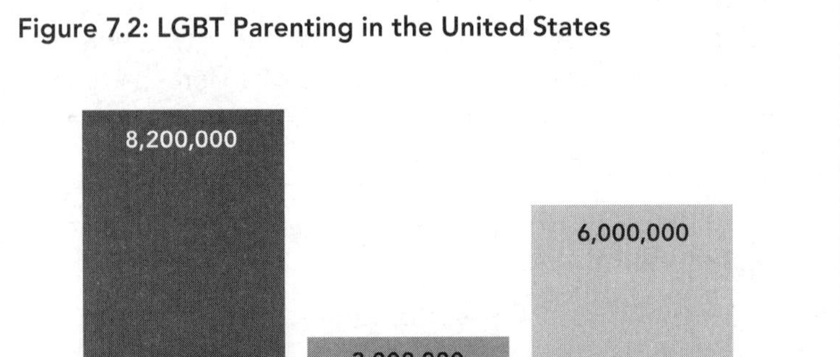

Sources: Gary J. Gates, "LGBT Parenting in the United States," Williams Institute, February 2013, williamsinstitute.law.ucla.edu/wp-content/uploads/LGBT-Parenting.pdf; Gallup Daily Tracking Survey, June–September 2012; General Social Survey 2008/2010; National Transgender Discrimination Survey.

likely than their different-sex counterparts to be raising an adopted child.

- Same-sex couples are six times more likely than their different-sex counterparts to be raising foster children.[57]

What states and cities have the highest number of same-sex couples with children?

States with the highest proportion of same-sex couples raising children are:

- Mississippi—26 percent.
- Wyoming—25 percent.
- Alaska—23 percent.
- Idaho—22 percent.
- Montana—22 percent.[58]

The five U.S. metropolitan areas with a population over 1 million that have the highest percentage of same-sex couples raising children are:

- Salt Lake City, UT—26 percent.
- Virginia Beach–Norfolk–Newport News, VA—24 percent.
- Detroit–Warren–Livonia, MI—22 percent.
- Memphis, TN–MS–AR—22 percent.
- San Antonio–New Braunfels, TX—22 percent.[59]

How many same-sex couples are raising adopted children?

- 14 percent of same-sex couples in the United States are raising adopted children, versus 3 percent of different-sex married couples.
- In the 21 states that had legal protections for LGBT people as of 2014, 17 percent of same-sex couples were raising adopted children.
- In the 29 states that did not have legal protections for LGBT people as of 2014, 11 percent of same-sex couples were raising adopted children.[60]

What laws govern adoption of children by LGBTQ parents?

- Adoption by single LGBT individuals is legal in all jurisdictions and has been since 2011.[61]
- Adoption by same-sex couples is legal in all 50 states and the District of Columbia and has been since 2016, when Mississippi became the 50th state to legalize this practice.[62]

What laws govern foster parenting by LGBTQ Americans?

According to the Movement Advancement Project:

- 41 states and the District of Columbia are silent on fostering by LGBT parents.
- 7 states—California, Massachusetts, New Jersey, New York, Oregon, Rhode Island, and Wisconsin—support fostering by LGBT parents.

- 1 state—Maryland—supports fostering by LGB parents.
- 1 state—Nebraska—restricts fostering by LGBT parents.[63]

What laws govern surrogacy for same-sex couples?

According to Creative Family Connections, a surrogacy agency based in Maryland:

- 10 states—California, Connecticut, Delaware, Maine, Nevada, New Hampshire, Oregon, Rhode Island, Texas, and Utah—permit surrogacy for same-sex married couples. Pre-birth orders (legal documents that assign parentage before a child's birth) are granted throughout the state, and both parents are named on the birth certificate.
- 23 states—Alabama, Arkansas, Colorado, Florida, Georgia, Hawaii, Illinois, Kansas, Kentucky, Maryland, Massachusetts, Minnesota, Missouri, New Mexico, North Carolina, North Dakota, Ohio, Pennsylvania, South Carolina, South Dakota, Vermont, West Virginia, and Wisconsin—permit surrogacy, but results may be dependent on various factors or the venue; in some, only a post-birth parentage order is available, meaning legal assignment of parentage occurs in a court after the child's birth.
- In 12 states—Alaska, Arkansas, Idaho, Indiana, Iowa, Louisiana, Montana, Nebraska, Oklahoma, Tennessee, Virginia, and Wyoming—surrogacy is practiced, but there are potential legal hurdles and results may be inconsistent.
- In 5 states—Michigan, Mississippi, New Jersey, New York, and Washington—and the District of Columbia, a statute or published case law prohibits compensated surrogacy contracts, or a birth certificate naming both parents cannot be obtained.[64]

In what ways are LGBTQ parents involved in their children's schools?

In the first study of LGBTQ families and schools, conducted in 2008, researchers compared LGBTQ parents to a national sample of K–12 parents and found that LGBTQ parents were more likely to:

- Volunteer at their children's schools (67 percent vs. 42 percent).
- Attend parent-teacher conferences (94 percent vs. 77 percent).
- Belong to a parent-teacher organization at the high school level (41 percent vs. 22 percent).[65]

In the same study:

- 42 percent of the children surveyed reported being harassed because of having an LGBTQ parent.
- 23 percent reported being harassed by parents of other students.
- 11 percent to 15 percent reported harassment from teachers.[66]

What economic challenges confront LGBTQ adults who are raising children?

LGBTQ parents face a variety of financial disadvantages:

- Single LGBT adults raising children are three times more likely than comparable non-LGBT individuals to report household incomes near the poverty threshold.
- Married or partnered LGBT individuals living in two-adult households with children are twice as likely as their non-LGBT counterparts to report household incomes near the poverty threshold.
- The median annual household income of same-sex couples with children under 18 in the home is lower than that of comparable different-sex couples: $63,900 versus $74,000, respectively.[67]

What professional associations support LGBTQ parenting?

The HRC Foundation has compiled a list of 13 national professional associations that support LGBT parenting:

- American Academy of Child and Adolescent Psychiatry
- American Academy of Family Physicians
- American Academy of Pediatrics

- American Bar Association
- American Medical Association
- American Psychiatric Association
- American Psychoanalytic Association
- American Psychological Association
- Child Welfare League of America
- National Adoption Center
- National Association of Social Workers
- North American Council on Adoptable Children
- Voice for Adoption[68]

What have studies concluded about the well-being of children with LGBTQ parents?

The Public Policy Research Portal at Columbia Law School conducted a review of 77 studies looking at the well-being of children with LGB parents and found:

- 74 of the studies concluded that children of gay or lesbian parents "fare no worse than other children."[69]
- Of the four studies that showed that the children faced disadvantages, 100 percent used samples of youth who had gone through family breakups, a cohort known to face added risks. Based on the children sampled, scholars have criticized these four studies as unreliable assessments.[70]
- According to a 2014 Williams Institute publication that reviewed 51 existing reports on trans Americans who are parents: "Research shows that transgender parent-child relationships and child development appear to be similar to those in any other family."[71]

I think *Will & Grace* probably did more to educate the American public [on LGBTQ issues] than almost anything anybody has ever done so far. And I think people fear that which is different. Now they're beginning to understand.

—*Vice President Joe Biden, May 6, 2012, in an interview on* Meet the Press[1]

As Vice President Biden suggested, the growing number of positive portrayals of LGBTQ characters in mainstream media has had a profound effect on Americans' views on—and understanding of—LGBTQ issues. For decades gay, lesbian, bisexual, and transgender characters were marginalized at best and more often mocked in films and on television. Then between 2001 and 2005, *Will & Grace* became the highest-rated sitcom among 18- to 49-year-olds, building on the momentum generated by the decision of Ellen DeGeneres to come out in 1997 on an array of platforms—including her own prime-time comedy series, *The Oprah Winfrey Show*, and the cover of *Time*. DeGeneres's coming out became a national phenomenon and marked a turning point in perceptions about LGBTQ people: legal scholar Kris Franklin coined "the Ellen effect" to describe "a watershed in the way the straight mainstream media conceived of lesbians and gay men as simultaneously culturally meaningful and not intimidating."[2]

During the first decade of the 2000s, the rise of social media gave LGBTQ Americans and their allies powerful new ways to connect, make their voices heard, and build new alliances. President Obama, for example, reached 150 million people with a 2013 tweet supporting marriage equality.[3] Yet growing visibility has also brought setbacks: in a 2015 *Variety* poll, 60 percent of Americans said they would choose not to see an action film in which a lead character or lead actor was gay.[4] And finding such films remains a challenge: As Sarah Kate Ellis, CEO of GLAAD, has noted, "America's major film studios lag far behind other media when it comes to nuanced portrayals of LGBT people. . . . Hollywood's movie studios seem to be operating in a time warp."[5]

TELEVISION

What are some milestones in the portrayal of LGBTQ characters on television?

- The first gay male character to appear regularly on television was Peter, a gay set designer on ABC's short-lived 1972 series *Grant's Tomb*.[6]
- The first gay couple to appear regularly on television were Gordon and George in *Hot L Baltimore*, a 1975 ABC series created by Norman Lear that chronicled the lives and loves of residents at a seedy Baltimore hotel.[7]
- Between 1977 and 1981, Billy Crystal played Jody Dallas on the ABC comedy series *Soap*. Although Dallas began as a flamboyant gay man, he later attempted suicide, realized he was bisexual, became involved with a woman, and fathered a child.[8]
- The first lesbian character to appear regularly on a prime-time television series was Marilyn McGrath of ABC's *Heartbeat* in 1989.[9]
- To celebrate the fact that she had gotten a raise, Abby Perkins (played by Michele Greene) kissed C.J. Lamb (played by Amanda Donohoe) on the February 7, 1991, episode of the hit series *L.A. Law*—marking the first time a same-sex couple had kissed on network television. The scene provoked negative reactions from advertisers who threatened to withdraw their sponsorship of the program.[10]
- The first "passionate" kiss by a male couple on prime-time TV occurred on *Dawson's Creek* on May 24, 2000.[11]
- *Will & Grace* premiered on NBC in the fall of 1998. It was the first prime-time television program to feature an openly gay male character as the lead. The program

aired from 1998 to 2006, was the highest-rated sitcom among 18- to 49-year-olds from 2001 to 2005, and received 83 Emmy nominations and 16 Emmy wins.[12]

How did television personalities such as Ellen DeGeneres and Anderson Cooper handle the process of coming out publicly?

Ellen DeGeneres came out in 1997, when she was starring in her hit TV comedy series *Ellen*, creating a media firestorm:

- DeGeneres's character on *Ellen* came out to 42 million viewers just after DeGeneres herself came out on *The Oprah Winfrey Show*. Her coming out resulted in a *Time* cover story, a *New York Times* editorial, and a two-part *20/20* newsmagazine special.
- DeGeneres's current daily talk show, *The Ellen DeGeneres Show*, which has been running since 2003, has won her 27 Emmys and made her the highest-paid celebrity on TV. *Forbes* ranked DeGeneres at number 12 on its 2015 list of the world's highest-paid celebrities, as well as number 50 on its list of the world's most powerful women.
- As of June 2016, DeGeneres was ranked seventh in the world on Twitter and had 24,810,742 Facebook fans.[13]
- In a 2015 interview, DeGeneres acknowledged that she almost didn't come out: "I didn't think I was going to come out, period," she said, adding: "[W]hat I had been saying to myself was, 'Would I still be famous, would they still love me if they knew I was gay?' And my fear was that no, no they wouldn't, and then it made me feel ashamed that I was hiding something. It made me feel ashamed that I couldn't feel honest and really be who I am, and I just didn't want to pretend to be somebody else anymore so that people would like me."[14]

"The fact is, I'm gay, always have been, always will be . . ."[15] With those words, Anderson Cooper, the prominent Emmy-winning CNN journalist, quietly came out on July 2, 2012, on Andrew Sullivan's blog, becoming America's first openly gay prime-time anchor.[16] Cooper, however, was not the first TV news personality to come out:

- Hank Plante, formerly of KPIX in San Francisco, came out in 1978, making him one of the first openly gay TV reporters in the country.[17]
- Rachel Maddow, the first openly LGBTQ person to host a major prime-time news program in the United States, began by hosting *The Rachel Maddow Show* on the Air America radio network in 2005 before moving in 2008 to MSNBC, which is currently home to her daily program.[18]
- CNN weekend anchor Don Lemon came out in his 2011 memoir *Transparent*, which addresses intersections and tensions between his African American and gay identities.[19]
- Thomas Roberts became the first openly gay anchor of a network news broadcast when he hosted *NBC Nightly News* on July 18, 2015.[20]

Has Ellen DeGeneres had a measurable impact on raising awareness of LGBTQ issues?

- Following the February 12, 2008, murder of Lawrence King—a 15-year-old student shot at an Oxnard, California, middle school by a 14-year-old male classmate whom King had asked to be his valentine—DeGeneres made a plea on her television show: "[S]omewhere along the line," she said, "the killer got the message that it's so threatening and so awful and horrific that Larry would want to be his valentine that killing Larry seemed to be the right thing to do. And when the message out there is so horrible that to be gay you can be killed for it, we need to change the message."[21]
- King's murder initially received scant coverage in the mainstream press, but the video of DeGeneres making her plea to "change the message" received more than a million hits on the show's YouTube page between 2008 and 2009 and helped catapult King's murder into the national headlines.[22]

- The killer, Brandon McInerney, was tried as an adult and sentenced to 21 years in prison. King's family received $273,000 in a civil suit from four defendants, including the McInerney family and the school district.[23]

What is Logo TV, and how many households have access to it?

The first advertiser-supported commercial television channel in the United States geared to the LGBTQ community, Logo TV launched on June 30, 2005.

- As of February 2015, Logo reached approximately 51,337,000 American households—44.1 percent of households with television.[24]
- *RuPaul's Drag Race*, which entered its eighth season in 2016, is the highest-rated program to date on the Viacom-owned channel.[25]

What is the status of television representations of LGBTQ people?

According to GLAAD's "Where We Are on TV Report," which analyzed the number of LGBT characters as well as overall diversity on television during the 2015–16 season:

- Of 881 regular characters on 118 prime-time TV shows on the major networks, 35 (4 percent) were identified as LGB. An additional 35 recurring or occasional LGB characters were counted. There were 0 transgender regular or recurring characters on prime-time network programs.
- Of the 70 regular and recurring LGB characters on prime-time network shows:
  - 47 percent were gay men.
  - 33 percent were lesbians.
  - 17 percent were bisexual women.
  - 3 percent were bisexual men.
  - 69 percent were white, 19 percent were black, 7 percent were Latino/a, and 6 percent were Asian–Pacific Islander (API).
- On cable programs, 84 regular characters were LGBTQ-identified, as were 58 recurring characters. Of these 142 characters:

- 41 percent were gay men.
- 22 percent were lesbians.
- 23 percent were bisexual women.
- 13 percent were bisexual men.
- 1 percent were transgender women (two characters).
- 1 percent were transgender men (one character).
- 71 percent were white, 11 percent were black, 8 percent were Latino/a, 4 percent were API, and 5 percent were from other backgrounds.

- On streaming services such as Netflix and Amazon Prime, an analysis of 23 original series found 43 LGBTQ-identified regular characters and 16 recurring LGBTQ characters. Of these 59 characters:
  - 39 percent were gay men.
  - 36 percent were lesbians.
  - 15 percent were bisexual women.
  - 5 percent were bisexual men.
  - 7 percent were transgender women (4 characters).
  - 0 percent were transgender men.
  - 73 percent were white, 12 percent were black, 12 percent were Latino/a, 2 percent were API, and 2 percent were from another background.[26]

What representations of transgender people on television have received critical acclaim?

Laverne Cox of Netflix's *Orange Is the New Black* broke new ground in 2014 when she became the first transgender person to be nominated for an Emmy.[27]

- The first actor to win an Emmy for portraying a trans character was Bradley Whitford, who won the 2015 Outstanding Guest Actor in a Comedy category for his depiction of Marcy on Amazon's *Transparent*.[28]
- A week later, *Transparent* star Jeffrey Tambor won the 2015 Emmy for Outstanding Lead Actor in a Comedy Series for his portrayal of Maura Pfefferman, a trans woman who comes out to her family late in life.[29]
- Vanessa Redgrave was nominated for a 1987 Emmy for

playing transgender tennis star Renée Richards in the 1986 CBS movie *Second Serve.*[30]

- Tom Wilkinson was nominated for an Emmy for his role as transitioning transgender factory worker Ruth in the 2003 HBO movie *Normal.*[31]

FILM

What are the most commercially successful films with LGBTQ themes?

The top 10 highest-grossing LGBTQ films in the United States are:

1. *The Birdcage* (1996): $124,060,553.
2. *Interview with a Vampire* (1994): $105,264,608.
3. *The Imitation Game* (2014): $91,125,683.
4. *Brokeback Mountain* (2005): $83,043,761.
5. *The Talented Mr. Ripley* (1999): $81,298,265.
6. *Philadelphia* (1993): $77,446,440.
7. *In & Out* (1997): $63,856,929.
8. *The Crying Game* (1992): $62,548,947.
9. *Bruno* (2009): $60,054,530.
10. *The Hours* (2002): $41,675,994.[32]

- These films were nominated for a total of 45 Academy Awards; they won eight.
- The most-awarded film on this list is *Brokeback Mountain*, which won Oscars for Best Director, Best Adapted Screenplay, and Best Score but not Best Picture, for which it was also nominated.
- Two other films with gay themes—*Midnight Cowboy* and *American Beauty*—have won Best Picture Oscars.[33]

Which members of the LGBTQ community have won Academy Awards?

More than a dozen openly LGBTQ people have won Oscars:

- In 2016, Sam Smith won the Best Original Song Oscar for "Writing's on the Wall," from the James Bond film *Spectre*. In his acceptance speech, he dedicated his award "to the LGBT community around the world."[34]

- Dustin Lance Black won the Best Original Screenplay Oscar in 2009 for *Milk*, a film about the pioneering gay activist Harvey Milk.[35]
- Melissa Etheridge won the Best Original Song Academy Award in 2007 for "I Need to Wake Up," from *An Inconvenient Truth*.[36]
- Spanish filmmaker Pedro Almodóvar won the Oscar for Best Foreign Language Film in 2000 for *All About My Mother* and the Best Original Screenplay Oscar for *Talk to Her* in 2003.[37]
- Alan Ball won the Best Original Screenplay Oscar for *American Beauty* in 2000.[38]
- John Corigliano won an Academy Award in 2000 for Best Original Score for *The Red Violin*.[39]
- Angelina Jolie, who is openly bisexual, won the Best Supporting Actress Oscar for *Girl, Interrupted* in 1999.[40]
- Bill Condon won the Best Original Screenplay Oscar in 1999 for *Gods and Monsters* (which starred openly gay actor Ian McKellen, who was nominated for the Best Actor Oscar, and which was based on the novel by openly gay author Christopher Bram).[41]
- Elton John won the Best Original Song Oscar in 1995 for "Can You Feel the Love Tonight" from Disney's *The Lion King*, with lyricist Tim Rice.[42]
- Howard Ashman won the Oscar for Best Original Song twice: in 1990 for "Under the Sea" from Disney's *The Little Mermaid*, and posthumously in 1992 for "Beauty and the Beast" from the film of the same name, with composer Alan Menken.[43]
- Debra Chasnoff won an Oscar in 1992 for Best Documentary Short for *Deadly Deception* and thanked her life partner, Kim Klausner, when she accepted the award.[44]
- Stephen Sondheim won an Oscar in 1991 for Best Original Song for "Sooner or Later," performed by Madonna in *Dick Tracy*.[45]
- In 1985, Rob Epstein and Richard Schmeichen won the

Oscar for Best Documentary Feature for *The Times of Harvey Milk*—the first gay-themed film made by openly gay filmmakers to win an Academy Award.[46]

- John Gielgud won the Best Supporting Actor award in 1982 for *Arthur*. He is generally considered the first openly gay actor to win an Oscar. Although he rarely discussed his sexual orientation in interviews, he publicly acknowledged his longtime partner, Martin Hensler, in 1988.[47]
- Linda Hunt, an out lesbian, won the Best Supporting Actress Oscar for *The Year of Living Dangerously* in 1982, making her the first person to win an Academy Award for portraying a character of the opposite gender. (Hunt played the male Chinese Australian photographer Billy Kwan.)[48]

Two LGBTQ actors have come out after having won Academy Awards:

- Jodie Foster won the Best Female Actor Oscar for *The Accused* (1988) and *The Silence of the Lambs* (1991) and came out in 2013.
- Joel Grey won the Oscar for Best Male Actor in a Supporting Role for *Cabaret* (1972) and came out in 2015 at the age of 82.[49]

What straight-identified actors have won Academy Awards for playing LGBTQ characters?

The following straight actors have won Oscars for playing an LGBTQ character; all but one portray characters who die at the end of the film:

1. William Hurt, *Kiss of the Spider Woman* (1985).
2. Tom Hanks, *Philadelphia* (1993).
3. Hilary Swank, *Boys Don't Cry* (1999).
4. Nicole Kidman, *The Hours* (2002).
5. Charlize Theron, *Monster* (2003).
6. Philip Seymour Hoffman, *Capote* (2005).
7. Sean Penn, *Milk* (2008).
8. Natalie Portman, *Black Swan* (2010).

9. Christopher Plummer, *Beginners* (2010).
10. Jared Leto, *Dallas Buyers Club* (2013).[50]

How many LGBTQ-themed films exist? What are some of the most essential titles?

- As of June 2016, *Wikipedia* listed 2,246 feature and documentary films from around the globe that "deal with or feature significant LGBT characters or issues, and may have same-sex romance or relationships as an important plot device."[51]
- *The Advocate*, founded in 1967 and now the oldest and largest LGBTQ publication in the United States, asked its readers and staff in 2014 what the most essential films are for LGBTQ audiences. "Then the arguing began," and the editors came up with a list of 175 films. These are the top 10:

    1. *Brokeback Mountain* (2005).
    2. *Milk* (2008).
    3. *Paris Is Burning* (1990).
    4. *Cabaret* (1972).
    5. *The Boys in the Band* (1970).
    6. *Philadelphia* (1993).
    7. *Bound* (1996).
    8. *Desert Hearts* (1985).
    9. *Boys Don't Cry* (1999).
    10. *Parting Glances* (1986).[52]

What was the quantity and diversity of LGBTQ characters in films released by major Hollywood studios in 2015?

In 2016, GLAAD issued a report examining feature film releases from seven major Hollywood studios, as well as films from four major subsidiary studios.

- Of the 126 films analyzed, 22 (17.5 percent) contained characters identified as lesbian, gay, bisexual, or transgender.

- Of the inclusive films, 77 percent featured gay male characters, 23 percent featured lesbian characters, and 9 percent included bisexual characters. One film was trans-inclusive: Warner Brothers' *Hot Pursuit*.
- GLAAD counted 47 LGBT characters among all mainstream releases in 2015. Male characters outnumbered females by a ratio of more than three to one.
- The racial diversity of LGBT characters decreased markedly in films tracked in 2015:
    - 25.5 percent of LGBT characters were people of color, compared to 32.1 percent the previous year.
    - Of the 47 LGBT characters counted, 34 were white, 5 were Latino/a, 4 were black/African American, and 3 were Asian–Pacific Islander.
    - One character was nonhuman: Fabian in Lionsgate's *Un Gallo con Muchos Huevos*.[53]

INTERNET

What have studies revealed about Internet usage among LGBTQ people?

In a 2011 quantitative and qualitative study of Internet usage among young gay men aged 18 to 24:

- 100 percent of respondents who sat for in-depth interviews reported using the Internet to search for health information.
- 87.5 percent said that the Internet played an active role in connecting to other people, in particular other gay or bisexual youth.[54]

A large, nationally representative survey of 1,197 LGBT adult Americans conducted by the Pew Research Center in 2013 found that 80 percent of respondents use social networking sites, as compared to 58 percent of the general public. Additional findings are shown in Figure 8.1 on page 136.

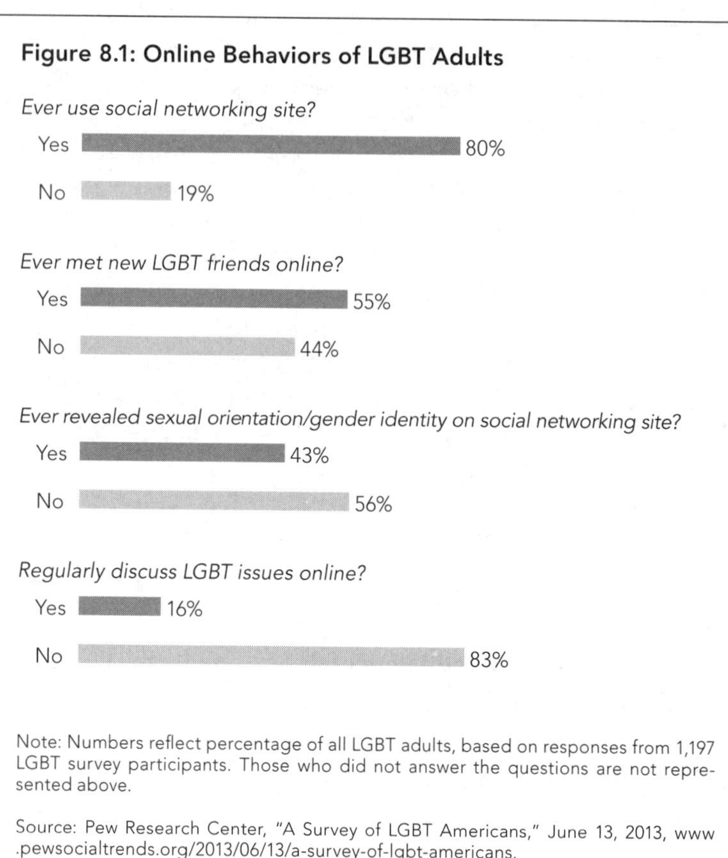

Note: Numbers reflect percentage of all LGBT adults, based on responses from 1,197 LGBT survey participants. Those who did not answer the questions are not represented above.

Source: Pew Research Center, "A Survey of LGBT Americans," June 13, 2013, www.pewsocialtrends.org/2013/06/13/a-survey-of-lgbt-americans.

How important is the Internet in the coming-out process?

- In a 2009 study on coming out and the media, 72 percent of respondents in the sample used some kind of media as their primary means of gathering information during the coming-out process. 70 percent used the Internet; 49 percent reported that the Internet was their primary source.[55]
- In June 2016, a YouTube search for "coming out" yielded 19,400,000 hits.[56]

How many people have come out on Facebook?

In data that Facebook released in October 2015, the company reported that:

- More than 6 million people in the United States have come out on Facebook since its creation in 2004. (The company defines coming out as changing one's profile to express same-sex attraction or an alternative gender.)
- In 2015 alone, 800,000 people had come out by October.
- 26 million Americans superimposed a rainbow flag filter on their profile picture in the days surrounding the Supreme Court's 2015 decision affirming same-sex marriage. This action—taken by figures ranging from Arnold Schwarzenegger to Elizabeth Warren—garnered more than half a billion "likes" and comments from Facebook users around the globe. (The rainbow filter was created by two Facebook interns during an internal hackathon at the company.)[57]

How many people did President Obama reach with his tweet about marriage equality?

On June 26, 2013—the day the Supreme Court struck down the Defense of Marriage Act (DOMA)—President Barack Obama tweeted: "Today's DOMA ruling is a historic step forward for #MarriageEquality. #LoveIsLove." Figure 8.2 on page 138 shows the number of people, in millions, who witnessed Obama's tweet, along with other media events from a variety of platforms.

MUSIC

Can listening to pro-LGBTQ song lyrics change people's views?

In a 2014 study of 292 individuals whose demographic closely mirrored U.S. Census data, participants who listened to Lady Gaga's gay anthem *Born This Way* put more weight on genetic explanations of gay origins when evaluating gay-rights policies,

Figure 8.2: Number of People Who Witnessed Major Media Events

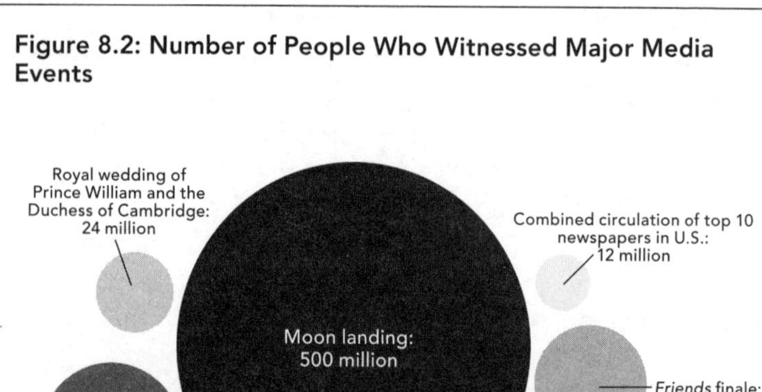

Source: "Finding a Voice Through Social Media: The LGBT Community," Salzburg Academy on Media and Global Change, 2013, www.salzburg.umd.edu/unesco/social-media-and-lgbt-community.

as compared to those who listened to an instrumental version of the song or those not exposed to any stimuli.[58]

Who are some out LGB Grammy winners?

- In 1987, Elton John was a co-winner of the Grammy for Best Pop Performance by a Duo or Group with Vocal for "That's What Friends Are For."
- Howard Ashman won two Grammys in 1991 for his lyrics for *The Little Mermaid*. He also won two posthumous Grammys in 1993 for his lyrics for *Beauty and the Beast*.
- In 1993, Melissa Etheridge won the Grammy for Best Rock Performance by a Female Vocalist for "Ain't It Heavy."

- Also in 1993, k.d. lang won the Grammy for Best Pop Performance by a Female Vocalist for "Constant Craving."
- Frank Ocean won the Grammy for Best Urban Contemporary Album for *Channel Orange* in 2013 and was co-winner of the Grammy for Best Rap/Sung Collaboration for "No Church in the Wild."
- At the 57th Grammy Awards in February 2015, British singer/songwriter Sam Smith became the first openly gay man to win Album of the Year for his album *In the Lonely Hour*. He also won three other Grammys: Best New Artist, Song of the Year, and Best Pop Vocal Album. In his acceptance speech, Smith thanked the man who broke his heart for inspiring the album.[59]

Do LGBTQ Americans spend more on music than straight listeners?

Nielsen's *2015 LGBT Consumer Report* found that in every area of music purchasing—paid music streaming, CDs, digital albums, vinyl/cassettes, music festivals, small live music events, and DJs at known clubs—LGBT households spent more than their straight counterparts.[60]

How many rappers are openly LGBTQ?

Wikipedia lists 32 LGBT rappers as of June 2016. Among them are Deadlee, a major player in the homo hip-hop music scene, who married his partner in 2013 and attacked Eminem, DMX, and 50 Cent as "homophobic," and Meshell Ndegeocello, an out bisexual who has been nominated for 10 Grammy awards and is credited with having "sparked the neo-soul movement."[61]

PRINT MEDIA: NEWSPAPERS AND BOOKS

How many LGBTQ books, bookstores, and newspapers are in the United States?

- A search for LGBTQ books on Amazon.com in June 2016 yielded 25,523 titles.[62]
- In 2016, there were 13 LGBTQ bookstores in the United

States, according to Lambda Literary Foundation. A list compiled in 1996 by the online site Queer Resources Directory included 69 LGBT bookstores in the United States.[63]

- In January 2016, *Wikipedia* listed 102 LGBTQ printed newspapers, magazines, and journals in the United States. When the first edition of this book was released in 1994, there were 125 newspapers serving the LGBT community.[64]

Who are some of the most highly acclaimed LGBTQ authors?

The Lambda Literary Awards—established in 1989 by L. Page "Deacon" Maccubbin, owner of Lambda Rising Bookstore in Washington, D.C.—"identify and celebrate the best lesbian, gay, bisexual and transgender books of the year and affirm that LGBTQ stories are part of the literature of the world."

- Lillian Faderman is the only writer to have won awards in seven different categories.
- Michael Nava has won five awards in the Gay Mystery category.
- Ellen Hart has won five awards in the Lesbian Mystery category.
- Alison Bechdel has won four awards in the Humor category, as well as two in the memoir/biography category. One of Bechdel's graphic novel memoirs, *Fun Home*, was the basis for the Broadway play of the same name, which won five Tony Awards, including Best Musical, in 2015. The first Broadway musical with a lesbian protagonist, *Fun Home* tells the story of Bechdel's coming out and chronicles her relationship with her gay father.[65]
- Colm Tóibín is the only writer to have won two awards in the Gay Fiction category.
- Paul Monette is the only writer to have won two awards in the Gay Nonfiction category.[66]

What trends have emerged regarding LGBTQ-themed books for young adults?

In 2014, mainstream publishers released 47 LGBT books for young adults. This is a 59 percent increase from 2013, when only 29 LGBT young adult books were published by mainstream publishers.[67]

How has *New York Times* coverage of LGBTQ issues evolved?

In a study of how the owners and editors of print media affect coverage of LGBTQ issues, researchers looked at a 1966 note from one of the owners of the *New York Times* to her son, the editor at the time. The note stated that articles about homosexuality should not appear on the newspaper's front page and that "parents and grandparents" would find it distasteful to be faced with "all this talk of perversion."

- The researchers then looked at the number of articles in which homosexuality was mentioned on the front page of the *Times* and found that the newpaper's owners "actively intervened to suppress coverage of lesbians and gays until 1987."[68]
- After a 1987 meeting with GLAAD representatives, *New York Times* editors agreed to use the word "gay" instead of "homosexual." Founded in 1985 to protest the *New York Post*'s inflammatory coverage of AIDS and initially known as the Gay and Lesbian Alliance Against Defamation, GLAAD has grown to be "one of the most successful organizations lobbying the media for inclusion," according to *Entertainment Weekly*.[69]

What religious voices are featured in media reports about LGBTQ issues?

A three-year study conducted by GLAAD and the University of Missouri Center on Religion & the Professions reached the following conclusions about religious voices in mainstream media reports about LGBTQ issues in newspapers and on broadcast programs:

- Evangelical Christians, whose messages are consistently negative regarding LGBTQ issues, are consulted and interviewed at a higher rate than their percentage in the population: they were quoted in 34 percent of mainstream media reports but represent 26 percent of the U.S. population.
- Christian Evangelical organizations accounted for 50 percent of all organizations cited.
- 40 percent of all anti-LGBTQ statements by religiously identified representatives were made by Evangelical Christians; 12 percent were made by Catholics.
- More than 50 percent of Catholics consulted presented negative messages about LGBTQ people, which is inconsistent with the majority view of American Catholics. 71 percent of U.S. Catholics support same-sex marriage, while 73 percent support legal protections for LGBTQ people.
- The mainstream media used far fewer religious sources from mainline Protestant, Catholic, or Jewish sources, but those messages were predominantly positive.
- Pro-LGBTQ or LGBTQ-identified sources were generally presented without any religious affiliation, reinforcing the media framing of "religious versus gay." The study's authors conclude that this framing of religious voices "has the potential to distort perceptions of religion, of LGBT people, and of the 'morality' of pro- and anti-gay viewpoints."[70]

For more on LGBTQ people and religion, see the Religion chapter on page 153.

America's change of heart toward its gay citizens is the greatest awakening of mass conscience in the United States since the civil rights movement of the 1960s.

—*Jonathan Rauch, in the 2013 essay "A Gay Awakening"*[1]

In 1977, Harvey Milk offered a simple prescription for combating the virulent—and life-threatening—prejudice that members of the LGBTQ community faced on a daily basis: "I would like to see every gay doctor come out, every gay lawyer, every gay architect come out, stand up and let the world know," he said. "That would do more to end prejudice overnight than anybody would imagine." Milk—who became America's fifth openly gay elected official in 1977 and served 11 months on San Francisco's Board of Supervisors before being assassinated in 1978—turned out to be correct: the decision by millions of LGBTQ Americans to be open and honest about their sexual orientation has brought about a profound transformation in America's views on LGBTQ people. When, for example, Pew researchers conducted a 2013 survey to find out why onetime opponents of same-sex marriage had changed their mind on this issue, the top response was not, "I believe in equal rights" or "Same-sex marriage is inevitable," but rather, "I know someone who is gay."[2] As of 2015, 88 percent of Americans said they personally know someone who is lesbian or gay—up from 24 percent in 1985[3]—and more than half have a close friend or family member who is lesbian or gay. As one survey participant told Pew when asked why he decided to support same-sex marriage: "My best friend from high school is a gay man, and he deserves the same rights [that I have]." Harvey Milk couldn't have said it better.

ATTITUDES TOWARD LGBTQ AMERICANS

How has public opinion shifted since the 1970s?

- In 1972, when the General Social Survey began polling Americans on an array of social issues, 52 percent of respondents said they felt comfortable with an "admitted homosexual" teaching at a college or university. That number rose to 85 percent in 2012.[4]
- In 1977, 56 percent of Americans believed gay men and lesbians should have equal rights in terms of job opportunities. 89 percent of American held that view in 2008 (the last year Gallup asked the question).[5]
- When asked in 1977 if same-sex activity between two consenting adults should be legal or illegal, 43 percent of Americans said such conduct should be illegal. The number dropped to 28 percent in 2015—its lowest point over this 38-year span:[6]

Figure 9.1: Evolving Views on Gay and Lesbian Rights

Do you think gay or lesbian relations between consenting adults should or should not be legal?

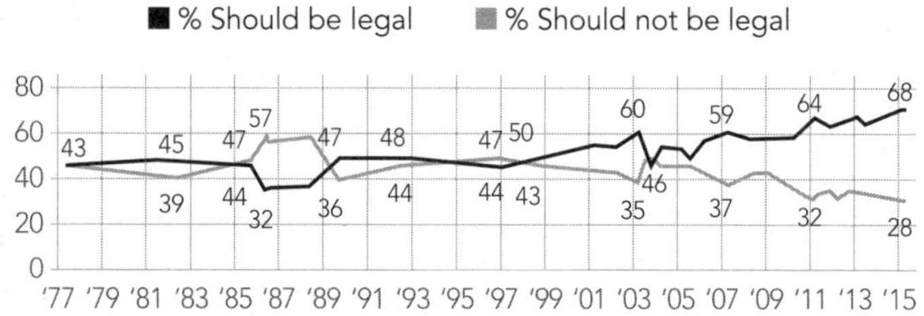

From 1977 to 2008, the question was posed as follows: Do you think homosexual relations between consenting adults should or should not be legal?

Source: Gallup, "Gay and Lesbian Rights," 2015, www.gallup.com/poll/1651/gay-lesbian-rights.aspx.

In a report on public-opinion trends on LGBT rights in the United States drawn from 325 surveys conducted between 1977 and 2014, the Williams Institute found:

- Public support for lesbians and gay men has doubled in the past three decades, more so than for any other group surveyed over the same time period. It appears that this trend is due to increased LGBTQ visibility and a cultural shift. The change has occurred among all age-groups, not just among younger Americans.
- While few polls have included questions about transgender people, the surveys that have addressed this segment of the population reflect a 40 percent increase in support between 2005 and 2011. 71 percent of participants in a 2013 Pew study said transgender people face a significant amount of discrimination.
- In 1978, 30 percent of Americans thought lesbians and gay men experience a lot of discrimination; in 2013, the number holding this view had risen to 68 percent. The only other group perceived to experience more discrimination than LGBT people is Muslims.[7]

What are some of the most significant trends regarding LGBTQ visibility and social acceptance?

- The percentage of Americans who believe "gay and lesbian relations are morally acceptable" rose from 40 percent in 2001 to 63 percent in 2015, according to Gallup.[8] 77 percent of American surveyed in 2012 said LGBT people should have health insurance and other employee benefits available to domestic partners or spouses. 78 percent said LGBT people should have inheritance rights.[9]
- 63 percent of respondents in a 2014 poll said LGBT people should be able to adopt children, up from 29 percent in 1992.[10]
- 78 percent of Americans report feeling comfortable around gay men and lesbians, according to a 2009 Gallup poll.[11]
- Support for LGBT people actively serving in the military went from 50 percent in 1993 to 70 percent in 2012.[12]

What have researchers learned about young adults' views on gay men and lesbians?

A 2015 study of undergraduates at a large Midwestern research university found that:

- 63.3 percent of students surveyed thought same-sex relations between adults are natural.
- 84.7 percent would vote for a well-qualified gay or lesbian presidential candidate.
- 92.2 percent would be friends with an effeminate man, and 93.3 percent would be friends with a masculine woman.
- 76.7 percent were in favor of same-sex marriage.
- When asked to rate how comfortable they would be with a roommate of the same sex who is gay or lesbian, with 1 being not comfortable at all and 7 being very comfortable, the mean rating was 5.16.[13]

What percentage of Americans favor nondiscrimination laws?

- According to the Public Religion Research Institute's 2015 *American Values Atlas*, 71 percent of Americans support laws that would protect LGBT people from discrimination.
- Residents of Rhode Island, Massachusetts, and Utah expressed the highest levels of support at 84 percent, 82 percent, and 82 percent, respectively.
- Residents of Alabama (57 percent), Arkansas (57 percent), and Mississippi (54 percent) expressed the lowest levels of support.[14]
- In a 2014 survey of 900 millennials (defined as adults between 18 and 34 at the time of the survey), 65 percent of respondents said they support comprehensive nondiscrimination protections for LGBT Americans. The breakdown among racial, ethnic, and political groups was as follows:

Figure 9.2: Percentage of Millennials (by Race/Ethnicity and Political Party Affiliation) Who Support Comprehensive Nondiscrimination Protections for LGBT Americans

Support for laws that protect LGBT people from discrimination in employment, housing, and other areas of life

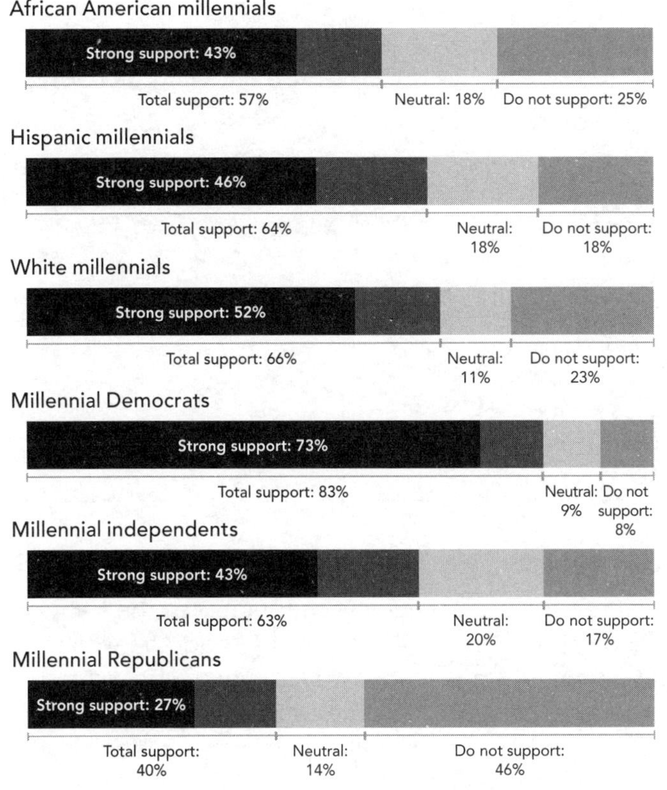

Sources: Sarah McBride and Zenen Jaimes Pérez, "Millennials Overwhelmingly Support Comprehensive LGBT Nondiscrimination Protections," Center for American Progress, April 7, 2015, www.americanprogress.org/issues/lgbt/news/2015/04/07/110523/millennials-overwhelmingly-support-comprehensive-lgbt-nondiscrimination-protections; Hart Research Associates, "America's Millennials: Still Looking for Change for Generation Progress," 2014.

What differences exist between rural and urban Americans' perceptions of LGBTQ people?

The 2013 Nebraska Annual Social Indicators Survey examined contrasts among the opinions of 1,608 rural and urban Americans in a "red state." Analyzing that data, researchers found varying levels of support for key issues of concern to LGBTQ people, as shown in Table 9.1 below:

Table 9.1: Rural Versus Urban Nebraskans' Views on LGBTQ Issues

	Rural	Urban	Total
Same-sex marriage	31.5%	50.3%	40.4%
Adoption	45.0%	67.4%	55.6%
Protection from housing discrimination	64.5%	79.5%	71.6%
Protection from job discrimination	68.6%	80.5%	74.2%

Source: Mathew Stange and Emily Kazyak, "Examining the Nuance in Public Opinion of Pro-LGB Policies in a 'Red State,'" *Sexuality Research and Social Policy* 13, no. 2 (2015): 142–57, doi: 10.1007/s13178-015-0213-x.

What have studies shown about attitudes toward trans people?

In a 2014 public opinion survey conducted by the Harris Poll:

- 75 percent of the 2,543 respondents agreed with the statement, "Transgender workers should be treated equally and fairly as all other workers."
- 65 percent agreed with the statement, "Federal law should be expanded to include protection from job discrimination based on sexual orientation and gender identity."[15]

In a two-part 2016 study assessing transphobia among undergraduate business students, two groups of students were asked to resolve a simulated dispute between coworkers over accommodating a trans employee's bathroom choice. Study participants were given three ways to respond: inclusion (i.e., establishing gender-neutral restrooms); hostility (refusing to accept the transgender employee's bathroom choice); or compliance (instructing the complaining employee to respect the trans employee's choice).

- Among the first group of students, the most popular response was compliance (selected by 38.7 percent of respondents), followed by hostility (34 percent).
- After reading a brief article about transgender employees, the second group chose inclusion as its most popular response (62 percent), though roughly one in six respondents still chose the hostile option.[16]

OPINIONS ON MARRIAGE

Where does the American public stand on same-sex marriage and related issues after the *Obergefell* decision?

- In a 2016 Gallup poll, 61 percent of Americans thought that same-sex couples should have the same marriage rights as opposite-sex couples—up from 27 percent in 1996.[17]
- After the Supreme Court legalized same-sex marriage in its *Obergefell v. Hodges* decision in June 2015, 59 percent of Americans opposed allowing a small business owner to refuse to provide products or services to gay or lesbian people, even if doing so violated the business owner's religious beliefs, according to the Public Religion Research Institute.[18]

How do opinions on same-sex marriage vary among different segments of the population?

- 71 percent of millennials (defined in this study as those born after 1981) were in favor of same-sex marriage in 2016, according to a Pew Research Center survey.[19]
- Support for same-sex marriage has grown among all religious groups surveyed between 2001 and 2015.

64 percent of white mainline Protestants favor same-sex marriage, as do 58 percent of Catholics. The approval rate was 39 percent among black Protestants and 27 percent among white evangelical Protestants.[20]
- In polls taken of LGBT Americans in 2013 and 2014, 38 percent of Republicans and 64 percent of Democrats said same-sex marriage should be the top priority for LGBT people. 7 percent of respondents said they opposed same-sex marriage, while 39 percent felt the issue was taking too much focus away from other issues important to LGBT people.[21]

For more data on marriage, see pages 108 to 119 of the Marriage and Family chapter.

VIEWS ON THE ORIGINS OF HOMOSEXUALITY

According to a 2013 Pew Research Center poll:
- 58 percent of Americans with a postgraduate degree believe people are born gay.
- 35 percent of Americans with a high school education or less believe the same.[22]

Views on this question have evolved dramatically over the past 40 years:
- In a 1977 Gallup poll, 13 percent of respondents said people are born gay or lesbian, while 56 percent believed being gay or lesbian is the result of upbringing or environment. 14 percent told pollsters that heredity and environment are both factors in determining sexual orientation.
- In a 1996 survey, 31percent of those questioned said people are born gay or lesbian, while 40 percent pointed to upbringing or environment. 13 percent felt that heredity and environment both play a role.
- In a 2015 poll, 51 percent of respondents told research-

ers that people are born gay or lesbian, while 30 percent cited upbringing or environment. 8 percent said heredity and environment are both factors.[23]

ATTITUDES AND EXPERIENCES OF LGBTQ AMERICANS

What levels of acceptance and rejection do LGBTQ Americans report?

In a comprehensive study of LGBTQ Americans conducted in 2013 by the Pew Research Center, 92 percent of respondents thought that society is more accepting of LGBTQ people than it was 10 years earlier. At the same time:

- 58 percent of those surveyed had been the subject of slurs or jokes, though only 16 percent within the previous year.
- 33 percent had been rejected by a family member or close friend.
- 30 percent had been threatened or physically attacked.
- 56 percent were out to their mothers and 39 percent were out to their fathers.
- 54 percent of all LGBT people said all or most of the important people in their life were aware that they are LGBT. The percentage was 28 percent for bisexuals, 71 percent for lesbians, and 77 percent for gay men. (A percentage was not given for transgender respondents.)
- The median coming-out age was 20, while 12 was the median age at which respondents thought they might be LGB.
- 67 percent of the women were in a committed relationship, as were 40 percent of the men.
- 7 percent thought being LGBT was a negative factor in their life.
- 18 percent of LGBT adults described themselves as "very happy," compared with 30 percent of the general public.[24]

How do LGBTQ Americans feel about social institutions and political parties?

In Pew's 2013 survey:

- Barack Obama was named the top public figure in advancing LGBT rights, followed by Ellen DeGeneres.
- The policy issue that ranked as the top priority was equal employment rights.
- 49 percent of respondents thought LGBT Americans should be able to achieve equality while maintaining a distinct culture and way of life—while 49 percent believed that the best way to achieve equality is to become part of mainstream culture and institutions such as marriage.[25]

> Today the war between homosexuality and religion rages on in the churches, mosques, and synagogues. Most conservative or orthodox or traditional religionists reject homosexual acts or the orientation itself as incompatible with ethical and righteous living. And worldwide these are the loudest voices and the most powerful and influential forces in society. But things are changing surprisingly rapidly . . .
>
> —*Joe Perez,* Gay Spirituality, *2014*[1]

Though opposition to LGBTQ Americans—and their spiritual and political concerns—remains vocal within many faith communities, shifts are occurring at a remarkable pace. More than half of LGBT Americans describe themselves as "highly" or "moderately" religious, and faith communities are taking concrete steps to embrace these worshippers. A record number of Christian churches—6,623 and growing—have gone on record to affirm their support for LGBT members, though this represents only 2 percent of the approximately 320,000 Christian churches nationwide.[2] In late 2015, the Union of Reform Judaism adopted a resolution to embrace transgender people by creating "inclusive and welcoming communities" and urging clergy members to deliver sermons on gender identity.

Despite such advances, LGBTQ Americans face a new challenge: according to the ACLU, as of June 2016 there has been state legislative action on 110 anti-LGBT religious exemption bills in states across the country.[3] These measures give businesses, government workers, organizations, and in some states, private individuals the right to refuse service to LGBTQ people. While Texas senator Ted Cruz has argued that opposition to these measures represents "a concerted assault . . . on the right of every American to seek out and worship God according to the dictates of his or her conscience,"[4] Tim Cook—the CEO of Apple and an openly gay man—counters that these bills "go against the very principles our nation was founded on, and they have the potential to undo decades of progress toward greater equality."[5] The relationship between LGBTQ people and religion in public life continues to be a high-stakes battleground.

FAITH EXPERIENCES OF LGBTQ PEOPLE

What percentage of LGBTQ Americans are religious?

Of the 3,242 LGBT interviewees who took part in a 2014 Gallup poll of 104,000 Americans:

- 24 percent considered themselves "highly religious," versus 41 percent of the non-LGBTQ population.
- 29 percent said they are "moderately religious"—as did 29 percent of the non-LGBTQ population.
- 47 percent classified themselves as "not religious," versus 30 percent of the non-LGBTQ population.[6]

How many LGB Americans identify as Christian?

In a Pew Research Center report from May 2015:

- 48 percent of LGB Americans identified as Christian, up from 42 percent in 2013.[7]
- In the general population, the number of Americans who identify as Christian declined from 78.4 percent to 70.6 percent between 2007 and 2014.[8]

How many gay men who were raised Christian maintain their religious identity as adults?

In a 2012 study of gay men's retention of a Christian faith tradition using data from 2010, 2,060 men were surveyed, with the following results:

- 83.6 percent were raised Christian.
- 43.2 percent identified as Christian at the time of the study.
- 28.9 percent identified as atheist or agnostic at the time of the study.

- 28 percent identified as spiritual but not Christian at the time of the study.

A second study on the same topic, composed of 326 gay men and completed in 2011, found:

- 89.8 percent were raised Christian.
- 38 percent identified as Christian at the time of the study.
- 50.5 percent identified as atheist or agnostic.
- 11.5 percent identified as spiritual but not Christian.[9]

A 2013 poll by the Public Religion Research Institute found that nearly a third of 18- to 33-year-olds who left the religion they were brought up in cited anti-gay teachings and the treatment of lesbian and gay people as major factors in their decision.[10]

Within American religious groups, what percentage of members have had same-sex experiences?

According to data from the General Social Survey, the following percentages of people from the religious groups listed below have had sex with someone of the same gender:

- Mormons: 5.2 percent.
- Evangelical Protestants: 6 percent.
- Mainline Protestants: 6.1 percent.
- Catholics: 6.7 percent.
- Members of historically black churches: 7.2 percent.
- Jews: 9.7 percent.
- Members of nonaffiliated religious groups: 11 percent.[11]

LGBTQ AMERICANS' PERCEPTIONS OF RELIGIOUS GROUPS

How do LGBTQ Americans view various religious groups?

In a study of 1,197 LGBT Americans conducted by the Pew Research Center, LGBT people reported the following attitudes toward religious groups:

Figure 10.1: How LGBT Americans View Major Religions

% saying each is generally . . . toward LGBT people

	Unfriendly	Friendly	Neutral
The Muslim religion	84	<1	13
The Mormon Church	83	2	13
The Catholic Church	79	4	16
Evangelical churches	73	3	21
The Jewish religion	47	10	41
Non-Evangelical Protestant churches	44	10	43

Source: Pew Research Center, "A Survey of LGBT Americans," June 13, 2013, www.pewsocialtrends.org/2013/06/13/a-survey-of-lgbt-americans.

RELIGIOUS GROUPS' ATTITUDES TOWARD LGBTQ AMERICANS

To what extent do members of various religious groups support LGBT rights and LGBT people?

Table 10.1, based on an average of surveys conducted in 2000, 2004, and 2008 by American National Election Studies (ANES)—the leading academically run national survey of voters in the United States—shows levels of support for various LGBT rights among a variety of religious groups.

Table 10.2 on page 158, based on data collected by ANES from voters in 2012, shows how religious Americans' views on LGBT issues evolved from previous surveys.

Table 10.1: Support for LGBT Rights Among Religious Americans, 2000 to 2008

	Age	Anti-discrimination laws (% supporting)	Military service (%)	Adoption (%)
White Evangelical Protestants	18–30	70	78	51
	31–45	61	74	37
	46–60	59	64	28
	61+	54	60	17
Black Protestants	18–30	65	79	46
	31–45	71	76	34
	46–60	71	68	31
	61+	62	54	21
White mainline Protestants	18–30	81	91	67
	31–45	72	87	63
	46–60	67	76	45
	61+	73	74	35
Catholics	18–30	79	80	63
	31–45	78	82	62
	46–60	80	85	54
	61+	74	75	39
Not religious	18–30	83	88	72
	31–45	81	84	66
	46–60	76	84	68
	61+	75	68	56

Source: Clyde Wilcox and Rentaro Iida, "Evangelicals, the Christian Right, and Gay and Lesbian Rights in the United States: Simple and Complex Stories" in David Rayside and Clyde Wilcox, eds., *Faith, Politics, and Sexual Diversity in Canada and the United States* (Vancouver: UBC Press, 2011).

Where do religious groups stand on inclusion of transgender people?

The following religions have issued an official statement of inclusion:

- Conservative Judaism
- Episcopal Church
- Metropolitan Community Church
- Reconstructionist Judaism
- Reform Judaism

Table 10.2: Support for LGBT Rights Among Religious Americans, 2012

	Percentage of sample	Anti-discrimination laws (% supporting)	Military service (%)	Adoption (%)	Same-sex marriage* (%)
White Evangelical Protestants	23.9%	67.4%	79.0%	43.9%	22.0%
Black Protestants	1.5%	90.9%	88.2%	54.7%	22.8%
White mainline Protestants	9.7%	75.1%	88.2%	67.3%	41.8%
Catholics	22.8%	80.4%	90.4%	65.4%	40.4%
Undifferentiated Christian	16.5%	71.8%	82.9%	51.4%	27.3%
Jewish	1.0%	87.3%	87.3%	83.6%	67.3%
Other religion	4.1%	82.4%	91.7%	55.0%	37.2%
Not religious	18.1%	80.9%	90.7%	78.5%	62.8%
Average	(NA)	79.5%	87.3%	62.5%	40.2%

* Note: the question allowed three answers: gay and lesbian couples should be allowed to marry; gay and lesbian couples should be allowed to form civil unions but not legally marry; and there should be no legal recognition of a gay or lesbian couple's relationship. The figures here reflect only those who agreed with the first option, full legal marriage.

Source: The raw data for this table came from the 2012 American National Election Studies Time Series Study (www.electionstudies.org) at the University of Michigan and Stanford University, which interviewed 5,914 voters prior to the 2012 election. Special thanks to Professor Shauna Lani Shames of Rutgers University for her assistance in creating this table for inclusion in this book.

- Unitarian Universalist Association
- United Church of Christ

The following religious groups are inclusive but have no official statement:

- Evangelical Lutheran Church of America
- Presbyterian Church (USA)
- United Methodist Church

The following religious groups have an official statement against inclusion:

- Assemblies of God
- Church of Jesus Christ of Latter-Day Saints (Mormon)
- Lutheran Church—Missouri Synod
- Southern Baptist Convention[12]

CHRISTIANITY

Christians constitute approximately 31 percent of the world's population.[13]

- According to the website gaychurch.org, 6,623 Christian churches in all 50 states and the District of Columbia are "LGBT-affirming"—meaning the church "does not view homosexuality in and of itself as a sin, and therefore they would welcome and treat a homosexual person no differently than any other person who walked through their church doors seeking Christ."[14]
- *Wikipedia* currently lists 74 LGBT-affirming Christian denominations worldwide.[15]

Catholicism

- Half the world's 2 billion Christians are Catholics.[16]
- In his book *The Changing Face of the Priesthood*, the Catholic priest Donald Cozzens estimates that between 23 percent and 58 percent of Catholic priests have a homosexual orientation.[17]
- According to the *Encyclopedia of Homosexuality*, there is evidence that at least 10 popes were gay or bisexual.[18]

- On June 26, 2016, Pope Francis stated that the Roman Catholic Church and Christians should seek forgiveness from gay people for the way the church has treated them. The Catholic Church still believes that homosexual acts are sinful but that having a gay orientation is not inherently wrong. Pope Francis said, "The question is: If a person who has that condition, who has good will, and who looks for God, who are we to judge?"[19]

United Church of Christ

- In 1969, the United Church of Christ, a small mainline Protestant denomination that represents less than 1 percent of Christians in the United States, adopted one of the first position statements on homosexuality, in which it called for the decriminalization of homosexual activities between consenting adults.[20]
- In 1972, the UCC became the first Christian denomination to ordain an openly gay candidate, Rev. William R. Johnson.[21]

Episcopalism

- In 1976, the General Convention of the Episcopal Church declared that "homosexual persons are children of God who have a full and equal claim with all other persons upon the love, acceptance, and pastoral concern and care of the Church."[22]
- In 2003, the first openly gay Episcopal bishop, Rev. Gene Robinson, was consecrated, and in 2009, the General Convention resolved that "God's call is open to all."[23]
- On July 1, 2015, the House of Deputies of the Episcopal Church, a voting body of clergy members and laypeople, voted 129–26 to allow same-sex couples to be married in church ceremonies.[24]

ISLAM

About 23 percent of the world's population practices Islam.[25]

- The Muslim Ottoman Empire, founded in 1299, decriminalized homosexuality in 1858—145 years before the United States took the same step in 2003.[26]
- In 20 of 50 Muslim-majority nations, homosexual relations are not illegal.[27]
- Organized activism by gay Muslims took root in major urban centers in Turkey in the late 1970s. In 1993, Turkish LGBT activists organized an international pride celebration in Istanbul, but authorities halted this demonstration at the last minute.[28]
- As of 2016, the PFLAG website listed 10 organizations that are supportive of LGBTQ Muslims around the world. (Founded in 1972, PFLAG provides support to family members and friends of LGBTQ people; the organization has 500 chapters and more than 200,000 members across the country.)[29]

HINDUISM

Hindus constitute about 15 percent of the world's population.[30]

- Hindu views of homosexuality and LGBTQ issues in general are diverse, and different Hindu groups have distinct views.[31]
- In 2009, the United Kingdom Hindu Council issued a statement that "Hinduism does not condemn homosexuality."[32]
- The *Kama Sutra*, an ancient Indian Hindu text, is widely considered to be the standard Hindu work on human sexual behavior. The *Kama Sutra* describes men who desire men as a "third nature," with two classifications: those who take the form or appearance of a woman and those who take the form or appearance of a man.[33]

BUDDHISM

About 7 percent of the world's population practices Buddhism.[34]

- Some scholars believe that early Buddhism placed no special stigma on homosexual relations, since the subject was not mentioned. In some Buddhist traditions—such as the practices of Buddhist monks in Japan—homosexuality was accepted and even flourished.[35]

- According to author Dharmachari Jnanavira, homoerotic relationships that developed in Buddhist institutions "served as the basis for wider same-sex sexual relationships between men throughout Japanese society from the thirteenth to the end of the nineteenth century."[36]
- The treatment of homosexuality varies by tradition and location among modern-day Buddhists. In the United States, numerous fellowships exist for LGBTQ Buddhists, including the Gay Buddhist Sangha, which describes itself as "a group of lesbian, gay, bisexual and transgender people [who] connect so that we can support each other in our practice as we explore the Buddha Way."[37]
- In interviews with 40,000 Americans conducted in 2014 and 2015 by the Public Religion Research Institute, 84 percent of Buddhists expressed support for same-sex marriage—more than any other religious group.[38]

JUDAISM

Jews represent 0.2 percent of the world population.[39]

- The Institute for Judaism, Sexual Orientation & Gender Identity currently lists 52 Jewish LGBT organizations.[40]
- Hebrew Union College–Jewish Institute of Religion began admitting openly LGBT students to its Reform rabbinical seminary in 1990. The Conservative movement's Jewish Theological Seminary followed suit in 2007 and ordained its first openly lesbian rabbi in 2011.[41]
- In November 2015, the Union of Reform Judaism, which has 1.5 million members in North America, overwhelmingly adopted a motion to embrace transgender people. The motion calls for advocating for the rights of transgender people while advising congregations to

"create inclusive and welcoming communities by training staff, organizing education programs, delivering sermons on gender identity, reviewing use of language in prayers, forms and policies, and providing gender-neutral facilities."[42]

MORMONISM (The Church of Jesus Christ of Latter-Day Saints)

Mormons represent approximately 0.2 percent of the world population.[43]

- The law of chastity of the Church of Jesus Christ of Latter-Day Saints (LDS Church) states that any sexual relations outside opposite-sex marriage are contrary to the will of God, and in principle forbids homosexual behavior.[44]
- Although the LDS Church has taught that homosexuality is a curable condition, it acknowledges that "individuals do not choose to have such attractions." The church teaches that regardless of the cause of same-sex attraction, "immoral relationships" must be abjured.[45]
- According to proponents of Proposition 8—a 2008 ballot measure to amend California's constitution to ban same-sex marriage in the state—half of the nearly $40 million raised in support of the proposition was donated by Mormons, and between 80 percent and 90 percent of the volunteers who worked to enact the measure were from the Mormon Church.[46] Proposition 8 passed by a margin of 52.2 percent to 47.8 percent. It was overturned in 2013.[47]
- In 2015, the Mormon Church distributed a handbook to its lay leaders establishing new anti-gay policies. This publication stated that children of same-sex couples cannot join the church until they turn 18, must disavow all same-sex relationships, and must obtain approval from the church's top leadership. Additionally, Mormons in same-sex marriages will be considered apostates and undergo disciplinary hearings.[48]
- In an act of protest against the new policies,

approximately 2,500 Mormons—including about 1,000 who took part in a protest on November 14, 2015—resigned from the Church of Latter-Day Saints.[49]

- Following the issuance of these new policies by the Mormon Church, at least 32 gay Mormon youths have committed suicide, according to Wendy Montgomery of San Francisco University's Family Acceptance Project.[50]

Additional data on American religious groups' acceptance of LGBTQ people are summarized in Figure 10.2.[51]

LGBTQ-AFFIRMING FAITH COMMUNITIES

What is the history of gay and lesbian churches? What faith institutions exist today specifically for LGBTQ people?

- The first known gay church was Charles Webster Leadbeater's Anglican-derived Liberal Catholic Church, founded in Sydney, Australia, in 1916.[52]
- The first American church organized primarily for homosexuals is thought to have been formed in Atlanta in 1946 by George Hyde, a youth minister in the independent Catholic Movement.[53]
- The Christian, nondenominational First Church of One Brotherhood was established in 1956 by Chuck D. Rowland, a co-founder of the Mattachine Society, to address the spiritual needs of religious gay men. Though the church launched with lofty ambitions, it ceased activities at the beginning of 1958.[54]
- The first LGBT synagogue, Beth Chayim Chadashim, was founded in Los Angeles in 1972.[55]
- Currently America's largest LGBT synagogue, New York City's Congregation Beit Simchat Torah has 1,100 members and was founded in 1973.[56]

What is MCC, and how broad is its reach?

The Universal Fellowship of Metropolitan Community Churches (MCC)—a Christian church whose primary outreach is to the

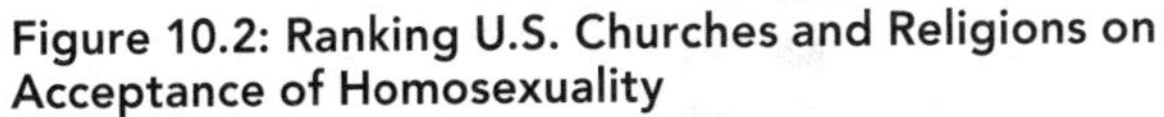

Figure 10.2: Ranking U.S. Churches and Religions on Acceptance of Homosexuality

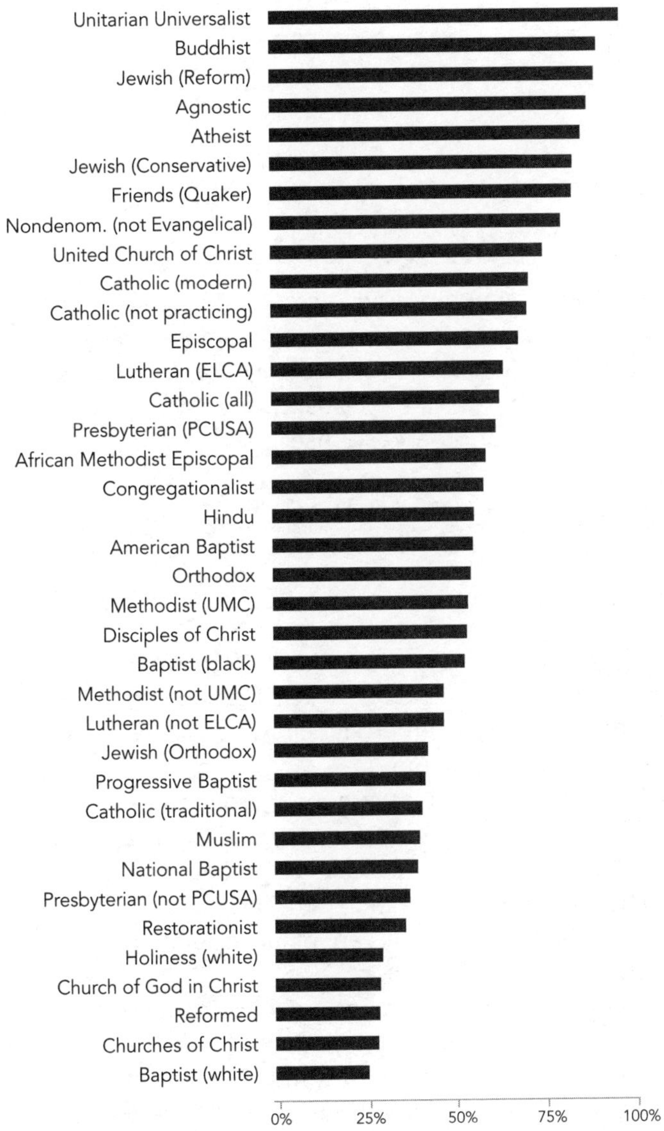

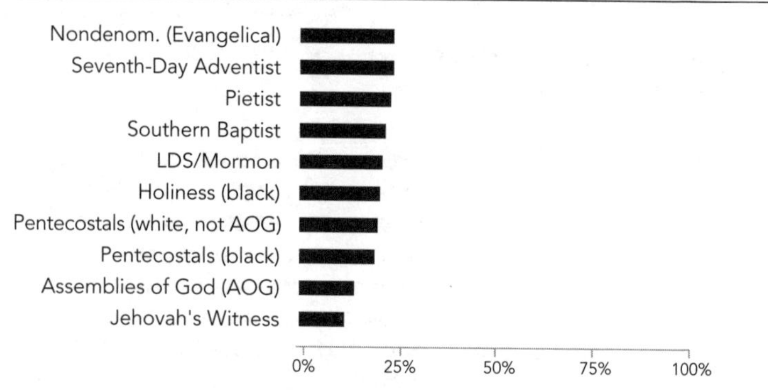

Percentage of members within each U.S. religion or church who agreed with the statement "Homosexuality is a way of life that should be accepted by society" (as opposed to those who said homosexuality should be discouraged, "don't know," or other responses).

Sources: Tobin Grant, "Ranking Religions on Acceptance of Homosexuality and Reactions to SCOTUS Ruling," June 30, 2015, Religious News Service, tobingrant.religionnews.com/2015/06/30/ranking-churches-on-acceptance-of-homosexuality-plus-their-reactions-to-scotus-ruling/#sthash.Xk8ANXkn.dpuf; Pew Religious Landscape Survey, 2007.

LGBT community—was founded in 1968 by Rev. Troy Perry. Today it is the world's largest LGBT denomination, with 160 affiliated churches, 45 emerging churches, and 7 oasis churches in 33 countries worldwide.[57]

- MCC is the largest international organization for public education about homosexuality and Christianity.
- MCC congregations have an aggregate annual operating budget in excess of $20 million.
- MCC Headquarters has an annual operating budget of approximately $2 million.
- The largest MCC churches are in Houston, Fort Lauderdale, and Toronto.
- MCC has members in every state in the United States and congregations in 39 states and the District of Columbia.
- 51.6 percent of MCC clergy are women.[58]

THE BIBLE

What does the Bible say about homosexuality?

- The word "homosexual" did not appear in any translation of the Bible until 1946.
- There are words in Greek for same-sex sexual activities, yet they never appear in the original text of the New Testament.
- The Bible says nothing about homosexuality per se as a sexual orientation but refers only to certain kinds of acts, primarily homosexual temple prostitution.[59]
- Notes Matthew Vines, author of *God and the Gay Christian*: "The Bible never directly addresses, and it certainly does not condemn, loving, committed same-sex relationships. There is no biblical teaching about sexual orientation, nor is there any call to lifelong celibacy for gay people."[60]

Here's a list of Bible teachings that literalists ignore while citing prohibitions against homosexuality:

1. Don't eat pork (Leviticus 11:7–8).
2. Shellfish are an abomination (Leviticus 19:9–12).
3. No cutting of the hair of your temples and beard (Leviticus 19:27).
4. Women should be silent in the church (I Corinthians 14:34–35).
5. Marry your brother's widow (Deuteronomy 25).
6. No hybrid food, livestock, or clothes (Leviticus 19:19).
7. No charging of interest (Leviticus 25:37).
8. Sex outside marriage is punishable by death (Leviticus 20:10).
9. Slavery is okay (Leviticus 25:44).
10. Death to those who take the Lord's name in vain (Leviticus 24:15–16).[61]

For statistics on conversion therapy, see pages 77 to 78 of the Health and Aging chapter.

RELIGIOUS EXEMPTIONS AND LAWS THAT AFFECT LGBTQ PEOPLE

How many religious schools have applied for exemptions under Title IX?

In 2014, the U.S. Department of Education (ED) extended protections provided by Title IX, the landmark 1972 law that prohibits gender-based discrimination in education, to transgender people. Title IX offers an exemption for religious organizations.

- Since 2014, 56 religious-affiliated schools have applied for exemptions from ED, which would legally allow them to discriminate against transgender people.[62]

What are Religious Freedom Restoration Acts, and in what states have they been considered or enacted?

In March 2015, Mike Pence—the governor of Indiana who in 2016 became the Republican nominee for vice president—signed into law the Religious Freedom Restoration Act (RFRA).

- This law allows individuals and companies to assert their right not to have their sincerely held religious beliefs impinged on. The law does not directly authorize discrimination in employment, housing, or public accommodations, but without protections for LGBT people, it could have discriminatory effects.[63]
- In the aftermath of Indiana's passage of its RFRA, at least four states and four cities, as well as numerous organizations and individuals, decided to boycott Indiana. On March 27, 2015, #boycottindiana trended to number one on Twitter.[64]
- A week later, Governor Pence signed into law changes to the bill that, while not outlawing anti-LGBT discrimination, clarified that the religious freedom law does not authorize such discrimination.[65]
- In the wake of the Supreme Court's 2015 decision to legalize same-sex marriage, at least 26 states considered some sort of religious-freedom-protection bill during the 2015 legislative session or will do so in 2016.[66]
- In March 2016, Georgia's State Senate and House of Representatives passed a religious freedom bill that

would have allowed businesses, nonprofits, and individuals to discriminate against LGBT people and others by citing religious grounds. Georgia's governor, Nathan Deal, vetoed the bill after multiple threats of boycotts by companies including Disney and the NFL.[67]

- On April 5, 2016, Mississippi governor Phil Bryant signed a bill that allows businesses, individuals, and religiously affiliated organizations to deny service to LGBT people, single mothers, and others who offend an individual's "sincerely held religious belief." The bill also directly targets transgender residents, effectively claiming that one's sex assigned at birth is immutable and will be the only gender recognized by the state. On July 1, 2016, U.S. District Judge Carlton Reeves struck down the controversial law, hours before it was slated to take effect.[68] Bryant responded by stating that he expects an "aggressive appeal" of the ruling.

For more on legislation that targets transgender Americans, see pages 202 to 205 of the Transgender chapter.

We have a lot to teach the world, because we are not constrained by what others think sex is supposed to look like.

—*Psychotherapist Ken Page, quoted in Hara Estroff Marano's "Gay Love, Straight Sense,"* Psychology Today, *2015*[1]

While it is common to hear that same-sex relationships are "just like straight ones," there are some profound differences—including the fact that same-sex relationships are more egalitarian. As Michael Kimmel points out in his book *The Gender of Desire*, members of lesbian and gay couples report initiating sex at identical rates, making their relationships significantly more equal than those of straight couples.[2] How gay men and lesbians meet partners and form relationships is different, as well, and evolving with technology. The advent of online dating and the spread of geosocial networking apps like Grindr and Scissr has redefined the process of forming relationships and finding partners. A striking 70 percent of single gay men and 47 percent of single lesbians have dated someone they met online,[3] compared to 15 percent of the general public who report using online dating sites or mobile dating apps.[4] This phenomenon transcends national borders. Since its launch in 2012, China's gay dating app Blued has grown to serve 22 million users, making it the most popular gay dating app in the world.[5] Meanwhile, institutions such as bathhouses, which proliferated in the 1970s and provided a discreet place for gay men to meet and have sex, are disappearing. While nearly 200 gay bathhouses drew crowds across America in the late 1970s, fewer than 70 exist today.[6] "The acceptance of gays has changed the whole world," reflects 75-year-old Dennis Holding, the owner of a Miami bathhouse. "It's taken away the need to sneak into back-alley places."

RELATIONSHIPS AND SEXUAL ACTIVITY

What percentage of LBT women are in a relationship?

A 2015 online survey of 8,566 self-selected lesbian, bisexual, and trans women conducted by Autostraddle—the world's most popular lesbian website—found that:

- 56 percent of respondents were in a monogamous relationship.
- 14.9 percent were in a nonmonogamous relationship. Of this group:
  - 71.2 percent talked with their partners about sex a few times a week.
  - 66.2 percent were mostly or very satisfied with their sex life.
  - 40 percent try something new in bed a few times a month or more.
  - 26 percent were in a long-distance relationship.
  - 22 percent were involved with two or more partners at the time of the survey.
- 29.1 percent were not in a relationship.[7]

How do LBT women define and organize their relationships?

When participants in the Autostraddle survey were asked about their preferred relationship style:

- 61.7 percent chose Monogamy—an exclusive relationship between two people.
- 22 percent chose Mostly Monogamy—which, in the words of the survey authors, "means many different things to many different people."
- 6 percent chose Open Relationship—two people in a committed relationship decide that they're allowed to hook up with other people, together or separately.
- 5.3 percent chose Polyamory—participants have multiple romantic and sexual partners, ideally with everybody involved being aware of and consenting to the arrangement.
- 1.4 percent chose Don't Ask, Don't Tell—partners are free to do whatever they want with whomever they want as long as it never becomes known to the other partner,

either via direct disclosure or other obvious behavior or relationship changes.

- 0.58 percent chose Polyfidelity—a closed relationship with sexual and emotional fidelity required of a group that is larger than two.
- 0.39 percent chose Triad—a closed relationship that involves three people instead of two.
- The breakdown of monogamous versus nonmonogamous relationships among respondents in relationships was as follows:[8]

Figure 11.1: Monogamous vs. Nonmonogamous Relationships Among Women

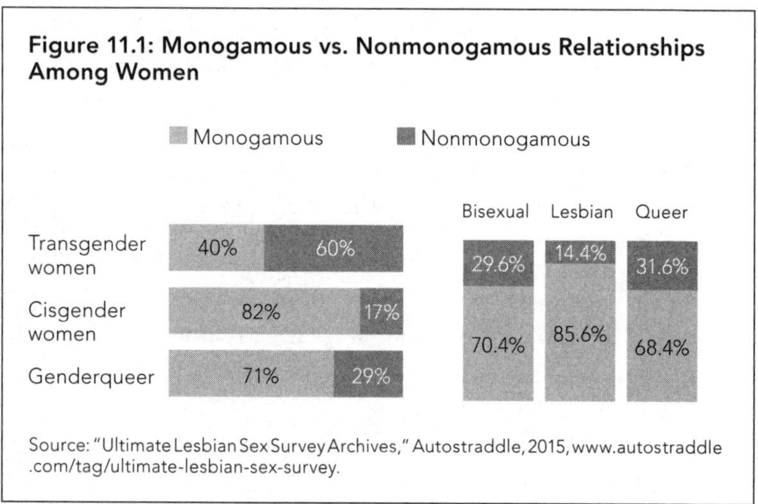

Source: "Ultimate Lesbian Sex Survey Archives," Autostraddle, 2015, www.autostraddle.com/tag/ultimate-lesbian-sex-survey.

What sexual activities are popular among gay men?

A 2011 scholarly study in which nearly 25,000 gay men reported on their most recent sexual experience found:

- More than 1,300 different sexual behaviors were described, with kissing on the mouth being the most common.
- More than 40 percent of respondents said their last partner was someone they were dating, their boyfriend, or their spouse/partner. In a similar study of straight men, the percentage was just over 50 percent.
- Less than 40 percent had engaged in anal intercourse.

- Of those who had engaged in anal sex, nearly 50 percent reported using a condom.
- 82 percent reported an orgasm.
- Older men reported the highest ratings of pleasure and arousal.[9]

How many gay and bisexual men are nonmonogamous?

In a 2010 study of New York City gay and bisexual men who were in a couple, 56 percent reported being nonmonogamous. These nonmonogamous couples adopted the following rules:

- 34 percent said they must use condoms for anal sex and agreed not to have sex with outside partners they know.
- 19 percent said they must talk about sex outside the relationship before it happens, discuss their status with outside partners, and use condoms for anal sex.
- 9 percent indicated they must play together, not have anal sex with outside partners, and not spend the night with outside partners.
- 37 percent had no clear set of rules.[10]

What is known about the sexual experiences of gay and bisexual men in rural communities?

A 2014 survey of 5,357 men who have sex with men (MSM) from rural communities, ranging in age from 18 to 81, found:

- 73.5 percent of the sample identified as gay; 26.5 percent identified as bisexual.
- 90 percent identified as white, 3.8 percent as Hispanic, 2.1 percent as black, and the remaining 2.3 percent as members of other racial and ethnic groups.
- 54.8 percent of respondents were not currently dating anyone.
- 23.5 percent had been in a relationship for five or more years.
- The most commonly reported lifetime sexual behavior was receiving oral sex (98.4 percent), followed by giving oral sex (98.2 percent) and mutual masturbation (96.1 percent).
- Sexual behaviors with female partners were least

common, with 55.1 percent and 22.1 percent of men reporting engaging in vaginal or anal intercourse, respectively.

- Within the past 30 days:
  - 66.7 percent of respondents had received oral sex.
  - 65.8 percent had given oral sex.
  - 39.5 percent had engaged in anal intercourse as the insertive partner.
  - 36.5 percent had engaged in anal intercourse as the receptive partner.
- A majority of men had received HIV or STD testing in the past year—78.6 percent and 51.5 percent, respectively.[11]

What health concerns can affect men who have sex with their age peers?

A 2012 study of 200 gay and bisexual men between the ages of 15 and 22 from Chicago and Miami, of whom 35.5 percent were African American and 34 percent were Latino, found that men who had sex with their age peers as opposed to older men were more likely to engage in risky sexual behaviors.[12]

What have researchers learned about straight-identified men who have sex with men?

According to a 2016 CDC study of data from 2011 to 2013 on adults aged 18 to 44, 2.8 percent of men engaging in same-sex sexual activity identify as straight.[13]

In a small 2010 study of straight-identified men who had at least one sexual encounter with a man in the past year:

- 61.9 percent were African American.
- 57.1 percent were HIV-positive.
- 28.6 percent were currently married to a woman.

Participants in the study did not believe their same-sex activity necessitated a reconsideration of their sexual orientation because:

- The activity was infrequent.

- Sex with men was seen as recreation or sport.
- Almost half participated in the sex for money.
- Respondents stated that the sexual activity was not their fault or was beyond their personal control, due to causes such as inebriation or an unplanned fight with a wife or female partner.[14]

Does social bonding lead straight men to have homoerotic impulses?

In a study conducted at the United Kingdom's University of Portsmouth, straight men were randomly divided into three groups and given word puzzles to complete: one with friendship/affiliative words, a second with sexual words, and a third with neutral words. The word puzzles looked like this:

Table 11.1: Examples of Priming Stimuli

	Intended prime	Puzzle stimuli
Affiliative	Cooperate	Co_pe_ _te
Sexual	Fornicate	For_ _ _ a _ e
Neutral	Sunlight	Sun_ _ _ ht

The men then took a survey to gauge their homoerotic motivation. Statements included: "The idea of kissing a man seems sexually arousing to me" and "I have fantasized recently about having sexual contact with a man." Researchers had previously measured participants' level of progesterone, a hormone that appears in both males and females and contributes to the formation of social bonds. The results of the testing showed:

- The group that was given the friendship/affiliative word puzzles showed 26 percent greater homoerotic motivation than the other two groups.
- Within the group that completed the friendship word puzzles, the men with the highest progesterone levels showed 41 percent greater homoerotic motivation

compared to the men with the highest progesterone levels in the two other groups.

- These findings led the study's chief author to conclude: "Compared to a control group, men's homoerotic motivation was not increased by priming them with sex, but thinking about friendship and bonding caused a measurable change in their attitude to the idea of having sex with other men."[15]

Who has the most orgasms?

In a peer-reviewed 2011 study that asked 1,497 single men and 1,353 single women how often they orgasm with a familiar partner on a scale of 0 to 100, researchers found that orgasms occurred:

- 85.5 percent of the time for straight men.
- 84.7 percent of the time for gay men.
- 77.6 percent of the time for bisexual men.
- 74.7 percent of the time for lesbians.
- 61.6 percent of the time for straight women.
- 58 percent of the time for bisexual women.[16]

PORNOGRAPHY

How many LBT women watch porn?

Of the 8,566 women who participated in the 2015 Autostraddle survey, 87 percent reported that they consume porn. Within that group:

- 45 percent watched straight porn videos online.
- 33 percent watched gay male porn videos online.
- 30 percent watched "lesbian videos created by/for straight people" online.
- 39 percent consumed porn once a week or more.[17]

How much money do male porn actors earn?

According to *Out* magazine, the salary for an exclusive contract with a male porn studio is about $24,000 a year. Most escorts use porn to advertise their sex work, which can be far more lucrative, with the hourly wage averaging around $250.[18]

What mental-health concerns have been documented for male porn stars and sex workers?

- According to an online survey of depression levels among men in the sex industry, the rate of suicidal ideation for male sex workers is more than double the national rate for adults.
- Between May 2012 and May 2013, more than a dozen gay male porn stars committed suicide.[19]

Is there a link between viewing pornography and sexual behavior?

According to a 2014 study of 821 nonmonogamous gay men, in the three months prior to the study interview:

- 99 percent viewed pornography; 96 percent viewed it on the Internet.
- 77.2 percent viewed pornography depicting unprotected anal intercourse.
- 42.6 percent engaged in unprotected insertive anal intercourse.
- 38.9 percent participated in unprotected receptive anal intercourse.

These findings led the survey authors to conclude: "Our data cannot establish the causality of the relationship between viewing pornography depicting unprotected anal intercourse and engaging in unprotected anal intercourse. Some MSM may watch pornography as part of a lifestyle that includes unprotected anal intercourse, with pornography viewing having little or no impact on sexual practices. For some MSM, however, the viewing of pornography depicting unprotected anal intercourse may affect sexual practices and attitudes, or reduce the perceived likelihood of adverse consequences associated with engaging in unprotected anal intercourse."[20]

How often are condoms used in sexually explicit male videos?

A 2014 study of five popular male porn websites found that 34 percent of sexually explicit male videos depicted unprotected anal sex, while 36 percent contained scenes in which condoms were used during anal sex.[21]

SEX WORKERS

What kinds and levels of discrimination do trans sex workers face?

A 2015 report on discrimination faced by transgender sex workers, drawing on data from the 2011 National Transgender Discrimination Survey (NTDS)—the largest published survey of transgender people in the United States, with 6,456 participants—found:

- While both trans men and trans women reported engaging in sex work, trans women were twice as likely to do so.
- Twice as many trans sex workers were unemployed or lived in extreme poverty than trans people who were not sex workers.
- 48 percent of trans sex workers had experienced homelessness at some point in their lives, compared to 14 percent of trans non–sex workers.
- 42.6 percent of black and black biracial trans sex workers were unemployed.
- More transfeminine than transmasculine sex workers were unemployed (27 percent versus 19 percent).
- 69 percent of trans sex workers said they had been denied a job, denied a promotion, or fired because of their gender identity, compared to 44.7 percent of trans non–sex workers. People who lost a job due to bias were almost three times as likely to engage in the sex trade.
- More than twice as many trans sex workers had been denied access to a homeless shelter than non–sex workers (39.5 percent versus 17.5 percent), and almost two-thirds of trans sex workers said they had been harassed by homeless shelter staff.
- Trans sex workers reported being mistreated by medical professionals in a variety of settings, as shown in Figure 11.2.
- The study's authors urged decriminalizing sex work: "Being involved in a highly stigmatized and often crimi-

Figure 11.2: Percent of Transgender People Reporting Mistreatment in a Medical Setting

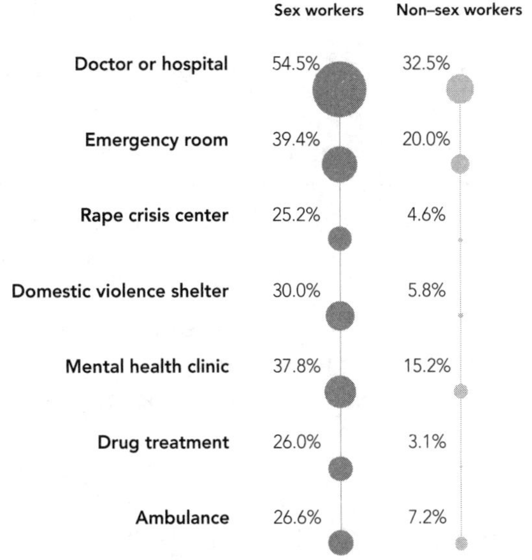

Source: "Meaningful Work: Transgender Experiences in the Sex Trade," Best Practices Policy Project, Red Umbrella Project, and National Center for Transgender Equality, 2015, www.bestpracticespolicy.org/wp-content/uploads/2015/12/Meaningful-Work-Full-Report.pdf.

nalized form of employment," they wrote, "deepens the marginalization that transgender people face."[22]

What are the experiences of youth who engage in survival sex work?

In a 2016 study of 283 New York City male and female youth, ages 15 to 26, who engage in sex work in order to meet basic survival needs:

- 99 percent said they use protection.
- 63 percent said they use protection all the time.
- When asked why he doesn't use protection all the time, one participant said: "I need the money, and some dudes throw in extra money for it."

- 29 percent of respondents had a current or previous sexually transmitted disease.
- Of that 29 percent, 21 percent were HIV-positive.
- 97 percent had seen a doctor in the last six months.[23]

What have researchers learned about male sex workers in the United States?

A New York City community-based survey from 2005 of sexually active nonmonogamous gay, bisexual, and other men who have sex with men found that 43 percent of participants had been paid for sex, paid for sex, or both.[24]

In a 2010 quantitative look at 1,932 male sex workers from the United States who had profiles on Rentboy.com, which at that time was the largest U.S. website advertising male sex workers:

- The average age was 28.
- The average charge for an outcall was more than $200 per hour.
- The sex workers were 54 percent white, 22 percent black, 14 percent Latino, 8 percent multiracial, and 1 percent Asian.
- Race played no role in pricing, but escorts who advertised "masculine behavior" charged prices that were approximately 17 percent higher than those who advertised less masculine behavior.
- 78 percent claimed to have an athletic or muscular build.
- 19 percent advertised that they exclusively practice safe sex.
- New York City had the largest number of sex workers, with more than 300.[25]

Following an investigation by the Department of Homeland Security, the office of Rentboy.com was raided by the U.S. attorney's office in New York on August 25, 2015. Rentboy.com had been operating for 18 years and, according to federal prosecutors, brought in 500,000 daily users and grossed $10 million over the last five years.[26]

What is the status of efforts to decriminalize sex work?

In a survey of 100 countries' laws on prostitution, the website ProCon.org found that sex work is legal in 49 countries, illegal in 39, and of limited legality in 12. (Canada is an example of "limited legality" for prostitution: selling sex is legal, but buying sex became illegal in December 2014.)[27]

- In 2015, Amnesty International called for the global decriminalization of all aspects of adult sex work that does not involve coercion, exploitation, or abuse.[28]
- Other groups that support this position include the World Health Organization, UNAIDS, the Global Alliance Against Trafficking in Women, the Global Network of Sex Work Projects, the Global Commission on HIV and the Law, and Human Rights Watch.[29]

In the United States, prostitution is legal in eight counties in Nevada under a state law that allows any county with a population under 700,000, as of the last decennial census, to license brothels if it so chooses.[30]

- As of 2012, there were four male prostitutes in Nevada who would accept clients of either gender. They worked at the Kit Kat Guest Ranch, which had no male sex workers on its staff as of June 2016.[31]

INTERNET

How popular are online dating and hookup sites?

Adam4Adam.com, which bills itself as "the world's largest gay hookup site," was launched in 2003 and is currently ranked at number 2,452 globally and at number 691 in the United States by Alexa.com, which analyzes online traffic. Though it has lost ground to phone apps like Grindr, Adam4Adam.com still has 1,675,658 unique page views on a daily basis and an estimated value of $3,944,928.[32]

According to research on gay men's online behavior published in *AIDS and Behaviour* and backed by the Australian National Health and Medical Research Council and LaTrobe University:

- 14 percent of the 4,215 Australian gay men who took part in this study met their long-term partners online in 2001.
- By 2014 that number had jumped to 80 percent.[33]

What have researchers learned about online dating among trans people?

In a 2010 study of personal ads posted by trans people in ten major American cities on Craigslist.com, a free classified advertising website that had 40 million visitors per month in the United States and was the eighth-largest English-language website in the world at the time of the study:

- 77.6 percent of the ads contained photos of the person posting the ad.
- The median age was 29.7.
- 90 percent of the ads' posters clearly indicated their identity as trans men or trans women.[34]

How widespread is the use of social networking apps?

Grindr, a geosocial networking app for gay men, was launched in 2009 with a few thousand dollars from its founder, Joel Simkhai. The company, which describes itself as the largest all-male mobile social network in the world, boasts that it has "supplanted the gay bar and online dating sites as the best way for gay men to meet the right person, at the right time, in the right place." Some stats about the app:

- The company was valued at $155 million as of 2016.
- In 2016, a Chinese gaming company bought a 60 percent stake in the company.
- Revenue for 2014 was $32 million, up 29 percent from $25 million in 2013.
- Grindr has 2 million regular visitors every day in 196 countries.
- The average daily time spent on the app is 54 minutes.
- 70 million messages are sent every day.[35]

When Grindr polled a sample of its daily users in 2014, it found that:

- 75 percent of users had their first sexual experience in their teens.
- 72 percent said the first person they came out to was a friend; 22 percent said a family member.
- 68 percent were out at work.
- 53 percent had had a sexual encounter with a woman.
- 18 percent were not out at all.
- 6 percent said they would never come out.[36]

In 2013, the New York–based nonprofit organization Community Health Project released the results of a survey of 725 gay men who meet their sexual partners through geosocial networking apps such as Grindr, GROWLr, Manhunt, and Scruff and found:

- 81.9 percent believed AIDS to be a somewhat serious (52.5 percent) or serious (29.4 percent) problem for people they know.
- 80.9 percent of respondents knew that HIV is transmitted through "unprotected anal sex, vaginal sex, and—less frequently—oral sex."
- 68.1 percent were afraid to be infected or reinfected with HIV.
- The majority of respondents considered barebacking (i.e., engaging in anal sex without a condom) dangerous and believed barebackers were informed of the risk.
- 46.4 percent reported that they engage in barebacking sometimes, often, or always.[37]

In countries where homosexuality is taboo—such as China, India, and Pakistan—geosocial networking apps can be the most effective way for gay men to meet one another, especially in rural areas with no gay bars or organizations.

- Turkey blocked Grindr in 2013 as a "protection measure," a move that activists challenged in the country's constitutional court.[38]
- China's most popular gay dating app, Blued, was launched by an ex-policeman in 2012. As of 2015, Blued had 22 million users, according to a statement issued

by the company, making it the most popular gay dating app in the world. Half of Blued's users were between 18 and 25 years old.[39]

What dating apps are popular among lesbians and bisexual women?

The website DigitPedia lists three primary geosocial networking apps for women—Scissr, Wapa, and HER (formerly Dattch)—along with a number of other apps that have fewer users, including Wingma'am and FindHrr.[40]

- HER founder Robyn Exton—who secured $2.5 million in funding and moved the company's headquarters from London to San Francisco in 2015—explained that HER "is about creating a space where lesbian, bi, queer, curious, flexisexual, pansexual and not-so-straight women can meet and find out what's going on in their lesbian world." Exton told *Fortune* in 2015 that traffic was growing by 30 percent per month but declined to quantify the number of app users.[41]
- SCISSR—founded in 2014 by Chicagoan Allison Ullrich and open to women over 18, who are allowed to upload three photos and write a bio of 300 words—was created "to provide women a fun solution to a true dilemma, in a safe environment without dudes or fake accounts."[42]

PRISON

What sexual experiences do LGBTQ prisoners have while incarcerated?

A small representative study of sex in U.K. prisons, in which 26 former prisoners were interviewed in 2014, found that:

- Almost all managed their sexual needs through masturbation.
- About a third of the study's male participants had consensual sex with other men.
- The self-identified heterosexual men who engaged in sex with other men did not perceive that the activity altered their sexual identity as heterosexual.

- Interviewees believed that prison officials were aware of sex happening but exercised discretion.
- The availability of condoms varied considerably among prisons.
- Most interviewees had access to heterosexual pornographic magazines in prison; access to and tolerance of gay porn varied significantly among prisons.
- Interviewees reported having between 1 and 35 sexual partners in prison.
- More than one-eighth of male interviewees reported being raped while in prison; none told prison officials.
- Gay and bisexual male interviewees reported that although they were "fairly" or "totally" open about their sexual orientation while in prison, they were discreet about their sexual activities and relationships.
- In contrast to sexually active male prisoners who felt the need to be discreet, female prisoners were more overtly affectionate and willing to be seen to be emotionally and socially reliant on other women prisoners.[43]

GAYDAR

What have researchers concluded about gaydar?

Studies about gaydar—defined as the ability to detect sexual orientation as if through radar—have reached conflicting conclusions:

- A 2012 study of college students who viewed black-and-white photo flashes of faces from which the hairstyle, jewelry, glasses, and other "self-presentational" aspects had been cropped out showed an average of 60 percent accuracy in identifying lesbian and gay subjects, with some participants achieving 80 percent accuracy. These results led the survey's authors, Joshua Tabak and Vivian Zayas, to conclude: "Even when viewing such bare faces so briefly, participants demonstrated an ability to identify sexual orientation. . . . [I]s gaydar real? Absolutely."[44]
- A 2015 study found that sexual orientation could not

be determined by viewing subjects' faces alone but required a stereotypical statement about the person pictured in order to make accurate identifications. These findings prompted the study's lead author, William Cox, to conclude that gaydar is a myth. "Most people think of stereotyping as inappropriate," he said. "But if you're not calling it 'stereotyping,' if you're giving it this other label and camouflaging it as 'gaydar,' it appears to be more socially and personally acceptable."[45]

> Sports are proving to be the final frontier for gay acceptance. A decade ago, most considered it improbable that entrenched attitudes about military service and civil marriage, as well as employment equality and cultural acceptance, would allow advancement in those arenas prior to the advent of acknowledgment by gay athletes. Nor would many have expected that broad and strong support for all would become the dominant societal standard so soon. Yet progress in sports has proven more elusive . . .
>
> —*Mark Lee in "Are Sports the Final Frontier for Gay Acceptance?,"* Washington Blade, *2014*[1]

In a national survey of LGBTQ Americans conducted by the Pew Research Center in 2013, 6 in 10 respondents characterized the world of professional sports as unfriendly toward LGBT people—while only 4 percent reported that they view professional sports as welcoming.[2] Among athletes, the negative impressions are even higher: 84 percent of respondents in an international study have experienced or witnessed discrimination on the basis of sexual orientation when playing sports, and one in four gay men reported abandoning team sports as kids because of bad experiences.[3] The statistics and milestones presented in this chapter chronicle the courage of individual athletes who have chosen to come out despite entrenched homophobia, as well as the incremental changes that are starting to occur within the worlds of professional and campus sports. This chapter also includes statistics on leisure and community activities, ranging from Pride events to LGBTQ rodeos, along with a look at LGBTQ consumer habits, shopping patterns, and travel trends.

SPORTS

Who are some famous sports figures that who are known to be LGBTQ?

- "Big Bill" Tilden (1893–1953)—the first American to win Wimbledon, the world's top-ranked player from 1920 to 1925, and winner of a remarkable 138 of 192 tennis tournaments during his record-breaking career—was arrested twice in California on "morals charges" and sentenced to two prison terms. Tilden included a statement about his sexual identity in his autobiography, *My Story*, published in 1948: "Greater tolerance and wider education on the part of the general public concerning this form of sex relationship," he argued, "is one of the crying needs."[4]
- In 1975, running back Dave Kopay (born 1942) came out as gay after retiring from the National Football League in 1972. Kopay played for Vince Lombardi with the Washington Redskins, as well as for four other teams during nine NFL seasons, and became the first major-team-sport athlete to tell the world he was gay.[5]
- In 1975, gay Canadian jockey John Damien (1933–1986) was dismissed when his sexual orientation became known to the Ontario Jockey Commission. He sued and the case dragged on for more than a decade; in 1986, Damien won a wrongful-dismissal verdict against the commission.[6]
- In 1976, John Curry (1949–1994), a popular British figure skater, was outed by a German tabloid. Even though this revelation caused a minor scandal in Europe, the press generally ignored Curry's sexual orientation and he became the first out LGBTQ person to win an Olympic Gold Medal when he emerged as the top skater at the 1976 Winter Olympics.[7]
- In 1977, Renée Richards (born 1934), a trans woman tennis player, won a lawsuit against the United States Tennis Association because she had been barred from competing as a woman in the 1976 U.S. Open.[8]

- Billie Jean King (born 1943), a former World Number 1 professional tennis player and winner of 39 Grand Slam Titles, was outed in 1981 by a former lover, who was suing her for palimony. King reported that within 24 hours of the lawsuit being filed, "I lost all my endorsements; I lost everything. I lost $2 million at least, because I had longtime contracts. I had to play just to pay for the lawyers. In three months I went through $500,000. I was in shock. I didn't make $2 million in my lifetime, so it's all relative to what you make."[9]
- Also in 1981, tennis great Martina Navratilova (born 1956), who won an unprecedented 59 Grand Slam titles—including a record nine Wimbledon singles championships, 167 singles, and 177 doubles championships—came out as bisexual in an article in the *New York Daily News*.[10]
- Glenn Burke (1952–1995), a retired outfielder for the Los Angeles Dodgers and the Oakland Athletics, came out in 1982. In so doing, Burke became the first-ever openly gay former Major League Baseball player.[11]
- In 1989, Bob Paris (born 1959), who won the weightlifting titles Mr. America and Mr. Universe in 1983, disclosed that he was gay.[12]
- In 1990, Justin Fashanu (1961–1998), a top British soccer player, revealed that he was gay. He became the first team-sport athlete to come out while still an active player and played until 1997. In 1998, Fashanu committed suicide after being accused of sexual assault in the United States. In his suicide note, he claimed the disputed sex had been consensual.[13]
- In 1993, Canadian Savoy Howe became the first out lesbian in women's boxing.[14]
- Greg Louganis (born 1960), a four-time Olympic gold medalist who made history at the 1982 world championships by becoming the first diver ever awarded a perfect 10 from all seven judges, announced in 1994 that he is gay. "I wanted my participation in the sport to

be about the sport. I didn't want it to be about being the 'gay diver,'" he told Outsports in 2012.[15]

  - Following his wins at the 1984 and 1988 Olympics, Louganis was not asked to appear on the cover of a Wheaties cereal box, a symbol of sports achievement since 1934. Louganis has said that homophobia was most likely the reason.[16]
  - After 41,000 people signed a petition supporting a campaign for Louganis to join the ranks of athletes who have endorsed the "breakfast of champions," General Mills announced that Louganis's photo would appear on Wheaties boxes beginning in May 2016.[17]

- In 1995, Ian Roberts (born 1965), one of Australia's most popular rugby players, posed nude for a gay magazine and came out. He was the first major Australian athlete to disclose that he is gay.[18]
- Muffin Spencer-Devlin (born 1953), a three-time tournament winner on the Ladies Professional Golf Association Tour in the 1980s, came out as a lesbian in a 1996 *Sports Illustrated* article—making her the first female or male professional golfer to come out while still playing.[19]
- In 1998, Mike Muska, an openly gay man and former collegiate track and field coach, was named athletic director at Oberlin College, an NCAA Division III school in Ohio, becoming the first openly gay male administrator at that level in college sports.[20]
- In 1999, Cyd Zeigler and Jim Buzinski launched the first website devoted to sports news and information for LGBTQ sports fans and athletes: Outsports.com.[21]
- In 2000, an openly gay high school football captain from Massachusetts, Corey Johnson, received national attention for coming out, with coverage on ABC and in the *New York Times*.[22]
- In 2005, Sheryl Swoopes (born 1971), a Women's National Basketball Association player and three-time

most valuable player (MVP), came out as a lesbian at the height of her career.[23]

- 11 openly gay athletes participated in the Athens Olympics in 2004: two Americans (Guenter Seidel and Robert Dover), two Britons (Carl Hester and Rob Newton), one Frenchwoman (Amelie Mauresmo), one Czech (Martina Navratilova), one Spaniard (Conchita Martinez), one New Zealander (Blyth Tait), one Dutchman (Johan Kenkhuis), and two Germans (Imke Duplitzer and Judith Arndt). Kenkhuis emerged as the lone medalist from the group.[24]
- In 2005, Keelin Godsey, a member of the track and field team at Bates College in Lewiston, Maine, began transitioning to male, becoming the first openly transgender athlete to compete at the NCAA level.[25]
- In 2007, John Amaechi (born 1970), a former NBA player, came out in his memoir, *Man in the Middle*—making him the first former NBA player to reveal that he is gay.[26]
- In 2010, Kye Allums became the first openly trans man to play for a college women's basketball team. His coach and teammates at George Washington University, which has a Division 1 women's basketball team, embraced Allums's public announcement. The NCAA told the university that Allums was eligible for the women's team because he had not undergone hormone treatments.[27]
- Orlando Cruz, a Puerto Rican boxer, became the first professional boxer to be openly LGBTQ while still boxing after coming out in an interview with the Associated Press in 2012. At the time, Cruz was the World Boxing Organization's Number 4 featherweight fighter and had a record of 18–2–1, with nine knockouts.[28]
- By 2013, the National Hockey League, Major League Baseball, Major League Soccer, the National Basketball Association, and the National Football League had all adopted nondiscrimination policies that included sexual orientation.[29]

- In May 2013, Jason Collins rocked the world of professional sports by declaring on the cover of *Sports Illustrated*: "I'm a 34-year-old NBA center. I'm black. And I'm gay." The first openly gay man in any of the four major American team sports, Collins had been in the NBA for 12 years and went on to play with the Nets for one season before announcing his retirement from basketball in 2014. In 2014, *Time* magazine featured Collins as one of the "100 Most Influential People in the World."[30]
- In August 2013, defensive end Michael Sam came out to his football teammates at the University of Missouri and came out publicly on ESPN prior to the 2014 NFL draft. He made history when he became the first openly gay man ever drafted by an NFL team, the St. Louis Rams. Yet as of May 2016, despite having been named Defensive Player of the Year by the Southeastern Conference, Sam had been released by the Rams and had not been signed to another NFL team. "I think if I never would have came out, never would have said those words out to the public, I would still be currently in the NFL," Sam told an interviewer in 2016.[31]

What are the Gay Games?

The Gay Games, originally named the Gay Olympics, were founded in San Francisco in 1982 by former decathlete Dr. Tom Waddell. This is the world's largest sporting and cultural event organized by and specifically for LGBTQ athletes, artists, and musicians.

- The event's name had to be changed due to a lawsuit filed by the International Olympic Committee and the United States Olympic Committee less than three weeks before the inaugural Gay Games of 1982.[32]
- There have been nine iterations of the Gay Games since its founding. At the most recent, held in Cleveland/Akron in 2014, an estimated 10,000 athletes from more than 60 nations participated in 37 sports and cultural events.[33]

EVENTS

How many LGBTQ events take place worldwide? What are some of the best attended?

Wikipedia lists 667 annual LGBT events worldwide, including film festivals, Pride parades, Mr. Leather contests, sporting events, and parties.[34]

- The International Gay Rodeo Association lists 20 events in North America for 2017.[35]
- According to estimates from organizers, police, and media accounts, the largest LGBTQ Pride events, calculated by the number of attendees, include:
    1. São Paulo Pride Parade (2006)—3 million people.
    2. Madrid Europride Festival (2007)—2.3 million.
    3. New York City Pride Parade (2016)—2 million.
    4. San Francisco Pride Parade (2014)—1.7 million.
    5. New York City Pride Parade (2015)—1.6 million.
    6. Cologne Europride Parade (2002)—1.4 million.
    7. Toronto Pride Festival (2012)—1.2 million.
    8. Madrid National Pride (2012)—1.2 million.[36]

TRAVEL

LGBT consumers spend an estimated $65 billion per year on vacations.[37]

- Industry analysts regard LGBT consumers as "Teflon travelers," meaning they are "less prone to cancel in the wake of geopolitical or natural disasters and more willing to part with a bigger portion of their disposable income on vacations than the general population is."[38]

How often do LGBTQ Americans travel for leisure and business purposes?

In a 2014 survey of 3,502 LGBT Americans:

- 29 percent are frequent leisure travelers, taking five or more leisure trips per year.
- 14 percent are frequent business travelers, taking five or more business trips per year.
- 82 percent took a vacation within the last 12 months.

- 89 percent would not travel to a country that has laws against LGBT people.
- 82 percent considered Russia an unsafe travel destination.
- 62 percent of lesbian and bisexual women and 56 percent of gay and bisexual men spent no money on gambling in casinos.[39]

What are the most popular destinations for LGBTQ travelers?

The top leisure destinations for lesbian, gay, and bisexual travelers surveyed by Community Marketing & Insights in 2014 were:

1. New York City
2. San Francisco
3. Las Vegas
4. Chicago
5. LA/West Hollywood[40]

The top international leisure destinations for LGBT travelers in 2014 were:

1. Canada
2. England
3. France
4. Mexico
5. Germany[41]

When LGBT survey participants were asked what country would be their "dream destination," the most popular responses were:

1. Australia—15 percent.
2. Italy—7 percent.
3. New Zealand—6 percent.
4. Japan—5 percent.
5. Ireland, Germany, Greece, France, Spain, and the United Kingdom—3 to 4 percent.[42]

What are some U.S. destinations with particularly strong connections to LGBTQ history?

The following sites throughout the U.S. have been designated as National Historic Landmarks or listed on the National Register of Historic Places:

- Dr. Franklin E. Kameny Residence in Washington, D.C.
- James Merrill House in Stonington, CT.
- Carrington House in Fire Island Pines, NY.
- Cherry Grove Community House & Theater in Cherry Grove, NY.
- Bayard Rustin Residence in New York, NY.
- Julius' Bar in New York, NY.
- The Furies Collective house in Washington, D.C.
- Edificio Comunidad de Orgullo Gay de Puerto Rico (commonly known as Casa Orgullo, or Pride House) in San Juan, Puerto Rico.
- Henry Gerber House in Chicago, IL.
- The Stonewall National Monument in New York, NY.[43]

COMMUNITY

What is the history and status of LGBTQ community centers?

The first LGBT community center, originally known as the Los Angeles Gay & Lesbian Center, was founded in 1969.

- It is now the world's largest provider of programs and services for LGBT people, with seven facilities throughout L.A.
- In 2010, the center received a $13.3 million, five-year grant from the U.S. Department of Health and Human Services Administration on Children, Youth and Families to create a model program for LGBTQ youth in foster care. This was the largest-ever grant by the federal government to an LGBTQ organization.
- Today there are more than 200 such centers across 45 states, Puerto Rico, and the District of Columbia.[44]

According to a 2014 report on 111 U.S. LGBTQ community centers:

- 37,900 individuals are served in a typical week.
- Center patrons are disproportionately male, people of color, transgender, and/or low income.
- 50 percent of the budget for large centers comes from government grants.
- 21 percent of these centers rely entirely on volunteers.
- 57 percent have five or fewer paid staff members.
- 76 percent of the budget for large centers is spent on program-related expenses.[45]

How do gay men feel about being part of a community?

In Logo's 2015 nationally representative quantitative survey of 1,000 gay men:

- 85 percent of gay men ages 18 to 49 agreed that "even as gay people become more accepted, we should have places that are just for us," and that "it's sad to see gay neighborhoods and bars disappear."
- 95 percent of respondents agreed that "younger gay men are embracing their gay identity more so today than in the past."
- 92 percent of gay men hoped community members become more accepting of each other.
- 91 percent described a need for more open dialogue among gay men.
- 87 percent wished the gay community "was as united during the rest of the year as we are during Pride."[46]

We make assumptions every day about other people's genders without ever seeing their birth certificates, their chromosomes, their genitals, their reproductive systems, their childhood socialization, or their legal sex. There is no such thing as a "real" gender—there is only the gender we experience ourselves as and the gender we perceive others to be.

—*Julia Serano, trans activist, writer, performer, and biologist, in* Whipping Girl: A Transsexual Woman on Sexism and the Scapegoating of Femininity, *2007*[1]

My documents match now, but they didn't for most of my life. I lived in terror of losing my life, my freedom, my employment, and my friends.

—*Anonymous participant in the National Transgender Discrimination Survey, 2011*[2]

The stories—and the struggles—of transgender Americans are receiving unprecedented attention, in forums ranging from front-page articles in the *New York Times* to award-winning television series like *Orange Is the New Black* and *Transparent*. The Pentagon made headlines in 2016 when it rescinded the ban on trans service members; women's colleges have begun admitting trans students; and Olympic gold medalist Bruce Jenner's transition to Caitlyn Jenner has sparked a national conversation about gender identity and the importance of living as one's authentic self.

Legal protections for trans people, however, are lagging behind this wave of visibility and openness. In the absence of a federal law that would prohibit discrimination in hiring and employment on the basis of gender identity and sexual orientation, legislators in numerous states are passing laws that severely restrict the rights of trans residents. Yet as quickly as states like North Carolina and Mississippi enact discriminatory laws such as HB 1523—which, among other sweeping provisions, allows Mississippi businesses to refuse to serve LGBT people while affirming the legality of "conversion therapy" and permitting schools to ban transgender students from wearing clothing that conforms to their gender identities—citizens, businesses, and political leaders across the political spectrum have denounced this surge of bigotry. Talk show host Montel Williams's statement is representative: "As a human being, a Christian, a conservative, an American who served 22 years in the military," he wrote, "I find myself dumbfounded that Governor Bryant has signed HB 1523, a bill that is steeped in bigotry towards LGBT individuals and seems to create a sin test for public accommodation in Mississippi. . . . I urge the immediate repeal of HB 1523 while there is still time to clear Mississippi's good name."[3]

TRANS STATS: STARTING POINTS

As with most statistics regarding LGBTQ people, approximations of the size of the trans population are likely affected by underreporting based on stigma.

- HRC estimates that between 0.25 percent and 1 percent of Americans identify as trans.[4]
- The most frequently cited numerical estimate of the trans population is 700,000 in the United States and 15 million worldwide.[5]
- In June 2016, the Williams Institute released a report with updated figures. Based on the latest data available from the CDC, the report estimated that 0.6 percent of the U.S. population—or 1.4 million adults—identify as transgender. In addressing the fact that this figure is twice as high as their 2011 estimate of 700,000, the researchers said: "A perceived increase in visibility and social acceptance of transgender people may increase

the number of individuals willing to identify as transgender on a government-administered survey."[6]

The first trans person to visit the White House was We'wha, a Native American who shook hands with President Grover Cleveland in 1886.

- We'wha was a Zuni two-spirit—a term that reflects "the combination of masculinity and femininity which was attributed to males in a feminine role and females in a masculine role," writes Sabine Lang in *Men as Women, Women as Men: Changing Gender in Native American Cultures*.[7]
- In 2015, President Barack Obama appointed the first openly trans White House staff member, Raffi Freedman-Gurspan, to serve as an outreach and recruitment director in the Office of Presidential Personnel.[8]

BEYOND MALE AND FEMALE

The diversity of identities on the gender spectrum is vast and evolving as new configurations of gender and identity are named and embodied. In 2014, Facebook began giving its users more than 50 options to identify their gender. "All too often transgender people like myself and other gender-nonconforming people are given this binary option: do you want to be male or female? What is your gender? And it's kind of disheartening because none of those let us tell others who we really are," said Brielle Harrison, a Facebook software engineer who worked on the project. Some of the options end with an asterisk, which derives from computer language and represents a wildcard within an online search; in this context, the asterisk expands the boundaries of the identity being named. The 56 custom gender options include:

Agender
Androgyne
Androgynous
Bigender
Cis
Cis female

Cis male
Cis man
Cis woman
Cisgender
Cisgender female
Cisgender male
Cisgender man
Cisgender woman
Female to male
FTM
Gender fluid
Gender nonconforming
Gender questioning
Gender variant
Genderqueer
Intersex
Male to female
MTF
Neither
Neutrois
Nonbinary
Other
Pangender
Trans
Trans*
Trans female
Trans* female
Trans male
Trans* male
Trans man
Trans* man
Trans person
Trans* person
Trans woman
Trans* woman
Transfeminine
Transgender
Transgender female
Transgender male
Transgender man
Transgender person
Transgender woman
Transmasculine
Transsexual
Transsexual female
Transsexual male
Transsexual man
Transsexual person
Transsexual woman
Two-Spirit[9]

To move beyond the restrictions imposed by "he" and "she," hundreds of nonbinary pronouns have been proposed—some as early as the mid-1800s. Among the most popular are "zie," "ey," and "they." (Proponents of the singular "they" have included Geoffrey Chaucer, William Shakespeare, and Jane Austen.)[10]

DOCUMENTING THE EXPERIENCES OF TRANS PEOPLE IN AMERICA

The largest-ever study of the experiences and opinions of transgender and gender-nonconforming people was conducted in

2011, under the joint auspices of the National Gay and Lesbian Task Force and the National Center for Transgender Equality. More than 6,400 Americans participated in this landmark project, known as the National Transgender Discrimination Survey (NTDS). Respondents reported being:

- 25 percent bisexual.
- 23 percent straight.
- 23 percent gay, lesbian, or same-gender-loving.
- 23 percent queer.
- 4 percent asexual.
- 2 percent something else, such as trans-attracted.[11]

What forms of discrimination do trans people face?

The National Transgender Discrimination Survey reported that:

- 90 percent of participants in the study experienced harassment or discrimination on the job.
- 71 percent hid their gender or gender transition to avoid discrimination.
- 57 percent faced significant family rejection as a result of being trans.
- 57 percent said they were delaying their gender transition to avoid discrimination.
- 19 percent reported having been refused an apartment.
- 11 percent had been evicted because of their gender identity.
- 19 percent reported experiencing homelessness. Among homeless respondents:
    - 55 percent experienced harassment by homeless shelter workers or residents;
    - 22 percent were sexually assaulted by residents or staff; and
    - 29 percent were turned away altogether.
- Trans people were four times more likely to live in extreme poverty compared to members of the general population.
- The unemployment rate for trans people in the United States is double the national average.

- 22 percent reported being denied equal treatment by a government agency.
- 29 percent reported police harassment or disrespect.[12]

What evidence of resilience did the study authors chronicle?

- Among 25- to 44-year-old respondents, 22 percent were in school, compared to 7 percent of their counterparts in the general population.
- Of the 19 percent who had faced housing discrimination, 94 percent were currently housed.
- Of the 26 percent who reported having lost a job due to bias, 58 percent currently had a job.
- 76 percent of respondents reported being able to get hormone therapy.
- 78 percent reported feeling more comfortable at work after transitioning.[13]

ANTI-TRANS LEGISLATION

What aspects of life for transgender citizens are targeted by the anti-trans legislation that has been enacted in North Carolina and Mississippi?

- On March 23, 2016, North Carolina governor Pat McCrory signed HB2, a law that prohibits trans people from using public bathrooms and locker rooms that are not consistent with the gender on their birth certificates, while restricting cities from passing nondiscrimination laws. HB2 also created a statewide antidiscrimination policy—which does not mention LGBT people.[14]
- In response, more than 180 companies and a number of national political leaders—Republicans as well as Democrats—publicly opposed the measure, while dozens of performers canceled planned appearances in the state.[15]
- A study by the Williams Institute at UCLA School of Law found that HB2 could cost North Carolina up to $5 billion a year if it is not repealed.[16]

On April 5, 2016, Mississippi governor Phil Bryant signed into law HB 1523, allowing businesses to refuse to serve transgender, lesbian, gay, and bisexual people. The law permits Mississippians to:

- fire people who do not adhere to their religious beliefs;
- refuse to let transgender students at public schools wear clothing that conforms to their gender identities;
- deny housing based on religious beliefs; and
- force LGBT foster children to undergo conversion therapy.[17]

According to a 2016 report from the Williams Institute:

- HB 1523 legalizes discrimination against the more than 60,000 LGBT people who live in Mississippi, including 11,500 transgender youth and adults and 3,500 same-sex couples.
- 44 percent of Mississippi's LGBT residents are raising children—a higher percentage than in any other state.
- Statewide, 75 percent of Mississippi residents support protections from discrimination for LGBT people.[18]

In a lawsuit challenging the constitutionality of HB 1523, attorney Roberta Kaplan argued that the law violates not only the Due Process and Equal Protection Clauses, but also the Establishment Clause of the First Amendment by enshrining into law special protections for people who hold three religious beliefs:

- marriage is between a man and a woman;
- sexual relations outside a heterosexual marriage are improper; and
- a person's gender must be the same as the sex assigned at birth.

Kaplan argues that because the law grants those who hold these religious beliefs the right to discriminate against LGBT people with regard to marriage licenses, adoption and fertility services, access to health care, and public accommodation in restaurants, hotels, and other venues, "[I]t is hard to imagine a clearer violation of the First Amendment than HB 1523."[19] U.S.

District Judge Carlton Reeves struck down the law on July 1, 2016, hours before it was slated to take effect; in response, Governor Bryant stated that he was "disappointed" and looked forward to an "aggressive appeal."[20]

What is the status of anti-trans legislation in other states?

As of April 2016, more than 100 anti-trans bills were being considered in 22 state legislatures.[21] Among them:

1. Bills targeting trans students in sports were pending in Illinois, Indiana, Minnesota, Missouri, Oklahoma, South Dakota, Tennessee, Virginia, and Wisconsin.
2. Bills limiting access to gender-segregated public facilities were being considered in Massachusetts, Missouri, Virginia, and Washington.
3. A bill prohibiting transition-related treatment for prisoners was pending in South Carolina.
4. A bill preventing trans people from amending their birth certificates was being considered in Virginia.
5. A bill defining "sex" to exclude trans people from state legal protections in employment and education was also pending in Virginia.
6. A bill requiring trans people to disclose their surgical history when applying for a marriage license was introduced in Oklahoma.[22]
7. In Kansas, lawmakers introduced legislation that offers a $2,500 bounty to any non-trans person who "catches" a trans person in the "wrong" restroom.[23]

What challenges do transgender people face in updating identity documents?

Many transgender people seek to revise the gender marker on their identity documents so that it matches the gender they live every day. According to data from the 2011 National Transgender Discrimination Survey:

- 41 percent of respondents were living with IDs that did not match their gender.
- Of those who have transitioned, only 21 percent had

been able to update all their IDs and records to reflect their new gender.

- 33 percent of those who have transitioned had updated no records to reflect their new gender.[24]

The map on page 206 shows which states do and do not allow gender markers to be changed on birth certificates.

PROTECTIONS

What are some examples of policies that protect trans people from discrimination at the state and local level?

According to the ACLU, the following states have enacted laws that "clearly prohibit discrimination against transgender people," though the level of protection varies from state to state:

1. California
2. Colorado
3. Connecticut
4. Delaware
5. Hawaii
6. Illinois
7. Iowa
8. Maine
9. Maryland
10. Massachusetts
11. Minnesota
12. Nevada
13. New Jersey
14. New Mexico
15. New York
16. Oregon
17. Rhode Island
18. Utah
19. Vermont
20. Washington
21. The District of Columbia[25]

At least 200 cities and counties have banned discrimination on the basis of gender identity.[26]

FEDERAL LAWS AND POLICIES

What are some developments that demonstrate the disparate ways in which the U.S. government treats trans people?

- The first winning legal case of a trans person granted asylum in the United States was *Hernandez-Montiel*

Figure 13.1: Laws for Changing Gender Markers on Birth Certificates

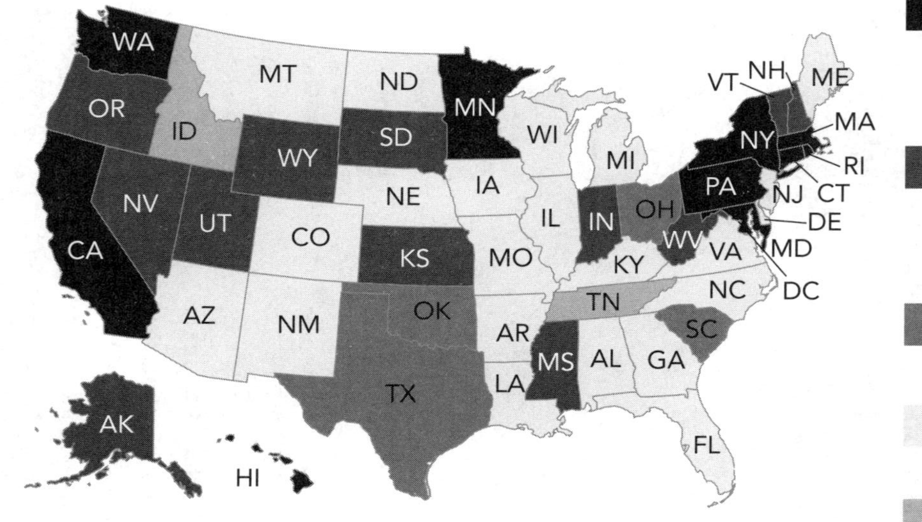

- State issues new birth certificate and does not require sex-reassignment surgery or court order to change gender marker (10 states and D.C.)
- State is unclear regarding surgical/clinical requirements and/or may require a court order to change gender marker (12 states)
- State has unclear, unknown, or unwritten policy regarding gender marker changes (4 states)
- State requires proof of sex-reassignment surgery to change gender marker (22 states)
- State does not allow for amending the gender marker on the birth certificate (2 states)

Source: Movement Advancement Project, "Birth Certificate Laws," updated September 2016, www.lgbtmap.org/equality-maps/identity_document_laws/birth_certificate.

v. INS (2000). Geovanni Hernandez-Montiel had been raped and persecuted by the police in Mexico and won his case, on appeal, because he was labeled a "gay man with female sexual identity." The U.S. Court of Appeals for the Ninth Circuit determined that Hernandez-Montiel's expression of his gender identity through his attire was a manifestation of his fundamental identity, and persecution on this basis qualified him for asylum.[27]

- Passed in 2009, the Matthew Shepard and James Byrd Jr. Hate Crimes Prevention Act includes gender identity as a basis for prosecuting hate crimes.[28] (For more on the Matthew Shepard and James Byrd Jr. Hate Crimes Prevention Act—and on violence against trans people—see pages 225 to 226 in the Violence chapter.)
- On the 2010 U.S. Census form, there were boxes for two genders: male and female. The existence of trans people was not acknowledged.[29]
- In 2012, the U.S. Citizenship and Immigration Services issued a groundbreaking policy statement specifying the requirements for updating the gender designation on immigration identity documents and allowing trans people to do so.[30]
- According to a 2015 investigative report, roughly 1 in 500 detainees held by U.S. Immigration and Customs Enforcement (ICE) is transgender. A report by the Government Accountability Office found that 1 in 5 substantiated cases of sexual abuse in ICE facilities involved trans detainees, who face long stints in solitary confinement, denial of hormones, and widespread transphobia.[31]
- In June 2015, the U.S. Department of Homeland Security released a series of guidelines for ICE about respecting transgender individuals' gender identity. The guidelines directed ICE staff to house transgender immigrants in sex-segregated housing that corresponds with the person's gender identity.[32]
- In August 2015, the National Institutes of Health

awarded $5.7 million for a five-year, multicenter study, the first in the United States to evaluate the long-term outcomes of medical treatment for transgender youth.[33] One topic to be examined in this study is the effect of puberty-blocking medications, which allow parents and children with gender variance more time to make decisions about transitioning and which can cost up to $50,000 for up to six years of treatment.[34] (For more on trans youth, see pages 254 to 255 of the Youth and Education chapter.)

- In November 2015, the U.S Department of Housing and Urban Development proposed new rules to protect trans people in federal housing that is assisted or insured.[35]
- As of January 2016, the Equal Employment Opportunity Commission had filed three lawsuits on behalf of MTF trans employees:
    - The first lawsuit was settled in 2015 for $150,000.
    - The second suit was settled in 2016 for $115,000.
    - The third lawsuit is pending.[36]

HEALTH AND MEDICINE

What health care services do trans people receive under state and federal programs?

- On July 12, 2012, the Department of Health and Human Services (HHS) clarified that provisions in the Affordable Care Act prohibiting sex discrimination in health insurance apply to trans people.[37]
- In January 2016, HHS ruled for the first time that trans people are entitled to gender-confirming surgery under Medicare.[38]
- Six states—California, Maryland, Massachusetts, New York, Oregon, and Vermont—have updated their Medicaid rules to provide hormone therapy for trans people. These therapies, which generally consist of testosterone for patients seeking to become more mas-

culine and estrogen plus androgen blockers for patients seeking a feminizing effect, are among the most commonly used treatments for trans people.[39]

What have researchers learned about the effects of hormone therapy?

In a 2011 study of the long-term effects of hormone therapy on 966 female-to-male (FTM) and 365 male-to-female (MTF) trans people, participants came from university gender clinics and the median amount of time for follow-up was 18.5 years. The results showed that:

- In the FTM population, there was no significant difference in the mortality rate.
- The mortality rate in the MTF population was 51 percent higher than in the general population, but the increased death rate was primarily due to HIV infection, suicide, drug abuse, cardiac arrest, and other unknown factors.[40]

To what extent are transgender issues included in medical schools' curricula?

- In a 2013 paper, Dr. Joshua Safer of the Boston University School of Medicine noted: "Because medically appropriate high-quality care for transgender individuals is not taught in most medical curricula, too few physicians have the requisite knowledge and comfort level for treatment of transgender individuals."[41]
- In 2014, the Association of American Medical Colleges (AAMC) released the first guidelines to help medical schools integrate transgender cultural competency at the institutional and curricular levels.[42]
- A 2015 study showed that a single lecture on transgender care resulted in significant increases in resident physicians' confidence and knowledge. After the lecture, the percentage of residents who felt sufficiently knowledgeable to assist with hormonal therapy for FTM patients rose from 5 percent to 76 percent, and from 5 percent to 71 percent for MTF patients.[43]

What are some milestones in the evolution of medical care for transgender patients?

- In 1966, the first university-based surgery clinic in the United States opened at Johns Hopkins University for those who sought gender confirmation surgery. It was followed closely by programs at the University of Minnesota, Northwestern University, and Stanford. Since the American Medical Association did not sanction these clinics and government agencies did not support them, the initial funding came from a wealthy female-to-male transsexual, Reid Erickson, who founded the Erickson Educational Foundation in 1964.[44]
- In 1979, the Harry Benjamin International Gender Dysphoria Association, founded in 1978 and now known as World Professional Association for Transgender Health (WPATH), released the first health care standards for trans patients.
  - Publication of these standards took the surgical process out of the hands of a few university gender clinics and widened options considerably, allowing trans people to change parts of their body while keeping genitalia intact.[45]
  - Dr. Harry Benjamin, for whom the organization was initially named, is known as "the founding father of transsexualism." Born in Germany in 1885, he lived most of his life in New York and treated some 1,500 trans patients over the span of nearly 60 years.[46]
- According to New York Presbyterian Hospital endocrinologist Wylie C. Hembree, the ratio of MTF to FTM patients used to be 10 to 1. The ratio is now nearly 1 to 1.[47]

What is "gender identity disorder"?

- The first two editions of the American Psychiatric Association's *Diagnostic and Statistical Manual of Mental Disorders (DSM)*, published in 1952 and 1968, respectively, did not address gender identity but did refer to transvestism—the practice, especially among men, of wearing clothing usually associated with the opposite sex for psychological gratification.[48]

- The diagnosis of "transsexualism" was first introduced in the third edition of the *DSM* in 1980.
- This diagnosis was replaced with "Gender Identity Disorder" in the *DSM-IV* of 1994.
- As a result of trans activists' objections to the pathologization of their existence, the term was replaced in 2013 in the fifth edition of the *DSM* with the diagnosis "Gender Dysphoria," which has the diagnostic criteria listed on page 212 for adolescents and adults (and closely related criteria for children).[49]

What are some turning points in the history of gender reassignment surgeries?

- One of the world's first gender reassignment surgeries took place in Germany in 1930. Lili Elbe—whose birth name was Einar Magnus Andres Wegener and who was probably born intersex—underwent four operations and died in 1931 from an infection that occurred when her immune system rejected the uterus that had been implanted in her.
- The 2015 film *The Danish Girl*, based on the novel of the same name by David Ebershoff and nominated for three Academy Awards, is a fictionalized account of Lili Elbe's story.[50]
- The first gender reassignment surgery in the United States was performed in 1966.[51]

How many gender confirmation surgeries are performed each year?

- The *Surgery Encyclopedia* estimates the number of gender reassignment procedures conducted in the United States each year at between 100 and 500, while the global number may be two to five times higher.[52]
- This surgery can cost between $5,000 and $100,000. The average cost is $15,500.[53]
- HRC currently lists 18 health-insurance providers that will cover gender reassignment surgery (also known

DIAGNOSTIC CRITERIA

Gender Dysphoria in Adolescents or Adults 302.85 (F64.1)

A. A marked incongruence between one's experienced/expressed gender and assigned gender, of at least 6 months' duration, as manifested by at least two of the following:

1. a marked incongruence between one's experienced/expressed gender and primary and/or secondary sex characteristics (or, in young adolescents, the anticipated secondary sex characteristics)
2. a strong desire to be rid of one's primary and/or secondary sex characteristics because of a marked incongruence with one's experienced/expressed gender (or, in young adolescents, a desire to prevent the development of the anticipated secondary sex characteristics)
3. a strong desire for the primary and/or secondary sex characteristics of the other gender
4. a strong desire to be of the other gender (or some alternative gender different from one's assigned gender)
5. a strong desire to be treated as the other gender (or some alternative gender different from one's assigned gender)
6. a strong conviction that one has the typical feelings and reactions of the other gender (or some alternative gender different from one's assigned gender)

B. The condition is associated with clinically significant stress or impairment in social, school, or other important areas of functioning.

Source: American Psychiatric Association, *Diagnostic and Statistical Manual of Mental Disorders*, Fifth Edition (2013).

as gender confirmation surgery), with an additional six insurers covering some trans health care.[54]

MEDIA

What are some recent developments regarding media coverage of trans issues?

16.9 million people tuned in to the April 2015 *20/20* segment in which Bruce Jenner, the retired Olympic-gold-medal-winning decathlete, spoke about transitioning to Caitlyn Jenner. Jenner was photographed by Annie Liebowitz for the July 2015 cover of *Vanity Fair*, which was published with the caption "Call me Caitlyn."[55]

Caitlyn Jenner was the first name on CBS News's 2016 list of "Transgender Celebrities You Need to Know." Additional names include:

- Laverne Cox—star of *Orange Is the New Black*.
- Chaz Bono—only child of Sonny and Cher.
- Lana Wachowski—joint director of *The Matrix*.
- Lily Wachowski—Lana's younger sibling and co-director of *The Matrix*.
- Andreja Pejić—model.
- Balian Buschbaum—former German Olympic pole vaulter.
- Christine Jorgensen—the first face of American trans people in the 1950s.
- Renée Richards—professional tennis player and trans activist.
- Jenna Talackova—Miss Universe Pageant representative for Canada.[56]

When Private Bradley Manning—the U.S. Army soldier convicted in July 2013 of violating the Espionage Act after disclosing more than 700,000 classified or unclassified documents to WikiLeaks—announced that he was transitioning to female, a media firestorm erupted.[57] In an analysis of 136 news stories published during a nine-month period in print media, online media, and blogs about Bradley Manning's transition to Chelsea Manning:

- 61 percent of the stories focused on Manning's coming out; attention to this topic waned once consensus was achieved on how to refer to her.
- One story in the online magazine *Queerty* was titled "CNN Guest Jokes Chelsea Manning Will Get 'Good Practice' Being a Woman in Prison."[58]
- On February 12, 2015, *USA Today* reported that the commandant of the U.S. Disciplinary Barracks at Fort Leavenworth, Kansas, wrote in a February 5 memo: "After carefully considering the recommendation that [hormone treatment] is medically appropriate and necessary, and weighing all associated safety and security risks presented, I approve adding [hormone treatment] to Inmate Manning's treatment plan." The decision to administer hormone therapy was a first for the military, which until July 2016 banned transgender people from serving but which provides health services, including hormone therapy, to trans veterans.[59]

For more on media coverage of trans issues, see pages 130 to 131 of the Media chapter.

PRISON

What percentage of the trans population has been incarcerated?

According to the National Center for Transgender Equality (NCTE), based on information gathered from the National Transgender Discrimination Survey, at some point in their life:

- 16 percent of trans people have been incarcerated—in contrast to 2.8 percent of the general population.
- 21 percent of trans women have been incarcerated.
- 47 percent of African American trans people have been incarcerated.
- 49 percent of homeless trans respondents have been incarcerated.[60]

In its first report on the incarceration of trans Americans, covering 2011 and 2012, the Federal Bureau of Justice Statistics found that:

- More than 3,200 trans people were imprisoned throughout the United States.
- Of this number, 39.9 percent reported sexual assault or abuse by another prisoner or a staff member within the previous year.[61]

How are conditions changing for trans people who are incarcerated?

In 2003, Congress unanimously passed the Prison Rape Elimination Act (PREA). After nearly a decade of study and review, the U.S. Department of Justice issued final regulations for the implementation of PREA in 2012. For the first time, these regulations—which the National Center for Transgender Equality described as "an historic step toward ending the crisis of sexual abuse in confinement"—addressed a number of trans-specific protections, including:

- a screening of all individuals at admission and upon transfer to assess their risk of experiencing abuse;
- the ability to shower privately if requested;
- staff training on LGBTQ issues;
- the guarantee of a case-by-case assessment regarding whether an individual is housed in male or female facilities; and
- a new policy stating that decisions regarding where an inmate is housed cannot be made solely on the basis of a person's anatomy or gender assigned at birth and must take into account the individual's views regarding personal safety.[62]

In February 2015, Ashley Diamond, a trans woman, sued the Georgia Department of Corrections, alleging that she had been denied medically necessary treatment, forced into solitary confinement, and sexually assaulted by prisoners in all-male Georgia state prisons.

- After Diamond filed her lawsuit, the Department of Justice filed a first-ever court brief arguing that blanket limits on medical care for transgender prisoners are unconstitutional.
- While in prison, Diamond was denied access to the hormone therapy she had been receiving for 17 years prior to her internment.
- As part of a historic settlement announced in 2016, the Georgia Department of Corrections "rescinded its 'freeze frame' policy that prevented many transgender inmates from receiving medically necessary treatment," according to a statement from the Southern Poverty Law Center, which defended Diamond. As a result, dozens of trans inmates across Georgia are receiving hormone therapy for the first time since entering custody.[63]

WORLD

Globally, what are some breakthroughs and setbacks that trans people have experienced in recent years?

- In 2010, France became the first country to remove transsexuality from its list of mental disorders.[64]
- In January 2016, the International Olympic Committee updated its guidelines and eliminated a requirement for trans athletes to have gender reassignment surgery before competing in the Olympics.[65]
- While homosexuality is outlawed in Iran, transgender Iranians are allowed to change their sex so that they can enter heterosexual relationships.[66]
- According to the organization Transgender Europe, there were 1,509 reported killings of trans people in 61 countries worldwide between January 2008 and March 2014. Eighty percent of these killings occurred in Latin America. Underreporting probably means that the actual number of killings is significantly higher.[67]
- 24 European countries require trans people to be steril-

ized as a prerequisite for changing their gender marker on identity documents and government records.[68]

What directives has the World Medical Association issued regarding the health of trans people?

At its 2015 conference in Moscow, the World Medical Association (WMA) released a statement on trans people that included the following directives:

1. Everyone has the right to determine one's own gender, and [the WMA] recognizes the diversity of possibilities in this respect. The WMA calls for physicians to uphold each individual's right to self-identification with regards to gender.
2. Gender incongruence is not in itself a mental disorder; however, it can lead to discomfort or distress, which is referred to as gender dysphoria (*DSM-5*).
3. Any form of coercive treatment or forced behavior modification must end.
4. Physicians should receive appropriate expert training at all stages of their career to enable them to recognize and avoid discriminatory practices, and to provide appropriate and sensitive transgender healthcare.
5. All forms of discrimination, stigmatization and violence against transgender people must end and appropriate legal measures to protect their equal civil rights must be provided.
6. No person, regardless of gender, ethnicity, socio-economic status, medical condition or disability, should be subjected to forced or coerced permanent sterilization. This also includes sterilization as a condition for rectifying the recorded sex on official documents following gender reassignment.[69]

What is Transgender Day of Remembrance?

Beginning in 1999, an annual Day of Remembrance has been held on November 20 to commemorate the lives of transgender people who have been murdered around the globe.

- The first event, a candlelight vigil in San Francisco, was organized by Gwendolyn Ann Smith in response to the death of Rita Hester, a trans woman of color who was killed in Massachusetts in 1998.
- In 2015—the 16th annual Transgender Day of Remembrance—89 lives were commemorated, including 57 from Brazil. The majority of those who had been murdered were transgender women.[70]

> This hatred for the LGBT community is something that the gunman learned right here at home, not outside our borders. This is the same hatred that led to the murders of over a dozen transgender Americans this year, most of them women of color. This is the same hatred that's been espoused by American lawmakers who have proposed over 100 anti-LGBT bills this year. And this is the same hatred that we all must come together to end once and for all.
>
> *—Sarah Kate Ellis, President and CEO of GLAAD, commenting on the gunman who murdered 49 people at Pulse, a gay club in Orlando, on June 12, 2016*[1]

In the 1960s, 82 percent of American men and 58 percent of American women believed that homosexuals posed a serious danger to this country, exceeded only by the menace of Communism and atheism.[2] Despite immense strides in public opinion about LGBTQ Americans, sexual minorities face bias and violence—including harassment, physical attacks, and murder—at alarming rates. It is difficult to determine whether the recent spike in numbers means there are more killings or whether higher statistics are the result of better reporting. Asks Sharon Stapel, former director of the Anti-Violence Project, an organization that tracks anti-LGBTQ violence: "Is it the more visible people are, the more vulnerable people are to violence? Or does it just represent a better identification of people killed? I wish we all knew the answer to that question."[3]

VIOLENCE AGAINST LGBTQ PEOPLE

What proportion of the LGBTQ community has experienced harassment or violence?

According to a national randomly selected sample of lesbian, gay, and bisexual adults:

- Nearly 50 percent of all LGB Americans have experienced verbal abuse.
- 23.4 percent have been threatened with violence.
- 20.9 percent have experienced a crime against their person or property based on their sexual orientation.
- 13.1 percent have been the victim of a violent crime.[4]

What are the deadliest attacks on the LGBTQ community in U.S. history?

In the early morning hours of Sunday, June 12, 2016, 49 people were shot and killed and 53 were injured at Pulse, an LGBTQ club in Orlando, Florida. This massacre marked not only the deadliest attack on the LGBTQ community but also the largest mass shooting in U.S. history. Of those murdered, 90 percent were Hispanic or of Hispanic descent.[5]

- "This had nothing to do with religion," Mir Seddique, the father of the gunman, Omar Mateen, told NBC News when asked to explain his son's actions. "[H]e saw two men kissing each other in front of his wife and kid and he got very angry."[6]
- In response to the shootings, President Barack Obama told the country: "This was an attack on the LGBT community. . . . And hatred towards people because of sexual orientation, regardless of where it comes from, is a betrayal of what's best in us."[7]

Prior to the Pulse massacre, the deadliest assault on the LGBTQ community was a 1973 fire in which 32 people were killed in a malicious arson attack at the UpStairs Lounge, a gay bar in New Orleans. According to the *New York Times*, "Churches refused to bury the victims' remains. Their deaths were mostly ignored and sometimes mocked by politicians and the media. No one was ever charged. A joke made the rounds in workplaces and was repeated on the radio: 'Where will they bury the queers? In fruit jars!'"[8]

Do recent statistics document an increase or decrease in anti-LGBTQ violence across the U.S.?

In 2015, the murders of 21 trans people—most of them women of color—were reported in the United States, the largest number of any year to date.[9]

In its most recent report on violence against LGBTQ people, covering incidents that occurred in 2014 and that were reported to 16 member organizations in 14 states, the National Coalition of Anti-Violence Programs found that:

- 1,359 incidents of anti-LGBT violence were reported, a 32 percent decrease from 2013.
- Hate-motivated violence against transgender people rose 13 percent.
- The number of homicides of LGBT people increased 11 percent.
- Of these homicide victims, 80 percent were people of color and more than half were transgender.
- 54 percent of the 2014 incidents were reported to the police. But only 6 percent of reported incidents were classified as bias crimes by the police—a substantial decrease from 24 percent in 2013.[10]

Among incidents committed by people known to the victims, 23.4 percent of offenders were landlords, tenants, and neighbors, as shown in Figure 14.1 on page 222.

In what ways have public figures incited or condoned anti-LGBTQ violence?

- A music video of Jamaican dance hall star and Grammy winner Buju Banton performing "Boom Bye Bye" includes these lyrics, in a Jamaican slang known as patois:

Figure 14.1: Violence Against LGBTQ Americans by People They Know

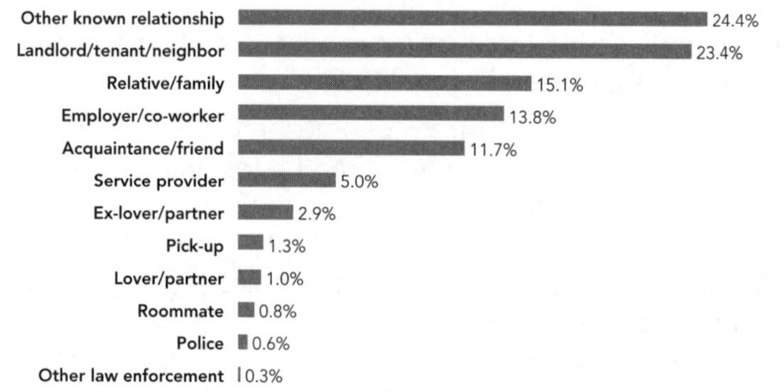

Source: National Coalition of Anti-Violence Programs, "Lesbian, Gay, Bisexual, Transgender, Queer, and HIV-Affected Hate Violence in 2014," June 2015, www.avp.org/storage/documents/Reports/2014_HV_Report-Final.pdf.

- *"Boom bye bye / inna batty bwoy head / Rude bwoy no promote no nasty man / dem haffi dead."*
- Translation: "*Boom [the sound of a gunshot], bye-bye / in a faggot's head / The tough young guys don't accept fags / they have to die.*[11]
- As of June 2016, the song had more than 18 million plays on YouTube.[12]
- In 2010—the same year Buju Banton won the Grammy for Best Reggae Album—28 gay Jamaicans were granted political asylum by the United States.[13]

□ In 2016, Manny Pacquiao—a world champion boxer and born-again Christian who was named the world's fourth most-influential sports star in 2012[14]—posted remarks on social media implying that gay people should be killed. After being fired by Nike for saying that gay people are "worse than animals," Pacquiao posted a picture on Instagram with a caption that quoted a passage from Leviticus that says men who have sex with men should be put to death.

- According to *Forbes*, Pacquiao's earnings in 2015 totaled $160 million, with $12 million coming from endorsements from Foot Locker, Wonderful Pistachios, Nestle's Butterfinger, Nike (which had had a relationship with Pacquiao since 2006), and other sponsors.[15]
- Early in 2016, Pacquiao said he planned to retire from boxing to become a full-time politician. In May 2016, he was elected to the Philippine Senate. When asked if his next target was the presidency, Pacquiao smiled and said, "Nothing, nothing, nothing."[16]

- In November 2015, then–U.S. presidential candidate Senator Ted Cruz appeared at a National Religious Liberties Conference where at least two pastors advocated killing LGBT people.[17]

At what rates do community college students harass or attack people they perceive to be LGBTQ?

In two studies of community college students, one in Salt Lake City (SLC) and one in San Francisco (SF):

- 5 percent of the SLC sample reported physically assaulting or threatening people they believed to be homosexual, while 10 percent of the SF sample reported assailant behavior against those they perceived to be gay or lesbian.
- 22.9 percent of SLC students reported calling homosexuals names, while 23.5 percent of the SF cohort reported verbally harassing gay men and lesbians.
- 97 percent of the SF students reported affiliation with a religious organization, while only 56.5 percent of the SLC students did.
- In both studies, most of the assailants acted in groups.[18]

BIAS AND HATE CRIMES

Who is most likely to harbor anti-LGBTQ bias?

In four studies of U.S. and German college students published in the April 2012 issue of the *Journal of Personality and Social Psychology*, researchers found that "participants who reported their heterosexuality despite having hidden same-sex desires were also the most likely to show hostility toward gay individuals."[19]

What traits are common to most perpetrators of hate crimes against LGBTQ people?

- The majority of anti-gay assailants are men in their late teens to early 20s who may otherwise have no criminal record.
- It is estimated that fewer than 5 percent of all hate-crime perpetrators belong to organized hate groups.[20]

What is the Hate Crimes Statistics Act?

Enacted in 1990, the Hate Crime Statistics Act (HCSA) requires the U.S. Department of Justice to collect data from law enforcement agencies across the country on crimes that "manifest prejudice based on race, religion, sexual orientation, or ethnicity" and to publish an annual summary of the findings.[21] According to statistics gathered by the FBI in accordance with the HCSA:

- In 2014:
  - 18.7 percent of reported hate crimes were against LGBTQ people. The largest bias motivation was race, which accounted for 48.3 percent of reported hate crimes.
  - 1,248 victims were targeted due to sexual-orientation bias.
  - 56.3 percent of these crimes were motivated by animus toward gay men.
  - 24.4 percent were victims of "mixed-group" bias, motivated by bias against lesbians, gay men, bisexuals, or transgender people.
  - 13.9 percent were victims of anti-lesbian bias.

- 3.8 percent were victims of anti-bisexual bias.
- The report did not document the number of victims of anti-transgender bias.[22]

- In 1996:
  - 11.6 percent of reported hate crimes were against LGBTQ people.
  - 1,281 victims were targeted due to sexual-orientation bias.
  - 73.4 percent of these crimes were motivated by animus toward gay men.[23]

What conclusions can be drawn by analyzing data gathered under the Hate Crimes Statistics Act?

Based on FBI statistics on hate crimes from 1995 to 2008, the Southern Poverty Law Center compared the rate of victimization of six minority groups based on their representation in the population and found that:

- LGBT people were victimized at 8.3 times the expected rate.
- Jews were victimized at 3.5 times the expected rate.
- African Americans were victimized at 3.2 times the expected rate.
- Muslims were victimized at 1.9 times the expected rate.
- Latinos were victimized at 0.6 times the expected rate.
- Whites were victimized at 0.2 times the expected rate.[24]

What is the Matthew Shepard and James Byrd Jr. Hate Crimes Prevention Act?

The Matthew Shepard and James Byrd Jr. Hate Crimes Prevention Act expanded federal hate crimes protections to include sexual orientation, gender, gender identity, and disability. It also provides multiple types of aid to local and state jurisdictions investigating and prosecuting hate crimes.

- This landmark civil rights legislation, which went into effect in 2009, was named after Matthew Shepard, a 21-year-old student at the University of Wyoming who was gay, and James Byrd Jr., a 49-year-old African American man living in Jasper, Texas. Both were murdered in acts of intolerance and hate.

- Byrd was walking home on June 7, 1998, when three white men stopped him and offered him a ride home. They beat him severely, chained him by his ankles to the rear bumper of their truck, and dragged him along the road for more than three miles. The men responsible for Byrd's murder were well-known white supremacists; two were sentenced to death, while the third was sentenced to life in prison.[25]
- On October 7, 1998, two young men in Laramie, Wyoming, offered 21-year-old Matthew Shepard, a freshman at the University of Wyoming, a ride home from a bar. Eighteen hours later, a cyclist found Shepard tied to a fence, beaten, burned, and comatose with a fractured skull. The cyclist initially mistook Shepard for a scarecrow. Shepard died six days later. His murderers were given life sentences, not the death penalty, largely because Shepard's parents sought life sentences for his killers.[26]

What impact has the Hate Crimes Prevention Act had on federal prosecution of hate crimes?

- Between 2009 and 2013, the Department of Justice charged 201 defendants on federal hate crimes or hate crimes–related charges, including the Shepard-Byrd Act and other federal hate crimes provisions—an increase of almost 50 percent from the previous five years.
- The department also convicted almost 50 percent more defendants on federal hate crimes or hate crimes–related charges, compared to the prior five years.[27]

How many states have hate crimes legislation?

- 44 states plus the District of Columbia have hate crimes laws. In addition:
  - 30 states and the District of Columbia include sexual orientation in their hate crimes laws.

- 17 states and the District of Columbia include gender identity.
- 14 states have existing hate crimes laws that do not cover sexual orientation or gender identity.

- The six states without hate crimes laws are Arkansas, Georgia, Indiana, Michigan, South Carolina, and Wyoming.[28]
- On May 13, 2015, the city of Laramie, Wyoming, passed the first nondiscrimination ordinance in Wyoming, banning discrimination based on sexual orientation and gender identity in housing, employment, and access to public accommodations. The 7–2 vote came three months after the Wyoming House of Representatives voted 33–26 to reject a bill that would have extended nondiscrimination protections based on sexual orientation and gender identity to all residents of the state.[29]

POLICE INTERACTIONS

At what rates do LGBTQ people experience harassment or violence when they interact with the police?

In a 2015 Williams Institute study of the relationship between LGBTQ people and the police:

- 21 percent of LGBT people who dealt with the police reported hostile attitudes.
- 14 percent reported verbal assault.
- 48 percent of LGBT people who dealt with the police after experiencing violence reported misconduct by the officers with whom they interacted, including unjustified arrest, use of excessive force, and entrapment.
- Two-thirds of Latina transgender women in Los Angeles who interacted with the police reported that they were verbally harassed; 21 percent reported being physically assaulted; and 24 percent reported that they were sexually assaulted.
- 46 percent of transgender people polled were uncomfortable seeking help from the police.[30]

In a 2010 study of active-duty police officers in the Chicago area:

- 90 percent of officers reported responding to an incident of same-sex domestic violence.
- 81.3 percent said their departments had no procedure in place to address the specifics of such incidents.[31]

PRISON

At what rates are LGBTQ prisoners sexually victimized?

According to a Bureau of Justice Statistics analysis of data from a 2011–12 survey of 92,449 adult inmates in U.S. federal and state prisons, sexual victimization by another inmate within the past year was reported by:

- 24.1 percent of prisoners who identify as transgender;
- 11.9 percent of non-heterosexual male inmates, compared to 1.0 percent of heterosexual male inmates; and
- 9.4 percent of non-heterosexual female inmates, compared to 3.6 percent of heterosexual female inmates.[32]

Sexual victimization by a member of the prison facility staff within the past year was reported by:

- 16.7 percent of prisoners who identify as transgender;
- 6.1 percent of non-heterosexual male inmates, compared to 2.0 percent of heterosexual male inmates; and
- 3.0 percent of non-heterosexual female inmates, compared to 1.4 percent of heterosexual female inmates.[33]

INTIMATE PARTNER VIOLENCE

What trends have been documented regarding violence between intimate partners?

- In representative samples of lesbians and of gay and bisexual men, the rates of intimate partner violence (IPV) were the same as for their heterosexual peers. Bisexual women were found to face a higher incidence of IPV.[34]

- Between 31 and 50 percent of transgender people experience intimate partner violence.[35]
- LGBTQ people who experience IPV face barriers to seeking help that are unique to their sexual orientation and gender identity.[36]

In a 2014 report, the National Coalition of Anti-Violence Programs found:

- 2,166 incidents of intimate partner violence in the LGBTQ community were reported in 2014, including 15 homicides.
- People of color make up more than half of all survivors of IPV.
- Physical violence was the most common form of IPV (20 percent), followed by threats and intimidation (16 percent) and verbal harassment (15 percent).
- The percentage of survivors who reported incidents to the police increased, from 35 percent in 2013 to 55 percent in 2014.
- 260 survivors sought orders of protection, with 85 percent receiving them, compared to 58 percent in 2013.[37]

I want you to go back to your offices after this conference and shut the door. Then I want you to remove all vestiges of your family, particularly your spouse. Put the pictures in the drawer and take off your wedding band. You cannot talk about your family and where you went on vacation. If your spouse or partner is seriously ill, you are afraid to acknowledge your relationships because you are afraid you might lose your job. Do all that and see how productive you are.

—Software engineer Louise Young, who was forced out of her job at an Oklahoma college after officials learned she had visited a lesbian bar, addressing a symposium at defense contractor Raytheon in 2001[1]

I don't consider myself an activist, but I realize how much I've benefited from the sacrifice of others. So if hearing that the CEO of Apple is gay can help someone struggling to come to terms with who he or she is, or bring comfort to anyone who feels alone, or inspire people to insist on their equality, then it's worth the trade-off with my own privacy.

—Tim Cook, CEO of Apple, in a 2014 coming-out article that made him the first openly gay CEO of a Fortune 500 company[2]

An estimated 8.2 million LGBT Americans are part of the U.S. workforce.[3] While 22 states, the District of Columbia, and many businesses offer workplace protections to some LGBTQ employees, the majority of states do not.[4] The consequences for workers like Patricia Dawson can be dire. An electrician from Hot Springs, Arkansas, Dawson was fired from her job after she transitioned from male to female. Her boss acknowledged that Dawson was one of his best employees but said her gender identity made her "too much of a distraction"—and under Arkansas law, it was legal for the company to fire her. With support from the ACLU, Dawson is suing, arguing that firing an employee on the basis of gender transition constitutes illegal sex discrimination under Title VII of the Civil Rights Act of 1964.[5]

At the national level, the Employment Nondiscrimination Act (ENDA), which would prohibit discrimination in hiring and employment on the basis of sexual orientation or gender identity by employers with at least 15 employees, has been introduced regularly in Congress since 1974 but has failed to secure enough support to become law. An expanded version of ENDA, the Equality Act—a piece of legislation introduced in 2015 that would broaden the Civil Rights Act to establish explicit protections for LGBT people against discrimination in employment, housing, and public accommodations—has not yet had a hearing in Congress. While the struggle for workplace equality continues, one major employment battle has been won: the world's largest employer, the U.S. Department of Defense, rescinded its "Don't Ask, Don't Tell" policy in 2011, allowing lesbians, gay men, and bisexuals—and, as of July 2016, transgender people—to serve openly in the armed forces.

FEDERAL EMPLOYMENT POLICIES

What is the history of the federal government's treatment of gay and lesbian employees?

- In 1953, President Dwight D. Eisenhower signed Executive Order 10450, mandating that "sexual perverts" be fired from federal jobs. Citing national security interests, the president also ordered private contractors doing business with the government to fire their homosexual employees and urged allies overseas to conduct similar purges in their countries.[6]
- Historian David Johnson, author of *The Lavender Scare*, estimates that at least several thousand gay men and

lesbians lost government jobs as a result of Eisenhower's order. "The real number is probably much higher," notes Johnson, "because most government workers who endured brutal interrogations about their sex lives chose to voluntarily resign rather than face further publicity."[7]

- During the McCarthy era, more people lost their jobs for being alleged homosexuals than for being Communists.[8]
- In 1976, the Carter administration issued a new standard for federal employment, stating that the private lives of federal employees were not relevant to federal personnel decisions.[9]
- On April 22, 1994, Secretary of State Warren Christopher issued a prohibition against discrimination in the State Department that included sexual orientation.[10]
- On May 28, 1998, President Bill Clinton issued Executive Order 13087, which amended a previous executive order to ban discrimination based on sexual orientation in hiring for the federal workforce, excluding the CIA, FBI, and NSA. In a statement regarding the order, Clinton wrote: "This Executive Order states Administration policy but does not and cannot create any new enforcement rights (such as the ability to proceed before the Equal Employment Opportunity Commission). Those rights can be granted only by legislation passed by the Congress, such as the Employment Non-Discrimination Act."[11]
- In 2010, the administration of President Barack Obama, through the Office of Personnel Management, added gender identity to the classes protected by federal Equal Employment Opportunity policies.[12]
- On July 21, 2014, President Obama signed Executive Order 13672, adding gender identity to categories protected against discrimination in hiring in the federal civilian workforce, and both sexual orientation and gender identity to categories protected against discrimina-

tion in hiring and employment on the part of federal government contractors and subcontractors.[13]

How has the Equal Employment Opportunity Commission (EEOC) ruled on job discrimination based on gender identity and sexual orientation?

- In 2012, the bipartisan EEOC ruled unanimously that Title VII of the Civil Rights Act of 1964 does not allow employers to discriminate on the basis of gender identity because doing so constitutes a form of sex discrimination.[14]
- In 2015, in a 3–2 vote, the EEOC concluded that Title VII of the 1964 Civil Rights Act also forbids employment discrimination on the basis of sexual orientation because this is a form of sex discrimination, which is explicitly forbidden. This statement by the EEOC is not binding on the courts and runs counter to many circuit court rulings that the EEOC characterized as dated. The EEOC's five commissioners serve five-year terms; a new president could appoint commissioners who could reverse this affirmation.[15]

DISCRIMINATION AND PROTECTION

How widespread is employment discrimination based on sexual orientation or gender identity?

According to data presented in a 2012 report from the Center for American Progress Action Fund:

- 17 percent of LGBTQ workers reported being fired because of their sexual orientation or gender identity.
- 13 percent reported being denied a promotion or receiving a negative job evaluation because of their sexual orientation or gender identity.
- 20 percent reported being harassed verbally or in writing on the job because they are gay or transgender.[16]
- In the largest survey of trans people to date, 78 percent of respondents reported experiencing at least one form

of harassment or mistreatment at work because of their gender identity.[17]

- In a large-scale, peer-reviewed study of discrimination against gay men in employment released in 2011, a researcher sent pairs of résumés to 1,769 job postings in seven U.S. states. One résumé described the applicant as the elected treasurer of a gay campus organization; the other listed experience in the Progressive and Socialist Alliance. The results revealed:
  - The equally qualified gay applicants were about 40 percent less likely than their non-gay-identified peers to get an interview.
  - In companies that had nondiscrimination ordinances, gay applicants were about 25 percent less likely to get an interview.
  - In companies that did not have nondiscrimination ordinances, gay applicants were 53 percent less likely to get an interview.[18]

What protections exist in federal law to combat anti-LGBTQ employment discrimination?

- 87 percent of the U.S. population believes—incorrectly—that it is illegal under federal law to fire someone for being LGBT.[19] While this is true for federal employees and for employees of federal contractors, federal law does *not* protect private sector or non-federal LGBTQ workers from discrimination.[20] As a result, in most states, employees of state and local governments, local school districts, and small businesses can be fired simply for being LGBTQ. Adds David Stacy, government affairs director for Human Rights Campaign: "With limited or no federal protections, an LGBT person can get legally married . . . but then be evicted from an apartment and denied a home loan."[21]
- The Employment Non-Discrimination Act (ENDA) was federal legislation proposed in the U.S. Congress that would ban employers with at least 15 employees from firing, refusing to hire, or discriminating against workers

or job applicants on the basis of sexual orientation or gender identity. ENDA was introduced without passage in every Congress since 1974 except the 109th, until it was abandoned in 2014.[22]

- In 2014, just after the Supreme Court issued its ruling in *Burwell v. Hobby Lobby*—a decision that allows a for-profit corporation with a limited number of shareholders to be exempt from a law to which its owners object on religious grounds—a coalition of LGBTQ legal organizations withdrew their support for ENDA because of a religious-exemption provision in the bill. The legal advocates described the provision as "unprecedented in federal laws prohibiting employment discrimination," adding that this provision "could provide religiously affiliated organizations—including hospitals, nursing homes and universities—a blank check to engage in workplace discrimination against LGBT people."[23]

What is the Equality Act?

In July 2015, the Equality Act was submitted to Congress to replace ENDA. This legislation would extend the Civil Rights Act of 1964 by establishing explicit, permanent protections against discrimination based on an individual's sexual orientation or gender identity in matters of employment, housing, access to public places, federal funding, credit, education, and jury service. In addition, it would expand protected places of public accommodations to include retail stores; transportation services like airports, taxis, and bus stations; and service providers such as accountants. It does not change the religious exemptions already in place in federal law.[24]

- In October 2015, Representative Jared Polis—a Colorado Democrat and an openly gay member of Congress—sought to bring up the Equality Act for its first-ever vote in the House. Polis's attempt was rebuffed by a House panel.[25]
- In January 2016, Representative Robert Dold of Illinois became the first Republican congressman to co-sponsor the bill.[26]

CORPORATE AMERICA

What percentage of corporate workplaces have created LGBTQ-friendly work environments?

The HRC Foundation creates an annual Corporate Equality Index (CEI) that rates companies on workplace equality for LGBTQ people. Companies must meet three criteria:

1. Have explicit nondiscrimination protections in place for sexual orientation and gender identity in all operations within the United States and globally.
2. Require all the company's U.S. contractors to abide by the company's nondiscrimination policies.
3. Prohibit company philanthropic giving to nonreligious organizations that have a written policy of discrimination on the basis of sexual orientation or gender identity.

In the 2016 Corporate Equality Index, 407 companies achieved a 100 percent rating.

- In 2002, the first year that the CEI rated companies, 13 businesses achieved a top score.
- In 2012, 189 businesses did.[27]

Other findings from the 2016 CEI include:

- 85 percent of the CEI-rated employers have an LGBTQ employee resource group or diversity council. In 2002, 40 percent did.
- 75 percent of Fortune 500 companies and 93 percent of the 851 businesses rated offer explicit gender-identity nondiscrimination in the United States, compared to just three companies in 2000.
- 40 percent of the Fortune 500 and 60 percent of the other businesses rated now offer transgender-inclusive health care coverage. In 2002, none did.
- More than 300 businesses have adopted gender-transition guidelines for their employees.[28]

What are the best companies for LGBTQ employees?

The magazine *DiversityInc.* listed these companies as the top U.S. workplaces for LGBTQ employees in 2015:

1. Wells Fargo
2. AT&T
3. Time Warner
4. Marriott International
5. Ernst & Young[29]

What impact do diversity and inclusion policies have on companies and employees?

In a 2011 Williams Institute study of the impact of diversity on the bottom line of the top 50 Fortune 500 companies and the top 50 federal government contractors, of the companies that have LGBT-related policies:

- 92 percent have linked diversity to corporate success—88 percent of the contractors and 96 percent of the Fortune 500 companies.
- 53 percent of employers in the study have "expressly linked either LGBTQ-related policies, or diversity that specifically includes LGBTQ people, to a positive impact on business." The reasons cited:
    - Ability to recruit and retain the best talent.
    - Increased variety of ideas and innovations.
    - Better ability to serve a diverse customer base.
    - Higher productivity and morale.
    - Ability to attract more public-sector clients.[30]

When Tim Cook, the CEO of Apple, revealed that he is gay in a column published by *Bloomberg Businessweek* in October 2014, he became the highest-profile CEO to come out, and the first out CEO of a Fortune 500 company. The *Financial Times'* list of 2015's "Leading 100 LGBT Executives" included CEOs of 16 other major companies.[31]

- Cook's decision to come out stands in contrast to the decision of the former CEO of BP, Lord John Browne, who resigned his CEO job in 2007, three months earlier than planned, in hopes of preventing a tabloid from reporting on his relationship with a man he had met through an escort service. Browne's early resignation cost him more than $30 million in stock and retirement benefits.[32]

- In 2014 Browne published *The Glass Closet: Why Coming Out Is Good Business*, a book that includes interviews with gay executives about their workplace experiences and the discrimination they encountered. He told *Bloomberg Businessweek*: "Studies show an inclusive environment can increase productivity up to 30 percent. When people can be themselves, they're not using half their brain trying to figure out how to be something they're not."[33]

How many LGBTQ workers hide their identity at work?

Despite progress in corporate America, many LGBTQ workers remain closeted at their jobs. "The Cost of the Closet," a 2014 HRC survey of more than 800 LGBTQ people across the United States, reported that:

- 53 percent of LGBTQ workers hide their sexual orientation or gender identity at work.
- 35 percent of LGBTQ employees feel compelled to lie about their personal lives while at work.
- More than one in five LGBTQ people report looking for other employment because they felt unwelcome for being who they are.

The survey points to some reasons why LGBTQ people feel uncomfortable at their jobs:

- 62 percent reported hearing jokes in the workplace about lesbians and gay men.
- 43 percent heard jokes about bisexuals.
- 40 percent heard jokes about trans people.[34]

MILESTONES IN LGBTQ LABOR UNION HISTORY

1970	The Executive Council of the American Federation of Teachers (AFT) approves a resolution protesting any personnel actions against homosexual behavior in private life.
1973	The AFT approves a resolution to support repeal of any laws that attempt to punish private acts.
1974	The San Francisco local Teamsters join queer activists in a boycott of Coors beer. The National Education Association adds sexual orientation to its nondiscrimination policy.
1975	An autoworker at General Motors leaves work for gender reassignment surgery and returns to much harassment. She sues, wins, and ends up working at the plant for 24 more years.
1982	The American Federation of State, County and Municipal Employees (AFSCME) and a division of the AFL-CIO pass resolutions calling for civil rights for gay people.
1997	Pride at Work, a national organization of LGBTQ unionists, is welcomed into the AFL-CIO as an official constituency organization.
1999	After a feasibility study, the "big three" automakers agree to the Union of Autoworkers proposal to add same-sex partner benefits to their contracts.

By this point, 18 percent of U.S. workplaces offer benefit equity to lesbian and gay employees.[35]

STATE GOVERNMENT

How have individual states acted to protect LGBTQ workers?

- In 1975, Pennsylvania became the first state to prohibit discrimination based on sexual orientation in public employment.[36]
- As of 2016, twenty states and the District of Columbia had enacted statewide bans against discrimination based on sexual orientation and gender identity in private employment.
- Wisconsin bans employment-related discrimination on the basis of sexual orientation but not gender identity, while New Hampshire's governor has issued an executive order that prohibits discrimination based on gender identity—but it only applies to public employment, access to state programs, and state contracting and can be revoked by a future governor.[37] The map on page 241 indicates which states offer employment protections to LGBTQ workers.

In 2014, the Williams Institute surveyed 221 state and local administrative agencies that had sexual-orientation and gender-identity nondiscrimination laws as of June 2009. The 123 responses provided data on 589 complaints of employment discrimination filed by LGBTQ state and local administrative workers. The survey found:

- There were three complaints per 10,000 LGB public sector workers and 4.2 complaints per 10,000 LGB private sector workers, across states.
- The researchers concluded, "Our analysis of these complaints shows that discrimination against public sector LGBTQ employees is pervasive. LGB employees of state and local governments are filing complaints under state

Figure 15.1: Employment Nondiscrimination Laws, by State

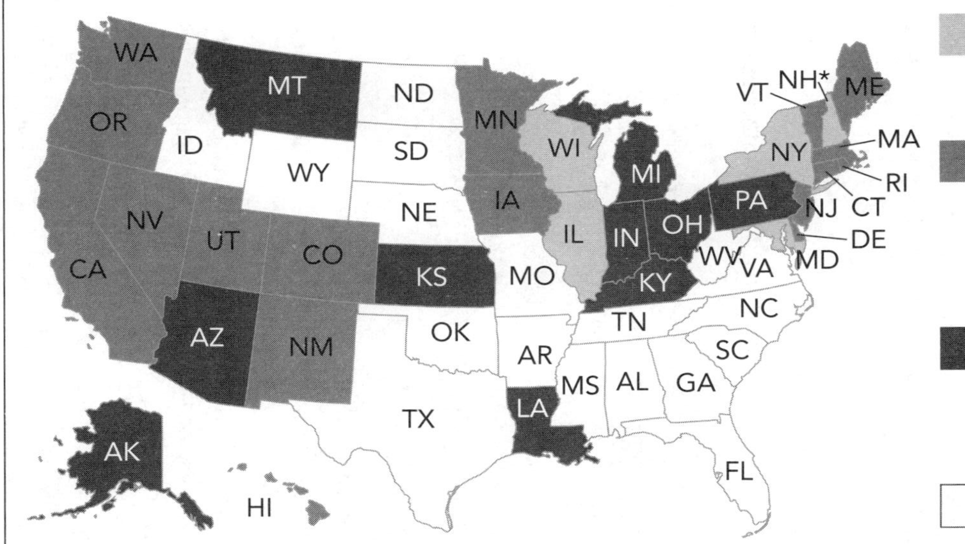

State law protects employees in both the private and public sectors from discrimination on the basis of sexual orientation.

State law protects employees in both the private and public sectors from discrimination on the basis of sexual orientation, as well as gender identity and/or gender expression.

State law/executive order protects public employees but NOT private sector employees on the basis of sexual orientation.

State has no law protecting workers from discrimination on the basis of sexual orientation or gender identity.

* Executive order protects public employees on the basis of gender identity and expression.

Source: Lambda Legal, "In Your State: Workplace Protections," accessed July 2016, www.lambdalegal.org/in-your-state.

nondiscrimination laws almost as frequently as LGB employees in the private sector. The rate at which LGB people file complaints under these laws is similar to the rate at which women and people of color file complaints under sex and race nondiscrimination laws."[38]

In states that do not protect workers from anti-LGBTQ discrimination, what are the consequences?

In 2015 the Williams Institute examined the consequences of not protecting LGBTQ workers in three states that do not have state laws prohibiting public and private employment discrimination against LGBTQ people. Table 15.1 summarizes the experiences of these workers.

LOCAL JURISDICTIONS

How many local jurisdictions have instituted protections for LGBTQ workers?

- On March 7, 1972, East Lansing, Michigan, became the first jurisdiction in the United States to provide protection against discrimination in employment based on sexual orientation.[39]
- As of January 2016, at least 225 cities and counties prohibit discrimination on the basis of gender identity for both public and private employees, according to HRC.[40]

LABOR DEMOGRAPHICS

In what occupational sectors are lesbians and gay men most represented?

According to data from the 2012 American Community Survey:

- The largest pecentage of gay men and lesbians work in the management, business, and financial sectors (24.3 percent and 18.9 percent, respectively), compared to 18.4 percent of straight men and 15.9 percent of straight women.

Table 15.1: Experiences of LGBTQ Workers in Three States Without Discrimination Protections

	Michigan	Montana	Texas
Number of LGBT workers	184,000	13,400	429,000
Income disparity between straight and gay male workers*	32%	61%	9%
Transgender workers reporting workplace discrimination	84%	N/A	79%
Public support for LGBTQ workplace protections	65%	67%	73%
Workforce covered by LGBTQ local nondiscrimination laws	16%	19%	14%
Estimated new complaints if LGBTQ protections are added to state laws	86	6	202

*Based on census data comparing men in same-sex couples to men in different-sex marriages.

Source: Williams Institute data on LGBTQ employment discrimination in Michigan, Montana, and Texas (2015), williamsinstitute.law.ucla.edu/wp-content/uploads/MI-Nondiscrimination-Feb-2015.pdf; williamsinstitute.law.ucla.edu/wp-content/uploads/MT-Nondiscrimination-March-2015.pdf; williamsinstitute.law.ucla.edu/wp-content/uploads/TX-Nondiscrimination-May-2015.pdf.

- 15.6 percent of gay men and 18.7 percent of lesbians work in the fields of education, legal affairs, arts and media, and community service, compared to 7.6 percent of straight men and 17.5 percent of straight women.[41]

MILITARY

Historically, what role have gay men, lesbians, and bisexuals played in the U.S. military?

- A significant number of historians concede that Friedrich Wilhelm von Steuben (1730–1794)—a Prussian-born American military officer who served as inspector general and major general of the Continental Army during the American Revolutionary War—was a lover of men. Steuben almost singlehandedly turned the American militia into a well-trained, disciplined, and professional army that was eventually able to defeat the British.[42]
- By some counts, up to 80 percent of all women who served in World War II had a lesbian or bisexual orientation.[43]

When did the U.S. military institute punishment of lesbian, gay, and bisexual soldiers?

- Punishment of LGB soldiers was first codified in U.S. military law during World War I.[44]
- The first official attempt to purge LGB service members from the military occurred in 1919 at the Naval Training Station in Newport, Rhode Island.[45]
- The prohibition on homosexual conduct was instituted in 1943, on the grounds that gay men, lesbians, and bisexuals were unfit for military service and a threat to unit cohesion. From 1943 to 1993, nearly 100,000 men and women were discharged from the military—in most cases, dishonorably—for alleged homosexuality.[46]

Who was the first service member to challenge the military ban on LGBT service?

Technical Sergeant Leonard Matlovich (1943–1988) was a Vietnam War veteran, race-relations instructor, and recipient of the Purple Heart and Bronze Star. In 1975, Matlovich became the first gay service member to out himself to the military to challenge the ban on LGB service members. He became one of the best-known gay men in America in the 1970s: he appeared on the cover of *Time* and was the subject of a TV movie.[47]

What is the connection between the military and the rainbow flag?

In 1977, Harvey Milk, California's first openly gay elected official, challenged Gilbert Baker—a gay man who had received an honorable discharge after two years of service in the U.S. Army—to create a symbol of pride for the gay community.

- Baker came up with the rainbow flag, which was first displayed in San Francisco's Gay Freedom Day Parade in June 1978.
- To commemorate the 25th anniversary of the Stonewall rebellion in 1994, Baker went on to construct the world's largest flag, which contained six colors of the rainbow and measured 30 feet wide by a mile long.[48]

How does the military treat openly LGB service members?

- In the fall of 1991, Bill Clinton, then a candidate for president, promised openly gay U.S. congressional leader Barney Frank that he would end the prohibition against LGB people in the military. On October 28, 1991, in response to a question from a student at a Harvard University forum, Clinton repeated his pledge.[49]
- After taking office and facing heated resistance to his promise to end the ban on LGB service members, Clinton offered the "Don't Ask, Don't Tell" (DADT) policy as a compromise. This policy prohibited military personnel from discriminating against or harassing closeted homosexual or bisexual service members or applicants,

while barring openly gay, lesbian, and bisexual persons from military service.[50]

- DADT became the official policy of the U.S. military on December 21, 1993.[51]
- In December 2010, a *Washington Post*–ABC News poll showed that 77 percent of Americans were in favor of allowing LGB personnel to serve openly in the military.[52]
- After the U.S. Department of Defense released a report saying there would be little disruption if the policy were repealed, Congress passed legislation in late 2010 repealing DADT, and President Obama signed the bill into law.[53]
- DADT was officially rescinded on September 20, 2011. During the time that DADT was in effect, the U.S. military discharged more than 13,000 service members for being "openly" LGB.[54]
- In 2006, the Government Accountability Office released a report stating that the costs of discharging and replacing service members fired for homosexuality or bisexuality during DADT's first nine years totaled at least $190.5 million.[55]
- In 2011, President Obama issued a policy that grants an honorable discharge to any veteran whose military service was terminated on the grounds of homosexuality unless there were aggravating circumstances. The Department of Defense reports that of the nearly 500 requests submitted under this policy, 80 percent have been granted.[56]
- On May 17, 2016, the Senate confirmed Eric Fanning as Secretary of the Army, making Fanning the first openly LGBT person to serve as secretary of one of the military services. During the Armed Services Committee nomination hearing, no committee member asked Fanning about his sexual orientation or objected to having an openly gay army secretary.[57]

What is the policy on military service by openly trans people?

- A 2013 study from the Williams Institute using data from the National Transgender Discrimination Survey of 6,456 transgender and gender-nonconforming people in the United States found that:
  - 20 percent of trans people had served in the military, compared to 10 percent of the U.S. general population.
  - 29 percent of trans women had served.
  - 36 percent of the trans veterans reported losing a job and 53 percent reported not getting hired for a job because of anti-trans bias. This rate was significantly higher than among veterans in the general population.
  - 54 percent of trans veterans reported being harassed on the job; 9 percent reported physical abuse; 8 percent reported sexual abuse.
  - Trans veterans are three times more likely to experience homelessness than members of the general population.[58]
- On June 30, 2016, the Pentagon announced the repeal of its ban on transgender service members, a decision that came after nearly a year of internal wrangling among the services on how to allow these troops to serve openly.[59]
- An estimated 15,000 transgender troops are currently serving in the ranks of the military.[60]

> Imagine walking into school each day and not hearing any stories through books or curriculum that depict the life that you are living? . . . Imagine that you attend a public school, but the "public" discussion that is accepted hardly ever mentions things you can relate to? That's how many LGBT students feel.
>
> —*Peter DeWitt in* Education Week, *July 10, 2015*[1]

> A lot of kids at my school think it's sick and nasty and will give me looks when I hold hands with my friend, and call us fags and lesbos. I am proud of who I am and I don't intend on changing. I just wish I wasn't viewed differently.
>
> —*Student quoted in HRC's 2012 report "Growing Up LGBT in America"*[2]

In 1991, the average age of coming out was 25; twenty years later, it had dropped to 16.[3] Schools and organizations that serve youth have begun to respond to this shift: the Boy Scouts, for example, began allowing openly gay youth to participate in scouting programs in 2013, and a year later—with 79 percent of its leadership approving—the organization rescinded its ban on openly gay adult leaders.[4] In Evansville, Indiana, a record-breaking 1,100 people attended the 2015 LGBT Pride Prom, an annual event geared to LGBTQ high school students and their allies that culminates in the crowning of a "prom king, queen, and in-between."[5] Despite such developments, many LGBTQ youth face severe levels of bullying and harassment at school, at home, and in their communities, coupled with relative invisibility within school curricula. As of 2016, only one state, California, has mandated the inclusion of LGBTQ topics within its textbooks and curricula.[6]

"It is clear," write the authors of GLSEN's 2013 *National School Climate Survey*, "that there is an urgent need for action to create safe and affirming learning environments for LGBT students."[7]

LGBTQ YOUTH: A SNAPSHOT

What is life like for LGBTQ young people?

In the largest nationally representative survey of LGBTQ-identified youth ever conducted, the Human Rights Campaign (HRC) polled more than 10,000 teenagers between the ages of 13 and 17 in 2012 and found:

- 91 percent of respondents were out to their closest friends.
- 64 percent were out to their classmates.
- 56 percent were out to their immediate family.
- 38 percent were out to their teachers.
- 25 percent were out to their extended family.
- 16 percent were out to their doctors.
- 11 percent were out to their coaches.
- 5 percent were out to their religious leaders.[8]

When the youth surveyed by HRC were asked what their biggest concern was:

- 26 percent cited nonacceptance by their families.
- 21 percent pointed to problems at school, including bullying—defined by StopBullying.gov as unwanted, aggressive, repeated behavior that involves a real or perceived power imbalance and that can take the form of verbal, social, or physical harassment.[9]
- 18 percent said fear of being out.[10]

Nine in ten LGBTQ youths say they hear negative messages about being LGBTQ.[11]

Four in ten LGBTQ youths say the community in which they live is not supportive of LGBTQ people; 63 percent say they will need to move to another town or part of the country to feel accepted.[12] When asked about the likelihood of achieving various life goals if they stay in their hometown, LGBTQ youth and their non-LGBTQ peers responded as follows:

Figure 16.1: Decline in Optimism Among LGBTQ Youth

Percentage decline in likelihood of life achievements if youth stay in city/town where they grew up

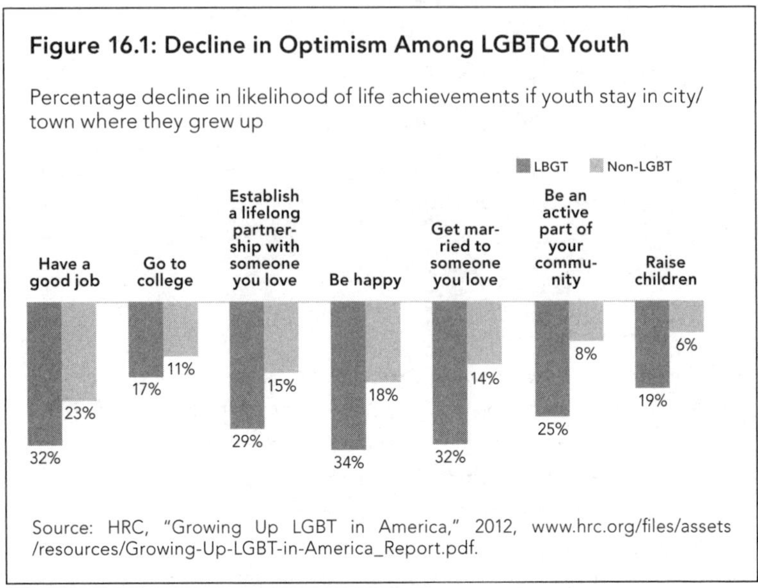

Source: HRC, "Growing Up LGBT in America," 2012, www.hrc.org/files/assets/resources/Growing-Up-LGBT-in-America_Report.pdf.

At the same time, 75 percent of LGBTQ youth say that most of their peers do not have a problem with their LGBTQ identity.[13]

SCHOOLS

What is the climate for LGBTQ students?

The Gay, Lesbian & Straight Education Network (GLSEN, whose website is glsen.org) is a national organization founded in 1990 that works "to assure that each member of every school community is valued and respected regardless of sexual orientation or gender identity/expression." In its 2013 National School Climate Survey, GLSEN found that:

- 85.4 percent of the 7,898 middle and high school students surveyed had been verbally harassed within the last year.
- 74.1 percent reported hearing "That's so gay" frequently or often at school.

- Most reported avoiding school functions and extracurricular activities (68.1 percent and 61.2 percent, respectively) because attending these events caused them to feel unsafe or uncomfortable.
- 55.5 percent of LGBTQ students experienced discriminatory school practices and policies.
- 35.4 percent avoided gender-segregated bathrooms and locker rooms in school because they felt unsafe or uncomfortable in these spaces.
- 33.1 percent reported hearing negative remarks about transgender people at school.
- 30.3 percent had missed at least one day of school in the past month because they felt unsafe or uncomfortable in their campus environment; 10.6 percent had missed four or more days for the same reasons.
- 28.2 percent had been disciplined at school for public displays of affection that were not similarly disciplined among non-LGBTQ students.
- 27.6 percent said their schools prevented students from attending a school dance with someone of the same gender.
- 18.5 percent reported taking classes that portrayed LGBTQ people, history, or events in a positive light.
- 17.8 percent had been hindered in establishing or promoting a GSA or school club supportive of LGBT issues.
- Among transgender students who took part in the survey, 31.6 percent were prevented from wearing clothing deemed "inappropriate" based on their legal gender.[14]

In a large U.S. study conducted from 2001 to 2009, between 12 percent and 28 percent of LGB youth reported being threatened or injured with a weapon on school property.[15]

How many students attend schools that have Gay-Straight Alliances (GSAs), and what is their impact?

- According to GLSEN's 2013 National School Climate Survey, 50.3 percent of students polled attend a school that has a GSA—a student-run club that provides a safe place for middle and high school students to meet, support each other, discuss issues related to sexual orientation and gender identity and expression, and work to end homophobia and transphobia.[16]

- The Gay-Straight Alliance Network lists more than 900 GSAs in California schools.[17]
- Students in schools with GSAs were less likely to hear homophobic slurs in school on a daily basis than students in schools without a GSA (57 percent versus 75 percent).[18]
- LGBTQ students at schools with GSAs were less likely to miss school because they felt unsafe.[19]

What is the FAIR Education Act, and when did California mandate inclusion of LGBTQ content in its public school curricula?

- In 2011, California became the first state to mandate inclusion of LGBTQ people in its social studies and history textbooks and curricula with passage of the Fair, Accurate, Inclusive, and Respectful (FAIR) Education Act.[20]
- The law's chief author, Senator Mark Leno, explained that the measure was intended to ensure that "the historical contributions of lesbian, gay, bisexual and transgender people are accurately and fairly portrayed in instructional materials by adding LGBT people to the existing list of under-represented cultural and ethnic groups already included in the state's inclusionary education requirements."[21]
- In addition to LGBTQ people, groups covered by the state's requirements now include African Americans, Asian Americans, European Americans, Mexican Americans, Native Americans, Pacific Islanders, and persons with disabilities.[22]
- As of 2016, California was the only state with a mandate to include LGBTQ people in its textbooks.[23]

How many states have laws stigmatizing LGBTQ people in the curricula?

- Laws stigmatizing LGBTQ people in the curricula, also known as "no promo homo" laws, are on the books in eight states: Alabama, Arizona, Louisiana, Mississippi, Oklahoma, South Carolina, Texas, and Utah. These local or state statutes expressly forbid teachers from discussing LGBTQ issues, including sexual health and HIV/AIDS awareness, in a positive light, if at all.[24]
- 12 states require discussion of sexual orientation in sex education. Of these, three require the teaching of inaccurate and negative information. In Alabama, for example, sex educators must teach that "homosexuality is not a lifestyle acceptable to the general public" and that "homosexual conduct is a criminal offense under the laws of the state"—despite the fact that the Supreme Court invalidated Alabama's sodomy law in its 2003 *Lawrence v. Texas* ruling.[25]

How many LGBTQ students participate in school sports?

According to a 2013 GLSEN study of 8,584 LGBTQ student athletes ages 13 to 20:

- LGBTQ students were about half as likely as their non-LGBTQ peers to play interscholastic sports (23.2 percent versus 47.8 percent).
- LGBTQ student athletes reported higher grade-point averages as sport-team members (3.2) and sport-team leaders (3.4) compared to nonathletes (3.0). LGBTQ student athletes were also more likely to report having higher self-esteem and feelings of belonging to their school.
- More than a quarter of LGBTQ student athletes reported that while playing on a school sports team, they were harassed or assaulted because of their sexual orientation (27.8 percent) or gender expression (29.4 percent).

- More than half of LGBTQ students who took a physical education class were bullied or harassed during P.E. because of their sexual orientation (52.8 percent) or gender expression (50.9 percent).
- 74.9 percent of LGBTQ students said they were uncomfortable talking to their P.E. teachers or coaches about LGBTQ issues.[26]

What are schools doing about bullying of LGBTQ youth?

- Nearly 6 in 10 LGBTQ students do not receive protections from bullying in school.[27]
- Of the 70.5 percent of school districts in the United States that have anti-bullying policies, only 42.6 percent include sexual orientation in the categories of students covered. 14.1 percent include gender and/or gender expression.[28]
- Having strict anti-bullying policies and Gay-Straight Alliances in place for three or more years significantly decreased suicidal thoughts and attempts among LGBTQ students, according to a 2014 Canadian study.[29]
- Only 10.1 percent of students polled for GLSEN's 2013 National School Climate Survey reported that their school has a comprehensive anti-bullying policy that includes both sexual orientation and gender identity/expression.[30]

What state and federal protections and support exist for transgender students?

Eighteen states and the District of Columbia have state laws that specifically protect trans students from bullying in public schools; 13 states and the District of Columbia protect trans students from discrimination in public schools.[31]

In May 2016, the Obama administration issued a guidance document confirming that transgender students are protected under Title IX, a federal law banning sex discrimination in education.

- These protections—which apply to students at public K–12 schools and at colleges and universities that receive federal funding—include respecting trans students' gender identity by using the students' preferred names and pronouns, and guaranteeing access to educational opportunities, sports teams, and sex-segregated bathrooms and other facilities that correspond with students' gender identity.
- In a statement accompanying the guidelines, Attorney General Loretta Lynch said, "This guidance gives administrators, teachers, and parents the tools they need to protect transgender students from peer harassment and to identify and address unjust school policies."
- In response, 11 states filed a federal lawsuit, charging that the guidelines could cause "seismic changes in the operations of the nation's school districts" and that the administration was seeking to "rewrite Title IX by executive fiat."[32]

What are some of the most pressing challenges that face LGBTQ students of color?

- In a 2009 study conducted by GLSEN, 80 percent of LGBTQ students of color reported hearing anti-gay slurs in U.S. schools. Only about 20 percent said that school personnel intervened when hearing the slurs.[33]
- In the same study, 80 percent of LGBTQ students of color reported being verbally harassed in the last year because of their sexual orientation.[34]
- 32 percent of LGBTQ Latino youth say they do not have an adult they can talk to about personal problems, while 13 percent of non-LGBTQ Latino youth say the same.[35]
- 86 percent of Latino youth surveyed cited the Internet as a source of positive messages on being LGBT. Additional sources of positive messages included peers (73 percent); movies, TV, and radio (59 percent); school

(50 percent); and family (26 percent). 3 percent of those surveyed cited religious leaders as a source of positive messages on being LGBT.[36]

The percentage of LGBTQ students of color who took part in GLSEN's 2009 study and who suffered physical violence in school because of their sexual orientation is:

- 54 percent of Native Americans.
- 45 percent of Latinos or Latinas.
- 45 percent of multiracial students.
- 41 percent of Asians or Pacific Islanders.
- 33 percent of African Americans.[37]

Less than half of LGBTQ students of color reported any harassment to school authorities; of students who did report harassment, less than half said that incidents were handled effectively.[38]

Only 18 percent of LGBTQ students of color reported attending a school with a policy that provides protections against harassment based on sexual orientation or gender identity or expression.[39]

How do LGBTQ educators respond to homophobic remarks in schools?

In a 2013 study of 350 American teachers and principals:

- Nearly 60 percent of LGBTQ teachers had heard homophobic slurs by other teachers.
- About half of LGBTQ teachers said they did not intervene or challenge homophobic language or bullying by students.
- LGBTQ teachers were less likely than straight teachers to say something in response to a homophobic remark in the classroom or staff room.
- 62 percent of LGBTQ teachers felt they would lose their job if they came out.[40]

Students report that when homophobic remarks are made, staff members "never intervene" 42.3 percent of the time:

Figure 16.2: LGBT Students' Reports of the Frequency of Intervention When Homophobic Remarks Are Made

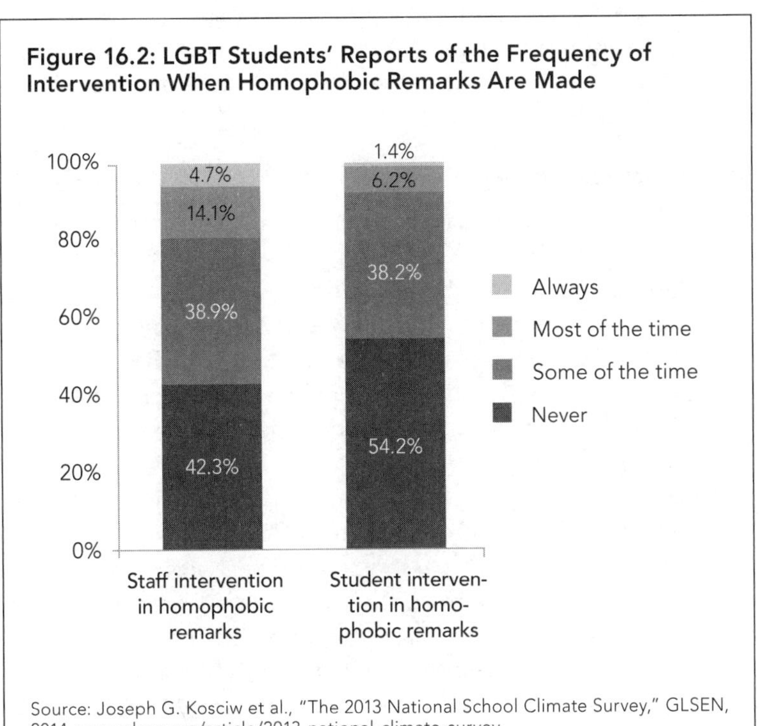

Source: Joseph G. Kosciw et al., "The 2013 National School Climate Survey," GLSEN, 2014, www.glsen.org/article/2013-national-climate-survey.

What is life like for LGBTQ students in rural areas?

- In a 2012 study, 97 percent of LGBTQ students in rural areas or small towns heard the word "gay" used in a negative way at school. Only 13 percent reported that school staff members intervened when biased comments were made.[41]
- 87 percent of rural students surveyed reported that within the past year, they had been verbally harassed

based on their sexual orientation. 22 percent reported that they had been physically assaulted.[42]

- Rural students were half as likely to have a Gay-Straight Alliance at their school as their suburban and urban counterparts: 27 percent of rural students versus 55 percent of suburban and 53 percent of urban students.[43]

How supportive are college environments for LGBTQ students?

- 148 colleges have LGBT centers, according to the College Equality Index (CEI), an organization focused on LGBTQ issues in higher education.
- The organization lists 14 colleges as trans-friendly.
- CEI lists four colleges that offer a major in LGBT studies: Evergreen State College, Hampshire College, Hobart and William Smith Colleges, and Sarah Lawrence College.[44]
- In 2016, the Tawani Foundation donated $1 million to the University of Victoria in British Columbia to create what is believed to be the first endowed professorship in trans studies at a major university. The Tawani Foundation was established by Jennifer N. Pritzker, an out trans, retired lieutenant colonel in the U.S. Army and billionaire heir to the Chicago Pritzker family fortune. The university's inaugural chair in transgender studies was Aaron Devor, a trans professor of sociology and the author of *Gender Blending*.[45]

Founded in 2001, the Point Foundation is the nation's largest scholarship-granting organization for LGBTQ undergraduate and graduate students; its website is pointfoundation.org.

- The foundation has invested $18 million in education and support of 300 LGBTQ scholars who have demonstrated academic excellence, leadership skills, community involvement, and financial need, including those who have lost financial and social support as a result of revealing their sexual orientation or gender identity or expression.[46]

How many religious colleges and universities have been granted waivers to bar LGBT students?

In 2014 and 2015, the U.S. Department of Education granted 27 colleges and universities in 17 states the legal right to bar students and staff who are transgender or in same-sex relationships by issuing waivers under Title IX, a 1972 law passed to combat sex discrimination.

- In 2014, the Obama administration issued guidance that the Title IX discrimination prohibition "extends to claims of discrimination based on gender identity or failure to conform to stereotypical notions of masculinity or femininity," meaning that entities receiving federal funding could not discriminate against transgender and gender-nonconforming people.
- The law permits waivers for educational institutions that are "controlled by a religious organization" so that these institutions do not have to comply with Title IX if doing so "would not be consistent with the religious tenets of such organization."[47]

For statistics on conversion therapy, see pages 77 to 78 of the Health and Aging chapter.

HOMELESSNESS

How many LGBTQ youth are homeless?

While LGBTQ youth are estimated to represent between 4 and 8 percent of the U.S. youth population, they represent between 20 and 40 percent of homeless youth.[48]

- 62 percent of homeless LGBTQ youth attempt suicide at least once, in contrast to 29 percent of their homeless non-LGBTQ peers, according to a 2009 report from the National Alliance to End Homelessness and other organizations.[49]
- 58 percent of homeless LGBTQ youth report being sexually assaulted, compared to 33 percent of non-LGBTQ homeless youth, according to a 2004 study.[50]

In a 2012 Web-based survey of homeless youth providers, which included 381 respondents at 354 agencies throughout the United States:

- LGBTQ youth represented 40 percent of young people served by these agencies.
- 68 percent of the LGBTQ youth clients had experienced rejection from their families.
- 54 percent of the youth had experienced family abuse.
- Fewer than 50 percent of respondents reported serving transgender clients 10 years ago, while more than 75 percent indicated doing so in 2012.
- The top three barriers to improving services for LGBTQ youth were the lack of state, local, and federal funding.[51]

The Thrive Youth Center in San Antonio, Texas, which opened in 2014, is one of the only homeless shelters in the United States exclusively for LGBTQ youth. Similar shelters exist in New York City and Los Angeles; plans for a new shelter to serve LGBTQ homeless youth in Omaha, Nebraska, were announced in early 2016.[52]

HEALTH RISKS

How do the health risks for LGB teens compare to those of their straight peers?

In August 2016, the CDC released the first nationally representative study on health risks that face lesbian, gay, and bisexual high school students. Approximately 15,600 students, ages 14 to 17, took the survey. The results showed that 8% of U.S. high school students identified as LGB—an estimated 1.3 million teenagers. Compared to their heterosexual peers, LGB students are significantly more likely to report:

- Being bullied at school or online (at school: 34 percent LGB vs. 19 percent heterosexual; online: 28 percent LGB vs. 14 percent heterosexual).
- Experiencing sexual dating violence (23 percent LGB vs. 9 percent heterosexual).

- Experiencing physical dating violence (18 percent LGB vs. 8 percent heterosexual)
- Being physically forced to have sex (18 percent LGB vs. 5 percent heterosexual).

The study also found that:

- More than 1 in 10 LGB students reported missing school during the past 30 days due to safety concerns.
- LGB students are up to five times more likely than other students to report using illegal drugs.
- 60 percent of LGB students reported having been so sad or hopeless that they stopped doing some of their usual activities.
- More than 40 percent of LGB students have seriously considered suicide, and 29 percent reported having attempted suicide during the past 12 months.[53]

How does family rejection affect LGB youth?

In a 2009 study by San Francisco State University, LGB youth who reported higher levels of family rejection during adolescence were:

- 8.4 times more likely to think about suicide than LGB peers who reported no or low levels of family rejection.
- 5.9 times more likely to suffer depression.
- 3.4 times more likely to use drugs.
- 3.4 times more likely to have unprotected sex.[54]

How many trans youth think about or attempt suicide?

Nearly half of young transgender people ages 15 to 21 who participated in a 2007 study reported that they seriously considered taking their lives, and 26 percent reported having attempted suicide.[55]

INTERNET USAGE

How do LGBTQ youth use the Internet?

- 62 percent of LGBTQ youth who took part in a 2013 GLSEN study searched online for information on sexuality, as opposed to 12 percent of their straight peers.

- 62 percent of LGBTQ youth have used the Internet to connect with other LGBTQ people in the past year.
- 29 percent of LGBTQ youth said they were more out online. Of those who were not out to peers, 52 percent used the Internet to connect with other LGBTQ people.
- On average, LGBTQ youth spent five hours per day online, approximately 45 minutes more than their straight peers.
- LGBTQ respondents reported being bullied while online 42 percent of the time as compared to 15 percent of the time for straight youth.
- 68 percent of LGBTQ youth in the 2013 study had engaged in volunteering as well as in Web- or text-based political activities during the past year.[56]
- 73 percent of LGBTQ youth who took part in a 2012 HRC survey said they are more honest about themselves online than they are in the real world.[57]

IT GETS BETTER

What is the It Gets Better Project, and what impact has it had?

- The It Gets Better Project, launched in 2010 by columnist Dan Savage with the goal of imparting hope to LGBTQ young people facing harassment, fear, and bullying, has become a worldwide movement, inspiring more than 50,000 user-created videos viewed more than 50 million times at www.itgetsbetter.org.
- As of 2016, at least 613,918 people had taken the It Gets Better Pledge, which states, in part: "I'll speak up against hate and intolerance whenever I see it, at school and at work. I'll provide hope for lesbian, gay, bisexual, transgender and other bullied teens by letting them know that it gets better."[58]
- Of LGBTQ youth surveyed in 2012, 77 percent said they believe things will get better.[59]

IMAGINING A WORLD FILLED WITH LOVE, NOT HATE

Jennifer Finney Boylan

When it comes to LGBT acceptance, things have gotten better in the aftermath of the *Obergefell* decision. But they haven't gotten better everywhere, and they haven't gotten better for everyone. If you're a person whose only issue is marriage equality, or someone living in a blue state, things are looking up. If you live somewhere else, or if you're a transgender person—especially a trans woman of color—things are as hard as they've ever been, and you stand a very good chance of being unemployed, or homeless, or being on the receiving end of violence. And this cannot stand. The right to live your life free of fear shouldn't be dependent on geography.

It would be nice if the movement for progress were a nonstop flight toward a better world. But things never work that way. For every advance, there is a new round of resistance. If you think about Prop 8 in California, that tremendous setback came in response to emerging freedoms. But that very defeat further inspired people to advocate for justice, and for love, and in time those forces carried the day. But it takes time, and it means enduring a tremendous amount of hatred in the meantime, and it just breaks people. Am I surprised? No. I'm never surprised by bigotry and prejudice. Those forces run pretty deep in human nature. Fortunately, so do the powers of love and forgiveness.

There still seems to be so much fear of trans people, including antipathy and hate. Our numbers are smaller, for one, so it's less likely that cis people will have a trans man or woman as a family member or friend, and it's that kind of connection to oppressed people that makes all the difference in terms of recognizing our humanity. But more importantly, trans people's struggle requires a kind of moral imagination that many people find a challenge. What I mean is that straight people know what it's like to be in love—so a movement based around the idea that "everyone deserves to love whom they love" is not a hard sell. But transness isn't about whom you love; it's about who you are. And many people just can't imagine what it must be like to find yourself in a body that doesn't feel like home. But they should try to imagine it. In the name of God they should try to imagine it. Because it's a very hard life, and this vulnerable, precious community deserves love and kindness and understanding—instead of being turned into whipping girls and boys for people whose stock in trade is hate. Everyone needs to open their hearts and treat their fellow man and woman with love.

I know that "open your heart and treat people with love" sounds like an easy thing to say, and I recognize that it's not. Treating other people with love is in fact the hardest thing in the world. But we can do it. One soul at a time.

This piece is adapted from a conversation that Jennifer Finney Boylan had with Washington Post *columnist Steven Petrow in June 2016, on the one-year anniversary of the Supreme Court's* Obergefell *decision. The authors extend their gratitude to Boylan and Petrow for granting permission to include these reflections in this book.*

ACLU
www.aclu.org

The Advocate
www.advocate.com

AIDS.gov
www.aids.gov

American Institute of Bisexuality
www.americaninstituteofbisexuality.org

American Military Partner Association
militarypartners.org

amfAR, The Foundation for AIDS Research
www.amfar.org

American Unity Fund
americanunityfund.com

Autostraddle
www.autostraddle.com

Bisexual Resource Center
www.biresource.net

Black Transmen
blacktransmen.org

The Center for HIV Law & Policy
hivlawandpolicy.org

CenterLink: The Community of LGBT Centers
www.lgbtcenters.org

Centers for Disease Control and Prevention
www.cdc.gov

Erasing 76 Crimes
76crimes.com

Freedom for All Americans
www.freedomforall americans.org

Funders for LGBTQ Issues
www.lgbtfunders.org

Gay & Lesbian Victory Fund
www.victoryfund.org

Gender Spectrum
www.genderspectrum.org

GLAAD
www.glaad.org

GLSEN (Gay, Lesbian & Straight Education Network)
www.glsen.org

GSA Network
gsanetwork.org

Human Dignity Trust
www.humandignitytrust .org

Human Rights Campaign
www.hrc.org

International Lesbian, Gay, Bisexual, Trans and Intersex Association
ilga.org

Intersex Society of North America
www.isna.org

It Gets Better Project
www.itgetsbetter.org

Kinsey Institute for Research in Sex, Gender, and Reproduction
www.kinseyinstitute.org

Lambda Legal
www.lambdalegal.org

Lambda Literary
www.lambdaliterary.org

LGBTQ Nation
www.lgbtqnation.com

LGBT Science
www.lgbtscience.org

Metropolitan Community Churches
mccchurch.org

Movement Advancement Project
www.lgbtmap.org

National Black Justice Coalition
nbjc.org

National Center for Lesbian Rights
www.nclrights.org

National Center for Transgender Equality
www.transequality.org

National Coalition of Anti-Violence Programs
www.avp.org

National LGBTQ Task Force
www.thetaskforce.org

Out & Equal Workplace Advocates
outandequal.org

Outsports: A Voice for LGBT Athletes
www.outsports.com

PFLAG
www.pflag.org

Point Foundation: The National LGBTQ Scholarship Foundation
www.pointfoundation.org

Pride@Work
www.prideatwork.org

Services and Advocacy for Gay, Lesbian, Bisexual & Transgender Elders
www.sageusa.org

TransWomen of Color Collective
www.twocc.us

Trans Youth Equality Foundation
www.transyouthequality.org

Transgender Law Center
transgenderlawcenter.org

Transgender Legal Defense & Education Fund
tldef.org

The Trevor Project
www.thetrevorproject.org

UNAIDS
www.unaids.org

U.S. Equal Employment Opportunity Commission
www.eeoc.gov

The Williams Institute
williamsinstitute.law.ucla.edu

WPATH, World Professional Association for Transgender Health
www.wpath.org

The majority of citations below include links to online versions of the documents we consulted; it is our hope that readers will use these links to delve more deeply into the issues addressed in the book. Wherever possible, we have included digital object identifiers; these provide a permanent link to the source and can be accessed by going to http://dx.doi.org and entering the identifier listed at the end of the citation. Please note that all information obtained via *Wikipedia* has been cross-referenced with at least one other source (and in many cases with multiple sources).

The Basics

1. Amin Ghaziani, *The Dividends of Dissent: How Conflict and Culture Work in Lesbian and Gay Marches on Washington* (Chicago: University of Chicago Press, 2008).
2. Camille Beredjick, "It Doesn't Matter What Percentage of Americans Are Gay," *Patheos*, August 8, 2014, www.patheos.com/blogs/friendlyatheist/2014/08/08/it-doesnt-matter-what-percentage-of-americans-are-gay.
3. Gallup, "Gay and Lesbian Rights," www.gallup.com/poll/1651/gay-lesbian-rights.aspx.
4. Gary J. Gates, "How Many People Are Lesbian, Gay, Bisexual, and Transgender?," Williams Institute, April 2011, williamsinstitute.law.ucla.edu/wp-content/uploads/Gates-How-Many-People-LGBT-Apr-2011.pdf.
5. Andrew R. Flores et al., "How Many Adults Identify as Transgender in the United States?," Williams Institute, June 2016, williamsinstitute.law.ucla.edu/wp-content/uploads/How-Many-Adults-Identify-as-Transgender-in-the-United-States.pdf.
6. Katherine B. Coffman, Lucas C. Coffman, and Ketih M. Marzilli Ericson, "The Size of the LGBT Population and the Magnitude of Anti-Gay Sentiment Are Substantially Underestimated," National Bureau of Economic Research, October 2013, practicingeconomist.files.wordpress.com/2013/10/w19508.pdf.
7. Emanuella Grinberg, "Census: More Same-Sex Couples in More Places," CNN, August 25, 2011, www.cnn.com/2011/US/08/25/same.sex.census.
8. U.S. Census Bureau, "Characteristics of Same-Sex Couple Households: 2014," www.census.gov/hhes/samesex.
9. Amira Hasenbush et al., "The LGBT Divide: A Data Portrait of LGBT People in the Midwestern, Mountain & Southern States," Williams Institute, December 2014, williamsinstitute.law.ucla.edu/wp-content/uploads/LGBT-divide-Dec-2014.pdf.

10. Ibid.

11. Gary J. Gates and Frank Newport, "LGBT Percentage Highest in D.C., Lowest in North Dakota," Gallup, February 15, 2013, www.gallup.com/poll/160517/lgbt-percentage-highest-lowest-north-dakota.aspx.

12. Ibid.

13. Frank Newport and Gary J. Gates, "San Francisco Metro Area Ranks Highest in LGBT Percentage," Gallup, March 20, 2015, www.gallup.com/poll/182051/san-francisco-metro-area-ranks-highest-lgbt-percentage.aspx.

14. Ibid.

15. Ibid.

16. Feargus O'Sullivan, "The 'Gaytrification' Effect: Why Gay Neighbourhoods Are Being Priced Out," *The Guardian*, January 13, 2016, www.theguardian.com/cities/2016/jan/13/end-of-gaytrification-cities-lgbt-communities-gentrification-gay-villages; Amelia Abraham, "The Future of Our Gay Neighborhoods," *Vice*, September 18, 2014, www.vice.com/read/the-future-of-the-gay-neighborhood-438.

17. Hasenbush et al., "The LGBT Divide."

Activism, Politics, and Law

1. Robert B. Marks Ridinger, ed., *Speaking for Our Lives: Historic Speeches and Rhetoric for Gay and Lesbian Rights (1892–2000)* (Binghamton, NY: Harrington Park Press, 2004).

2. "Out and About," *The Economist*, July 27, 1991, www.highbeam.com/doc/1G1-11056258.html.

3. Philip Elliott, "2015 Made History for LGBT Rights. Why Few Are Optimistic About 2016," *Time*, December 20, 2015, www.time.com/4143685/lgbt-rights-2016; Phil Reese, "2012 Proving Busy Year for Victory Fund," *Washington Blade*, April 26, 2012, www.washingtonblade.com/2012/04/26/2012-proving-busy-year-for-victory-fund.

4. Elliott, "2015 Made History for LGBT Rights. Why Few Are Optimistic About 2016."

5. Barry D. Adam, *The Rise of a Gay and Lesbian Movement* (Boston: Twayne, 1987).

6. Ibid.; Chuck Stewart, ed., *Proud Heritage: People, Issues, and Documents of the LGBT Experience* (Santa Barbara, CA: ABC-CLIO, 2014).

7. Adam, *The Rise of a Gay and Lesbian Movement.*

8. Nancy J. Knauer, *Gay and Lesbian Elders: History, Law, and Identity Politics in the United States* (New York: Routledge, 2016).

9. Ibid.

10. "Gay Liberation Front (GLF)," New York Public Library Online Exhibition Archive, web-static.nypl.org/exhibitions/1969/liberation.html.

11. "List of LGBT Rights Organizations in the United States," *Wikipedia*, en.wikipedia.org/wiki/List_of_LGBT_rights_organizations_in_the_United_States.

12. Ed O'Keefe, "Gay Rights Group Changing Its Name, Shifting Focus After Recent Victories," *Washington Post*, October 8, 2014, www.washingtonpost.com/news/post-politics/wp/2014/10/08/gay-rights-group

-changing-its-name-shifting-focus-after-recent-victories; National LGBTQ Task Force, "FY15 990," www.thetaskforce.org/static_html/downloads/devo/fy15_c3_public_990.pdf.

13. National LGBTQ Task Force, "Philadelphia to Host Nation's Largest LGBTQ Activist Conference in 2017," March 31, 2016, www.thetaskforce.org/philadelphia-to-host-nations-largest-lgbtq-activist-conference-in-2017.

14. Lambda Legal, "2015–2018 Strategic Plan," www.lambdalegal.org/about-us/strategic-plan.

15. "Lambda Legal," *Wikipedia*, en.wikipedia.org/wiki/Lambda_Legal; Lambda Legal, "History," www.lambdalegal.org/about-us/history.

16. National Center for Lesbian Rights, "Mission & History," www.nclrights.org/about-us/mission-history.

17. Log Cabin Republicans, "Our Mission," "Our History," and "Join a Chapter," 2016, www.logcabin.org.

18. Human Rights Campaign, Inc., "2014 HRC 990," hrc-assets.s3-website-us-east-1.amazonaws.com//files/images/campaign/HRC-990-2014.pdf; Human Rights Campaign, "2014 Anuual Report," hrc-assets.s3-website-us-east-1.amazonaws.com//files/assets/resources/HRC_2014_ANNUAL_FINAL.pdf.

19. ACT UP NY, "ACT UP Accomplishments—1987–2012," actupny.com/actions/index.php/the-community.

20. National Black Justice Coalition, "About Us" and "Issues," 2016, nbjc.org.

21. National Center for Transgender Equality, "History and 2013 Annual Report," www.transequality.org/sites/default/files/docs/resources/NCTE_Annual_Report_2013.pdf.

22. Freedom for All Americans, "About Freedom for All Americans," March 2016, www.freedomforallamericans.org/about; Kerry Eleveld, "The LGBT Movement Is in Chaos," *The Advocate*, March 4, 2016, www.advocate.com/current-issue/2016/3/04/lgbt-movement-chaos.

23. Mattachine Society of Washington, DC, "Our Mission," mattachinesocietywashingtondc.org/mission.

24. Lynne Yamaguchi Fletcher, *The First Gay Pope and Other Records* (Boston: Alyson, 1992).

25. Will Kohler, "46 Years Ago Today: First Lesbian & Gay Protest at the White House," Bilerico Project, April 17, 2011, bilerico.lgbtqnation.com/2011/04/46_years_ago_today_1st_lesbian_gay_protest_at_the.php.

26. Susan Stryker, *Transgender History* (Berkeley: Seal Press, 2008).

27. Adam, *The Rise of a Gay and Lesbian Movement.*

28. Associated Press, "Obama Names Stonewall National Monument; 1st for Gay Rights," *New York Times*, June 24, 2016, www.nytimes.com/aponline/2016/06/24/us/politics/ap-us-obama-gay-rights-monument.html.

29. "Lesbian and Gay Activists Meet in White House, First Time Ever," Today in Civil Liberties History, March 2016, todayinclh.com/?event=lesbian-and-gay-activists-meet-in-white-house.

30. "Anita Bryant and the Save Our Children Campaign," Gay History, August 13, 2009, gayhistory4u.blogspot.com/2009/08/religious-right-has-been-on-attack.html.

31. Amin Ghaziani, *The Dividends of Dissent: How Conflict and Culture*

Work in Lesbian and Gay Marches on Washington (Chicago: University of Chicago Press, 2008); John Cloud, "The Gay March: A New Generation of Protesters," *Time*, October 12, 2009, content.time.com/time/magazine/article/0,9171,1930526,00.html.

32. Megan Slack, "President Obama Honors Presidential Medal of Freedom Recipients," The White House, November 20, 2013, www.whitehouse.gov/blog/2013/11/20/president-obama-honors-presidential-medal-freedom-recipients.

33. Adam, *The Rise of a Gay and Lesbian Movement.*

34. DC Black Pride, "About Us: History," dcblackpride.org/2016/about.html.

35. "List of Largest LGBT Events," *Wikipedia*, en.wikipedia.org/wiki/List_of_largest_LGBT_events.

36. "2016 Gay Pride Calendar," www.gaypridecalendar.com.

37. HRC, "The History of Coming Out," www.hrc.org/resources/the-history-of-coming-out; "National Coming Out Day," *Wikipedia*, en.wikipedia.org/wiki/National_Coming_Out_Day.

38. "#TBT: They Died in the Closet," *The Advocate*, October 9, 2014, www.advocate.com/arts-entertainment/people/2014/10/09/tbt-they-died-closet; The White House, "Remarks by the President at Presidential Medal of Freedom Ceremony," November 20, 2013, www.whitehouse.gov/the-press-office/2013/11/20/remarks-president-presidential-medal-freedom-ceremony.

39. Gary J. Gates and Frank Newport, "LGBT Americans Skew Democratic, Largely Support Obama," Gallup, October 18, 2012, www.gallup.com/poll/158102/lgbt-americans-skew-democratic-largely-support-obama.aspx.

40. Eric Swank and Breanne Fahs, "Predicting Electoral Activism Among Gays and Lesbians in the United States," *Journal of Applied Social Psychology* 43, no. 7 (2013): 1382–93, doi: 10.1111/jasp.12095.

41. "List of the First LGBT Holders of Political Offices in the United States," *Wikipedia*, en.wikipedia.org/wiki/List_of_the_first_LGBT_holders_of_political_offices_in_the_United_States.

42. JJ Duncan, "Congressional Page Scandal Pt. 2: Gerry Studds," Zimbio, May 19, 2009, www.zimbio.com/America's+50+Most+Scandalous+Political+Scandals/articles/24/Congressional+Page+Scandal+Pt+2+Gerry+Studds.

43. "List of the First LGBT Holders of Political Offices in the United States," *Wikipedia*.

44. Ibid.

45. Ibid.

46. Ibid.

47. Ibid.

48. Scott Wong, "Gay Republicans Seek Breakthrough in 2016," *The Hill*, February 10, 2016, thehill.com/homenews/campaign/268861-gay-republicans-seek-breakthrough-in-2016.

49. Jane Laine, "LGBT Elected Officials and Their Roles in Changing America," in Wallace Swan, ed., *Gay, Lesbian, Bisexual, and Transgender Civil Rights: A Public Policy Agenda for a Divided America* (CRC Press: Boca Raton, 2015).

50. Elliott, "2015 Made History for LGBT Rights. Why Few Are Optimistic About 2016."

51. "List of the First LGBT Holders of Political Offices in the United States," *Wikipedia*.

52. Ibid.

53. Ibid.

54. Max Ehrenfreund, "The Number of White Dudes Becoming Federal Judges Has Plummeted Under Obama," *Washington Post*, February 18, 2016, www.washingtonpost.com/news/wonk/wp/2016/02/18/the-number-of-white-dudes-becoming-federal-judges-has-plummeted-under-obama.

55. "Victoria Kolakowski," *Huffington Post*, www.huffingtonpost.com/victoria-kolakowski.

56. "James Hormel," *Wikipedia*, en.wikipedia.org/wiki/James_Hormel.

57. U.S. Equal Employment Opportunity Commission, "Chai R. Feldblum, Commissioner," www.eeoc.gov/eeoc/feldblum.cfm.

58. Gay & Lesbian Victory Institute, "Presidential Appointments," March 2016, www.victoryinstitute.org/programs/presidential-appointments.

59. "List of the First LGBT Holders of Political Offices in the United States," *Wikipedia*.

60. Justin McCarthy, "In U.S., Socialist Presidential Candidates Least Appealing," Gallup, June 22, 2015, www.gallup.com/poll/183713/socialist-presidential-candidates-least-appealing.aspx.

61. Open Secrets, "Gay & Lesbian Rights & Issues: Lobbying, 2015," www.opensecrets.org/industries/lobbying.php?cycle=2016&ind=J7300.

62. Funders for LGBTQ Issues, "2014 Tracking Report," www.lgbtfunders.org/files/2014_Tracking_Report.pdf.

63. William B. Rubenstein, *Lesbians, Gay Men and the Law* (New York: The New Press, 1993).

64. John C. Gonsiorek and James D. Weinrich, *Homosexuality: Research Implications for Public Policy* (Newbury Park, CA: Sage Publications, 1991).

65. Gary David Comstock, *Violence Against Lesbians and Gay Men* (New York, Columbia University Press, 1991).

66. Fletcher, *The First Gay Pope and Other Records*.

67. Nico Lang, "Did Michigan Really Re-Criminalize Sodomy?" *The Advocate*, February 18, 2016, www.advocate.com/commentary/2016/2/18/did-michigan-really-re-criminalize-sodomy.

68. Ibid.

69. Ibid.

70. Shannon Minter, "Sodomy and Public Morality Offenses Under U.S. Immigration Law: Penalizing Gay and Lesbian Identity," *Cornell International Law Journal* 26, no. 3 (1993): 771–818, scholarship.law.cornell.edu/cgi/view content.cgi?article=1329&context=cilj.

71. Beth Rowen, "Important Supreme Court Decisions in Lesbian, Gay, Bisexual, and Transgender History," *Infoplease*, 2014, www.infoplease.com/gay-pride-month/supreme-court-decisions.html; "*Obergefell v. Hodges*," *Wikipedia*, en.wikipedia.org/wiki/Obergefell_v._Hodges; Leigh W. Rutledge, *The Gay Fireside Companion* (Boston: Alyson, 1989).

72. Fletcher, *The First Gay Pope and Other Records*.

73. Leigh W. Rutledge, *The Gay Decades: From Stonewall to the Present, the People and Events That Shaped Gay Lives* (New York: Plume, 1992).

74. Fletcher, *The First Gay Pope and Other Records*.

75. Ibid.
76. HRC, "Map of State Laws & Policies," www.hrc.org/state_maps.
77. Ibid.
78. HRC, "Map of State Laws & Policies."

AIDS

1. UNAIDS, "How AIDS Changed Everything," 2015, www.unaids.org/sites/default/files/media_asset/MDG6Report_en.pdf.

2. Edward Crocker Green and Allison Herling Ruark, *AIDS, Behavior and Culture: Understanding Evidence-Based Prevention* (Walnut Creek, CA: Left Coast Press, Inc., 2011); ACT UP NY, "ACT UP Accomplishments—1987–2012," actupny.com/actions/index.php/the-community.

3. Mark Joseph Stern, "Listen to Reagan's Press Secretary Laugh About Gay People Dying of AIDS," *Slate*, December 1, 2015, www.slate.com/blogs/outward/2015/12/01/reagan_press_secretary_laughs_about_gay_people_dying_of_aids.html.

4. AIDS.gov, "HIV in the United States: At a Glance," revised December 2, 2014, www.aids.gov/hiv-aids-basics/hiv-aids-101/statistics.

5. CDC, "HIV Among Gay and Bisexual Men," www.cdc.gov/hiv/group/msm.

6. Donald G. McNeil Jr., "U.S. Still in Danger of Losing War on AIDS, C.D.C. Director Says," *New York Times*, December 1, 2015, www.nytimes.com/2015/12/02/health/us-still-in-danger-of-losing-war-on-aids-cdc-director-says.html.

7. CDC, "HIV Surveillance Report: Diagnoses of HIV Infection in the United States and Dependent Areas, 2014," Volume 26, Table 1b, www.cdc.gov/hiv/pdf/library/reports/surveillance/cdc-hiv-surveillance-report-us.pdf.

8. CDC, "HIV Among African American Gay and Bisexual Men," 2016, www.cdc.gov/hiv/group/msm/bmsm.html.

9. Stern, "Listen to Reagan's Press Secretary Laugh About Gay People Dying of AIDS."

10. Ibid.

11. Ray Filar, "Silence = Death: Sarah Schulman on ACT UP, the Forgotten Resistance to the AIDS Crisis," *openDemocracy*, January 30, 2014, www.opendemocracy.net/transformation/ray-filar/silence-death-sarah-schulman-on-act-up-forgotten-resistance-to-aids-crisis; AP, "Poll Indicates Majority Favor Quarantine for AIDS Victims," *New York Times*, December 20, 1985, www.nytimes.com/1985/12/20/us/poll-indicates-majority-favor-quarantine-for-aids-victims.html.

12. Henry J. Kaiser Family Foundation, "HIV/AIDS at 30: A Public Opinion Perspective," June 1, 2011, kff.org/report-section/hivaids-at-30-section-1.

13. Ibid.

14. Ibid.

15. Ibid.

16. Ibid.

17. Ibid.

18. Liz Hamel et al., "HIV/AIDS in the Lives of Gay and Bisexual Men in

the United States," Kaiser Family Foundation, September 2014, kff.org/hivaids/report/hivaids-in-the-lives-of-gay-and-bisexual-men-in-the-united-states.

19. Ibid.

20. Ibid.

21. Stephanie Gallman, "FDA Lifts Lifetime Ban on Gay Men Donating Blood," CNN, December 21. 2015, www.cnn.com/2015/12/21/health/fda-gay-men-blood-donation-changes.

22. Julia Preston, "Obama Lifts a Ban on Entry into U.S. by H.I.V.-Positive People," *New York Times*, October 30, 2009, www.nytimes.com/2009/10/31/us/politics/31travel.html.

23. David Heitz, "HIV by the Numbers: Facts, Statistics, and You," *HealthLine*, 2014, www.healthline.com/health/hiv-aids/facts-statistics-infographic.

24. CDC, "HIV Surveillance Report: Diagnoses of HIV Infection in the United States and Dependent Areas, 2014," Volume 26, Table 22, www.cdc.gov/hiv/pdf/library/reports/surveillance/cdc-hiv-surveillance-report-us.pdf.

25. CDC, "HIV Surveillance Report: Diagnoses of HIV Infection in the United States and Dependent Areas, 2014," Volume 26, Table 26, www.cdc.gov/hiv/pdf/library/reports/surveillance/cdc-hiv-surveillance-report-us.pdf.

26. CDC, "HIV Among African American Gay and Bisexual Men."

27. Ibid.

28. Ibid.

29. Ibid.

30. Donald G. McNeil Jr., "San Francisco Is Changing Face of AIDS Treatment," *New York Times*, October 5, 2015, www.nytimes.com/2015/10/06/health/san-francisco-hiv-aids-treatment.html.

31. Katherine E. Baumann, Ashley Phillips, and Monisha Arya, "Overlap of HIV and Low Health Literacy in the Southern USA," *Lancet HIV* 2, no. 7 (2015): 269–70, doi: 10.1016/S2352-3018(15)00121-6.

32. Ibid.

33. CDC, "HIV Among Incarcerated Populations," www.cdc.gov/hiv/group/correctional.html.

34. National Institutes of Health, "HIV and Pregnancy," June 2016, aidsinfo.nih.gov/education-materials/fact-sheets/24/69/hiv-and-women.

35. Ibid.

36. CDC, "Likely Female-to-Female Sexual Transmission of HIV—Texas, 2012," *Morbidity and Mortality Weekly Report*, March 14, 2014, www.cdc.gov/mmwr/preview/mmwrhtml/mm6310a1.htm.

37. Sunnivie Brydum, "Why Transgender Women Have the Country's Highest HIV Rates," *HIV Plus*, April 2, 2015, www.hivplusmag.com/case-studies/2013/04/08/invisible-women-why-transgender-women-are-hit-so-hard-hiv.

38. CDC, "HIV Among Transgender People," 2016, www.cdc.gov/hiv/group/gender/transgender.

39. Ibid.

40. Andrew M. Seamen, "Few Gay, Bisexual Teen Males Being Tested for HIV," *Reuters*, August 26, 2015, uk.reuters.com/article/us-health-lgbt-teens-hiv-idUKKCN0QV2D520150826.

41. The Center for HIV Law & Policy, "When Sex Is a Crime and Spit Is a Dangerous Weapon," May 2016, www.hivlawandpolicy.org/resources/when

-sex-a-crime-and-spit-a-dangerous-weapon-a-teleconference-hiv-criminal-laws; Nicole Pasulka, "Should Not Disclosing Your HIV Status Be a Crime?" *Mother Jones*, June 21, 2012, www.motherjones.com/mojo/2012/06/criminal-transmission-hiv-law.

42. CDC, "HIV in the United States: At a Glance," 2015, www.cdc.gov/hiv/statistics/overview/ataglance.html.

43. Les Fabian Brathwaite, "And the Films Played On: 16 Essential Movies About AIDS," *Queerty*, December 1, 2013, www.queerty.com/and-the-films-played-on-16-essential-movies-about-aids-20131201.

44. "*The Normal Heart*," *Wikipedia*, en.wikipedia.org/wiki/The_Normal_Heart.

45. Susan Sontag, "The Way We Live Now," *New Yorker*, November 24, 1986, www.newyorker.com/magazine/1986/11/24/the-way-we-live-now.

46. "That's What Friends Are For," *Wikipedia*, en.wikipedia.org/wiki/That%27s_What_Friends_Are_For.

47. "*Angels in America: A Gay Fantasia on National Themes*," *Wikipedia*, en.wikipedia.org/wiki/Angels_in_America:_A_Gay_Fantasia_on_National_Themes.

48. Names Project Foundation, "The AIDS Memorial Quilt," www.aidsquilt.org/about/the-aids-memorial-quilt.

49. UNAIDS, "Global AIDS Update 2016," www.unaids.org/sites/default/files/media_asset/global-AIDS-update-2016_en.pdf.

50. UNAIDS, "Global Statistics 2016," www.unaids.org/en/resources/campaigns/HowAIDSchangedeverything/factsheet.

51. amfAR, "Statistics: Worldwide," updated June 2016, www.amfar.org/worldwide-aids-stats.

52. "How Achievable Is Immediate ART for All?" *Lancet HIV* 2, no. 9 (2015): e351, www.thelancet.com/pdfs/journals/lanhiv/PIIS2352-3018(15)00162-9.pdf.

53. UNAIDS, "How AIDS Changed Everything."

54. Ibid; UNAIDS, "The Gap Report 2014," www.unaids.org/sites/default/files/media_asset/UNAIDS_Gap_report_en.pdf.

55. Agence France-Presse, "Russian HIV-Aids Epidemic Worsening Under Kremlin Policies, Says Expert," *The Guardian*, May 14, 2015, www.theguardian.com/world/2015/may/15/russian-hiv-aids-epidemic-worsening-under-kremlin-policies-says-expert.

56. Kate Shannon et al., "Global Epidemiology of HIV Among Female Sex Workers: Influence of Structural Determinants," *The Lancet* 385, no. 9962 (2015): 55–71, doi: 10.1016/S0140-6736(14)60931-4.

57. UNAIDS, "The Gap Report 2014."

58. Ibid.

59. Ibid.

60. Ibid.

61. Ibid.

62. Ibid.

63. Catherine Yuk-ping Lo, *HIV/AIDS in China and India: Governing Health Security* (New York: Palgrave Macmillan, 2015).

64. World Health Organization, "Tuberculosis and HIV," www.who.int/hiv/topics/tb/en/index.html.

65. UNAIDS, "Fact Sheet 2016," www.unaids.org/en/resources/campaigns/HowAIDSchangedeverything/factsheet.

66. Nicoli Nattrass, *The AIDS Conspiracy: Science Fights Back* (New York: Columbia University Press, 2012).

67. UNAIDS, "UNAIDS Announces That the Goal of 15 Million People on Life-Saving HIV Treatment by 2015 Has Been Met Nine Months Ahead of Schedule," July 14, 2015, www.unaids.org/en/resources/presscentre/pressreleaseandstatementarchive/2015/july/20150714_PR_MDG6report; UNAIDS, "Global AIDS Update 2016."

68. World Health Organization, "HIV/AIDS: Data and Statistics," 2015, www.who.int/hiv/data/en.

69. UNAIDS, "Global AIDS Update 2016."

70. UNAIDS, "Fast-Track: Ending the AIDS Epidemic by 2030," November 18, 2014, www.unaids.org/sites/default/files/media_asset/JC2686_WAD2014report_en.pdf.

71. AIDSInfo.com, "FDA-Approved Medications," March 1, 2016, www.aidsinfo.nih.gov/education-materials/fact-sheets/21/58/fda-approved-hiv-medicines.

72. "An End to AIDS Is Possible, but Not Without an End to HIV," *Lancet HIV* 2, no. 8 (2015): e307, www.thelancet.com/pdfs/journals/lanhiv/PIIS2352-3018(15)00139-3.pdf.

73. McNeil, "San Francisco Is Changing Face of AIDS Treatment."

74. Anton Pozniak, "Making the Economic Case for Universal ART Access," *Lancet HIV* 2, no. 9 (2015): e358–59, doi: 10.1016/S2352-3018(15)00133-2.

75. INSIGHT START Study Group, "Initiation of Antiretroviral Therapy in Early Asymptomatic HIV Infection," *New England Journal of Medicine* 373, no. 9 (2015): 795–807, doi: 10.1056/NEJMoa1506816.

76. "Making the Most of a New HIV Self-Test," *Lancet HIV* 2, no. 6 (2015): e216, www.thelancet.com/pdfs/journals/lanhiv/PIIS2352-3018(15)00090-9.pdf.

77. CDC, "HIV Care Saves Lives Infographic," November 25, 2014, www.cdc.gov/vitalsigns/hiv-aids-medical-care/infographic.html.

78. Alice Park, "Truvada: 5 Things to Know About the First Drug to Prevent HIV," *Time*, July 17, 2012, healthland.time.com/2012/07/17/truvada-5-things-to-know-about-the-first-drug-to-prevent-hiv; Gilead Sciences, Inc., "About Truvada," www.truvada.com/treatment-for-hiv.

79. Ibid.

80. Josh Barro, "Is Truvada, the Pill to Prevent H.I.V., 99 Percent Effective? Don't Be So Sure," *New York Times*, July 16, 2014, www.nytimes.com/2014/07/17/upshot/is-truvada-the-pill-to-prevent-hiv-99-percent-effective-dont-be-so-sure.html.

81. Hamel et al., "HIV/AIDS in the Lives of Gay and Bisexual Men in the United States."

82. German Lopez, "The CDC Wants 1 in 4 Sexually Active Gay and Bisexual Men to Use an HIV Prevention Pill," *Vox*, December 1, 2015, www.vox.com/identities/2015/11/24/9793928/cdc-truvada-gay-bisexual-men.

83. Daniel Costa-Roberts, "8 Things You Didn't Know About Truvada,"

PBS NewsHour, April 12, 2015, www.pbs.org/newshour/rundown/8-things-didnt-know-truvadaprep.

84. Lopez, "The CDC Wants 1 in 4 Sexually Active Gay and Bisexual Men to Use an HIV Prevention Pill."

Bisexuality

1. Bisexual Resource Center, "What Is Bisexuality?," biresource.net/whatis.shtml.

2. "History of Bisexuality," *Wikipedia,* en.wikipedia.org/wiki/History_of_bisexuality#Timeline_of_bisexual_history; Steven Angelides, *A History of Bisexuality* (Chicago: The University of Chicago Press, 2001).

3. National Center for Injury Prevention and Control, Division of Violence Prevention, CDC, "The National Intimate Partner and Sexual Violence Survey: 2010 Findings on Victimization by Sexual Orientation," January 2013, www.cdc.gov/violenceprevention/pdf/nisvs_sofindings.pdf.

4. Eliel Cruz, "Report: High Rates of Violence, Discrimination Against Bisexual People," *The Advocate,* September 22, 2014, www.advocate.com/bisexuality/2014/09/22/report-high-rates-violence-discrimination-against-bisexual-people.

5. Carina Storrs, "Bisexuality on the Rise, Says New U.S. Survey," CNN, January 7, 2016, www.cnn.com/2016/01/07/health/bisexuality-on-the-rise.

6. Ibid.

7. Peter Moore, "A Third of Young Americans Say They Aren't 100% Heterosexual," YouGov US, August 20, 2015, today.yougov.com/news/2015/08/20/third-young-americans-exclusively-heterosexual.

8. Will Dahlgreen and Anna-Elizabeth Shakespeare, "1 in 2 Young People Say They Are Not 100% Heterosexual," YouGov UK, August 16, 2015, yougov.co.uk/news/2015/08/16/half-young-not-heterosexual.

9. Brian Dodge et al., "Beyond 'Risk': Exploring Sexuality Among Diverse Typologies of Bisexual Men in the United States," *Journal of Bisexuality* 12, no. 1 (2012): 13–34, doi: 10.1080/15299716.2012.645696.

10. HRC Foundation, "Supporting and Caring for Our Bisexual Youth," September 23, 2014, hrc-assets.s3-website-us-east-1.amazonaws.com//files/assets/resources/Supporting_and_Caring_for_Bisexual_Youth.pdf.

11. William E. Burleson, *Bi America: Myths, Truths and Struggles of an Invisible Community* (Binghamton, NY: Haworth Press, 2005).

12. Michael Schulman, "Bisexual: A Label with Layers; Tom Daley Comes Out as Bisexual, Igniting L.G.B.T. Debate," *New York Times,* January 3, 2014, www.nytimes.com/2014/01/05/fashion/Tom-Daley-Bisexual-LGBT.html.

13. Lena de Casparis, "Miley Cyrus on Sexuality, the New Frontier," *Elle UK,* October 2015, www.elleuk.com/now-trending/miley-cyrus-interview-october-2015; Social Blade, "Top 100 Instagram Users by Followers," June 2016, socialblade.com/instagram/top/100/followers.

14. Pew Research Center, "A Survey of LGBT Americans," June 13, 2013, www.pewsocialtrends.org/2013/06/13/a-survey-of-lgbt-americans.

15. HRC Foundation, "Bisexual Visibility in the Workplace," 2015, hrc-assets.s3-website-us-east-1.amazonaws.com//files/assets/resources

/Bisexuality_One_Page_Resource.pdf; HRC Foundation, "Degrees of Equality," hrc-assets.s3-website-us-east-1.amazonaws.com//files/assets/resources /DegreesOfEquality_2009.pdf.

16. Nicolette Severson et al., "Generational Changes in the Meanings of Sex, Sexual Identity and Stigma Among Latino Young and Adult Men," *Culture, Health & Sexuality* 15, no. 7 (2013): 804–18, doi: 10.1080/13691058.2013.783237.

17. Peter O'Dowd, "Sinema, First Openly Bisexual Member of Congress, Represents 'Changing Arizona,'" National Public Radio, January 1, 2013, www.npr.org/sections/itsallpolitics/2013/01/08/168362011/sinema-first -openly-bisexual-member-of-congress-represents-changing-arizona.

18. Aud Traher, "One Little Word Means the World," *The Advocate*, January 29, 2015, www.advocate.com/commentary/2015/01/29/op-ed-one-little -word-means-world.

19. Stephanie Fairyington, "How Oregon Changed Bisexual Visibility," *The Advocate*, May 19, 2015, www.advocate.com/politics/2015/05/19/how -oregon-suddenly-changed-bisexual-visibility.

20. Eliel Cruz, "CW Has First Bisexual Lead Character," *The Advocate*, February 26, 2015, www.advocate.com/bisexuality/2015/02/26/cw-has-first -bisexual-lead-character.

21. "Lena Kundera and Bianca Montgomery," *Wikipedia*, en.wikipedia .org/wiki/Lena_Kundera_and_Bianca_Montgomery.

22. "List of Media Portrayals of Bisexuality," *Wikipedia*, en.wikipedia .org/wiki/List_of_media_portrayals_of_bisexuality.

23. Wayne M. Bryant, *Bisexual Characters in Film: From Anaïs to Zee* (Binghamton, NY: Haworth Press, 1997).

24. "Fanny Hill," *Wikipedia*, en.wikipedia.org/wiki/Fanny_Hill.

25. Erich W. Steinman and Brett Genny Beemyn, eds., *Bisexual Men in Culture and Society* (Binghamton, NY: Haworth Press, 2002).

26. Burleson, *Bi America: Myths, Truths and Struggles of an Invisible Community.*

27. Ibid. and "Stephen Donaldson (activist)," *Wikipedia*, en.wikipedia .org/wiki/Stephen_Donaldson_(activist).

28. "History of Bisexuality," *Wikipedia*.

29. Bisexual Resource Center, "About Us," www.biresource.net/aboutus .shtml.

30. Clare Hemmings, *Bisexual Spaces: A Geography of Sexuality and Gender* (New York: Routledge, 2002).

31. Brett Genny Beemyn, "Marches on Washington," *glbtq Encyclopedia*, www.glbtqarchive.com/ssh/marches_washington_S.pdf.

32. Benoit Denizet-Lewis, "The Scientific Quest to Prove Bisexuality Exists," *New York Times*, March 20, 2014, www.nytimes.com/2014/03/23 /magazine/the-scientific-quest-to-prove-bisexuality-exists.html.

33. American Institute of Bisexuality, "Welcome to the American Institute of Bisexuality," www.americaninstituteofbisexuality.org.

34. "Celebrate Bisexuality Day," *Wikipedia*, en.wikipedia.org/wiki /Celebrate_Bisexuality_Day.

35. Ross Murray, "White House Holds Bisexual Leaders Roundtable,"

GLAAD, September 23, 2013, www.glaad.org/blog/white-house-holds-bisexual-leaders-roundtable.

36. Cassie Sheets, "10 Historical Bisexual Women Artists You Should Know," *SheWired*, February 1, 2016, www.shewired.com/identities/2016/2/01/10-historical-bisexual-women-artists-you-should-know.

37. Larry Rohter, "On Eve of Redefining Malcolm X, Biographer Dies," *New York Times*, April 1, 2011, www.nytimes.com/2011/04/02/books/malcolm-x-biographer-dies-on-eve-of-publication-of-redefining-work.html.

38. Judy Berman, "10 Famous Male Bisexuals Who Aren't David Bowie," *Flavorwire.com*, December 24, 2010, flavorwire.com/101310/10-famous-male-bisexuals-who-arent-david-bowie/view-all.

39. Christine Elizabeth Kaestle and Adrienne Holz Ivory, "A Forgotten Sexuality: Content Analysis of Bisexuality in the Medical Literature over Two Decades," *Journal of Bisexuality* 12, no. 1 (2012): 35–48, doi: 10.1080/15299716.2012.645701.

40. Alexandru Micu, "Study Finds Most Women Are Gay or Bisexual—A Personal Take," *ZME Science*, www.zmescience.com/research/studies/women-gay-or-bisexual-88234212.

41. Jordan E. Rullo, Donald S. Strassberg, and Michael H. Miner, "Gender-Specificity in Sexual Interest in Bisexual Men and Women," *Archives of Sexual Behavior* 44, no. 5 (2015): 1449–57, doi: 10.1007/s10508-014-0415-y.

42. A. M. Rosenthal et al., "The Male Bisexuality Debate Revisited: Some Bisexual Men Have Bisexual Arousal Patterns," *Archives of Sexual Behavior* 41, no. 1 (2012): 135–47, doi: 10.1007/s10508-011-9881-7.

43. Funders for LGBTQ Issues, "2014 Tracking Report: Lesbian, Gay, Bisexual, Transgender and Queer Grantmaking by U.S. Foundations," "2013 Tracking Report," "2012 Tracking Report," "LGBTQ Grantmaking by U.S. Foundations" (2011), "LGBTQ Grantmaking by U.S. Foundations" (2010), "LGBTQ Grantmaking by U.S. Foundations" (2009), www.lgbtfunders.org/resources/publications.cfm.

44. K. Bryant Smalley, Jacob C. Warren, and K. Nikki Barefoot, "Barriers to Care and Psychological Distress Differences Between Bisexual and Gay Men and Women," *Journal of Bisexuality* 15, no. 2 (2015): 230–47, doi: 10.1080/15299716.2015.1025176.

45. Maurizio Pompili et al., "Bisexuality and Suicide: A Systematic Review of the Current Literature," *Journal of Sexual Medicine* 11, no. 8 (2014): 1903–13, doi: 10.1111/jsm.12581.

46. CDC, "The National Intimate Partner and Sexual Violence Survey: 2010 Findings on Victimization by Sexual Orientation," January 2013, www.cdc.gov/violenceprevention/pdf/nisvs_sofindings.pdf.

47. Ron Suresha, "Where's the 'B' in National LGBTQ Organizations? The Bisexual Representation Report Card," *Huffington Post*, February 28, 2013 (updated February 2, 2016), www.huffingtonpost.com/ron-suresha/bisexual-representation-report-card_b_2748342.html.

Health and Aging

1. Kevin L. Ard and Harvey J. Makadon, *Improving the Health Care of Lesbian, Gay, Bisexual and Transgender People: Understanding and Eliminating Health Disparities,* National LGBT Health Education Center, 2012, www.lgbthealtheducation.org/wp-content/uploads/12-054_LGBTHealtharticle_v3_07-09-12.pdf.

2. John C. Gonsiorek and James D. Weinrich, eds., *Homosexuality: Research Implications for Public Policy* (Newbury Park, CA: Sage, 1991).

3. Ronald Bayer, *Homosexuality and American Psychiatry* (Princeton: Princeton University Press, 1987).

4. For an in-depth scientific discussion of the origins of sexual orientation and gender identity, see the website LGBT Science at www.lgbtscience.org.

5. Karen I. Fredriksen-Goldsen and Anna Muraco, "Aging and Sexual Orientation: A 25-Year Review of the Literature," *Research on Aging* 32, no. 3 (2010): 372–413, doi: 10.1177/0164027509360355.

6. SAGE, "Welcome Home: Improving Housing Security for LGBT Older Adults," February 2015, www.sageusa.org/files/SAGEHousingStrtgy_Brief_web.pdf.

7. Ibid.

8. Jason S. Schneider and Saul Levin, MD, "Uneasy Partners: The Lesbian and Gay Health Care Community and the AMA," *Journal of the American Medical Association* 282, no. 13 (1999): 1287–88, jama.jamanetwork.com/article.aspx?articleid=1842503.

9. Ibid.

10. Howard Wolinsky, "Paging Dr. Jekyll," *The Advocate*, June 28, 1994; David Dunlap, "A.M.A. States New Policy on Sexuality," *New York Times*, December 25, 1994, www.nytimes.com/1994/12/25/us/ama-states-new-policy-on-sexuality.html.

11. Trudy Ring, "Psychiatrists' Group Names First Out Gay Leader," *The Advocate*, May 21, 2013, www.advocate.com/health/mental-wellness/2013/05/21/psychiatrists-group-names-first-out-gay-leader.

12. World Medical Association, "WMA Statement on Natural Variations of Human Sexuality," October 2013, www.wma.net/en/30publications/10policies/s13.

13. Alison Gill, "Without Anyone Noticing, D.C. Passed a Remarkable LGBT Bill," *The Advocate*, February 8, 2016, www.advocate.com/commentary/2016/2/08/without-anyone-noticing-dc-passed-remarkable-lgbt-bill.

14. Lou Chibbaro Jr., "D.C. 'Cultural Competency' Bill Passes Committee," *Washington Blade*, December 11, 2015, www.washingtonblade.com/2015/12/11/d-c-cultural-competency-bill-passes-committee.

15. Gwendolyn P. Quinn, et al., "Lesbian, Gay, Bisexual, Transgender, Queer/Questioning (LGBTQ) Perceptions and Health Care Experiences," *Journal of Gay & Lesbian Social Services* 27, no. 2 (2015): 246–61, doi: 10.1080/10538720.2015.1022273.

16. Laura E. Durso and Ilan H. Meyer, "Patterns and Predictors of Disclosure of Sexual Orientation to Healthcare Providers Among Lesbians, Gay Men, and Bisexuals," *Sexual Research and Social Policy* 10, no. 1 (2013): 35–42, www.ncbi.nlm.nih.gov/pmc/articles/PMC3582401.

17. Lambda Legal, "When Health Care Isn't Caring: Lambda Legal's Survey on Discrimination Against LGBT People and People Living with HIV," 2010, www.lambdalegal.org/sites/default/files/publications/downloads/whcic-report_when-health-care-isnt-caring.pdf.

18. Jaime M. Grant, Ph.D. et al., "Injustice at Every Turn: A Report of the National Transgender Discrimination Survey," The National Center for Transgender Equality and The National Gay and Lesbian Task Force, 2011, www.transequality.org/sites/default/files/docs/resources/NTDS_Report.pdf.

19. HRC Foundation, "Healthcare Equality Index 2016," hrc-assets.s3-website-us-east-1.amazonaws.com//files/assets/resources/HEI_2016_FINAL.pdf.

20. Lila Shapiro, "Conversion Therapy Survey Reveals Real Harm in Gay 'Cure,'" *Huffington Post*, May 30, 2013, www.huffingtonpost.com/2013/05/30/conversion-therapy-survey_n_3354253.html.

21. American Psychological Association, "Just the Facts About Sexual Orientation and Youth," 2016, www.apa.org/pi/lgbt/resources/just-the-facts.aspx.

22. Jonathan Merritt, "How Christians Turned Against Gay Conversion Therapy," *The Atlantic*, April 15, 2015, www.theatlantic.com/politics/archive/2015/04/how-christians-turned-against-gay-conversion-therapy/390570.

23. Maya Rhodan, "9 Ex-Leaders of the Gay Conversion Therapy Movement Apologize," *Time*, July 31, 2014, time.com/3065495/9-ex-leaders-of-the-gay-conversion-therapy-movement-apologize.

24. Katie Rose Quandtaug, "'Ex-Gay' Conversion Therapy Group Rebrands, Stresses 'Rights of Clients,'" *Mother Jones*, August 8, 2014, www.motherjones.com/mojo/2014/08/ex-gay-group-attempts-rebranding-narth-conversion-therapy.

25. Movement Advancement Project, "Conversion Therapy Laws," May 2016, www.lgbtmap.org/equality-maps/conversion_therapy#sthash.Zdi9gVR1.dpuf.

26. Human Rights Campaign, "The Lies and Dangers of Efforts to Change Sexual Orientation or Gender Identity," 2016, www.hrc.org/resources/the-lies-and-dangers-of-reparative-therapy.

27. Kenneth Lovett and Denis Slattery, "EXCLUSIVE: Gov. Cuomo to Ban Use of Conversion Therapy on LGBT Youth by Public and Private Health Insurers," *New York Daily News*, February 7, 2016, www.nydailynews.com/news/politics/cuomo-announce-ban-conversion-therapy-lgbt-youths-article-1.2522458.

28. Neal Broverman, "Conversion Therapy Ban Introduced in Senate," *The Advocate*, April 28, 2016, www.advocate.com/politics/2016/4/28/conversion-therapy-ban-introduced-senate.

29. Bill M. Jesdale and Jason W. Mitchell, "Reported Excellent Health Among Men in Same-Sex and Mixed-Sex Couples: Behavioral Risk Factor Surveillance System, 1993–2010," *Journal of Homosexuality* 59, no. 6 (2012): 788–807, doi: 10.1080/00918369.2012.694755.

30. Community Marketing, Inc., "2012 LGBT Community Survey," www.equalitymi.org/files/uploads/cmi_6th_lgbt_community_survey_usv1.pdf.

31. Christopher Blackwell, "Reducing Alcohol Abuse in Gay Men: Clini-

cal Recommendations from Conflicting Research," *Journal of Social Service Research* 38, no. 1 (2012): 29–36, doi: 10.1080/01488376.2011.583836.

32. National LGBT Tobacco Control Network, "Cold Hard Truth," March 2016, www.lgbttobacco.org/truth.php.

33. Olivia Foster-Gimbel and Renee Engeln, "Fat Chance! Experiences and Expectations of Antifat Bias in the Gay Male Community," *Psychology of Sexual Orientation and Gender Diversity* 3, no. 1 (2016): 63–70, doi: 10.1037/sgd0000159.

34. Madina Agénor et al., "Sexual Orientation Identity Disparities in Awareness and Initiation of the Human Papillomavirus Vaccine Among U.S. Women and Girls: A National Survey," *Annals of Internal Medicine* 163, no. 2 (2015): 99–106, doi: 10.7326/M14-2108.

35. Christopher M. Fisher, Jay A. Irwin, and Jason D. Coleman, "LGBT Health in the Midlands: A Rural/Urban Comparison of Basic Health Indicators," *Journal of Homosexuality* 61, no. 8 (2014): 1062–90, doi: 10.1080/00918369.2014.872487.

36. Keith J. Horvath et al., "A Comparison of Mental Health, Substance Use, and Sexual Risk Behaviors Between Rural and Non-Rural Transgender Persons," *Journal of Homosexuality* 61, no. 8 (2014): 1117–30, doi: 10.1080/00918369.2014.872502.

37. Free & Equal: UN Human Rights Office, "Fact Sheet: Intersex," unfe.org/system/unfe-65-Intersex_Factsheet_ENGLISH.pdf.

38. Intersex Society of North America, "Frequently Asked Questions," 2016, www.isna.org/faq/healthy#fn1.

39. United Nations Human Rights Council, "Report of the Special Rapporteur on Torture and Other Cruel, Inhuman or Degrading Treatment or Punishment," February 1, 2013, www.ohchr.org/Documents/HRBodies/HRCouncil/RegularSession/Session22/A.HRC.22.53_English.pdf.

40. "Intersex," *Wikipedia*, en.wikipedia.org/wiki/Intersex.

41. Free & Equal: UN Human Rights Office, "Fact Sheet: Intersex."

42. Alessia Valenza, "Historic Moment for Trans and Intersex People as Malta Passes the Gender Identity, Gender Expression and Sex Characteristics Bill Act," International Lesbian, Gay, Bisexual, Trans and Intersex Association (ILGA), April 22, 2015, ilga.org/malta-gigesc.

43. Michael K. Lavers, "Chilean Officials Oppose Intersex Children 'Normalization' Surgery," *Washington Blade*, January 11, 2016, www.washingtonblade.com/2016/01/11/chilean-officials-oppose-normalization-surgery-for-intersex-children.

44. John E. Snyder, "Trend Analysis of Medical Publications About LGBT Persons: 1950–2007," *Journal of Homosexuality* 58, no. 2 (2011): 164–88, doi: 10.1080/00918369.2011.540171.

45. Robert W.S. Coulter et al., "Research Funded by the National Institutes of Health on the Health of Lesbian, Gay, Bisexual, and Transgender Populations," *American Journal of Public Health* 104, no. 2 (2014): e105–e112, doi: 10.2105/AJPH.2013.301501.

46. Jeffrey Neal et al., "Lesbian, Gay, Bisexual, and Transgender (LGBT) Content Representation on the Psychiatry Resident In-Training Examination, 2009–2013," *Journal of Gay & Lesbian Mental Health* 19, no. 3 (2015): 320–27, doi: 10.1080/19359705.2015.1039427.

47. Zack Ford, "Obamacare Drastically Increased the Number of LGBT Americans with Health Insurance," *ThinkProgress*, November 18, 2014, think progress.org/lgbt/2014/11/18/3593479/lgbt-obamacare-report.

48. Gary J. Gates, "In U.S., LGBT More Likely Than Non-LGBT to Be Uninsured," Gallup, August 26, 2014, www.gallup.com/poll/175445/lgbt-likely-non-lgbt-uninsured.aspx.

49. Ibid.

50. Ibid.

51. Ibid.

52. Department of Health and Human Services, "Healthy People 2020: Lesbian, Gay, Bisexual, and Transgender Health," 2010, www.healthypeople.gov/2020/topics-objectives/topic/lesbian-gay-bisexual-and-transgender-health/objectives.

53. SAGE, "Out & Visible: The Experiences and Attitudes of LGBT Older Adults, Ages 45–75," October 6, 2014, www.sageusa.org/files/LGBT_OAMarketResearch_Rpt.pdf.

54. Movement Advancement Project and SAGE, "Improving the Lives of LGBT Older Adults," March 2010, www.lgbtmap.org/file/improving-the-lives-of-lgbt-older-adults.pdf.

55. Fredriksen-Goldsen and Muraco, "Aging and Sexual Orientation."

56. Steven David and Bob G. Knight, "Stress and Coping Among Gay Men: Age and Ethnic Differences," *Psychology and Aging* 23, no. 1 (2008): 62–9, doi: 10.1037/0882-7974.23.1.62.

57. Richard G. Wight et al., "Internalized Gay Ageism, Mattering, and Depressive Symptoms Among Midlife and Older Gay-Identified Men," *Social Science & Medicine* 147 (2015): 200–8, doi: 10.1016/j.socscimed.2015.10.066.

58. Fredriksen-Goldsen and Muraco, "Aging and Sexual Orientation."

59. Arnold Grossman et al., "Domestic Harm and Neglect Among Lesbian, Gay, and Bisexual Older Adults," *Journal of Homosexuality* 61, no. 12 (2014): 1649–66, doi: 10.1080/00918369.2014.951216.

60. Ibid.

61. Fredriksen-Goldsen and Muraco, "Aging and Sexual Orientation."

62. Ibid.

63. Grossman et al., "Domestic Harm and Neglect Among Lesbian, Gay, and Bisexual Older Adults."

64. Ibid.

65. Fredriksen-Goldsen and Muraco, "Aging and Sexual Orientation."

66. Ibid.

International

1. Ban Ki-moon, "Secretary-General's Video Message to the Oslo Conference on Human Rights, Sexual Orientation and Gender Identity," United Nations, April 15, 2013, www.un.org/sg/STATEMENTS/index.asp?nid=6736.

2. James Ball, "More Than 2.7 Billion People Live in Countries Where Being Gay Is a Crime," *The Guardian*, May 16, 2014, www.theguardian.com/world/2014/may/16/countries-where-being-gay-is-a-crime.

3. Frank Bruni, "Gay and Marked for Death," *New York Times*, August 21,

2015, www.nytimes.com/2015/08/23/opinion/sunday/frank-bruni-gay-and-marked-for-death.html.

4. "ISIL Persecutes Gay, Lesbian, Trans People, Experts Tell UN," Al Jazeera America, August 24, 2015, america.aljazeera.com/articles/2015/8/24/isil-executed-30-people-for-sodomy-un-meeting-told.html.

5. "UN Security Council Holds First Meeting on LGBT Rights," Al Jazeera, August 24, 2015, www.aljazeera.com/news/2015/08/security-council-holds-meeting-lgbt-rights-150824201712751.html.

6. Aengus Carrol and Lucas Paoli Itaborahy, "State-Sponsored Homophobia: A World Survey of Laws," ILGA, May 2015, old.ilga.org/Statehomophobia/ILGA_State_Sponsored_Homophobia_2015.pdf.

7. M.V. Lee Badgett et al., "The Relationship Between LGBT Inclusion and Economic Development: An Analysis of Emerging Economies," Williams Institute and USAID, November 2014, williamsinstitute.law.ucla.edu/wp-content/uploads/lgbt-inclusion-and-development-november-2014.pdf.

8. Aengus Carroll, "State-Sponsored Homophobia," ILGA, 2016, ilga.org/downloads/02_ILGA_State_Sponsored_Homophobia_2016_ENG_WEB_150516.pdf.

9. "Iran: UK Grants Asylum to Victim of Tehran Persecution of Gays, Citing Publicity," *The Telegraph*, February 4, 2011, www.telegraph.co.uk/news/wikileaks-files/london-wikileaks/8305064/IRAN-UK-GRANTS-ASYLUM-TO-VICTIM-OF-TEHRAN-PERSECUTION-OF-GAYS-CITING-PUBLICITY.html.

10. Carroll, "State-Sponsored Homophobia."

11. Ibid.

12. Bible Hub, "Ezekiel 16:49: New Living Translation," biblehub.com/ezekiel/16-49.htm.

13. Louis Crompton, *Homosexuality & Civilization* (Cambridge, MA: Harvard University Press, 2003).

14. Crompton, *Homosexuality & Civilization*; Byrne Fone, *Homophobia: A History* (New York, Metropolitan Books, 2000); "Sodomy Law," *Wikipedia*, en.wikipedia.org/wiki/Sodomy_law.

15. Crompton, *Homosexuality & Civilization.*

16. Ibid.

17. "Sodomy Law," *Wikipedia.*

18. Crompton, *Homosexuality & Civilization.*

19. Vanessa Baird, *The No-Nonsense Guide to Sexual Diversity* (Oxford, England: New Internationalist Publications, 2007).

20. Ibid.

21. Joshua Hepple, "Will Sexual Minorities Ever Be Equal? The Repercussions of British Colonial 'Sodomy' Laws," *Equal Rights Review* (2012), www.equalrightstrust.org/ertdocumentbank/ERR8_Joshua_Hepple.pdf; Baird, *The No-Nonsense Guide to Sexual Diversity.*

22. Jeffrey Merrick and Bryant T. Ragan Jr., eds., *Homosexuality in Modern France* (New York: Oxford University Press, 1996).

23. Leigh W. Rutledge, *The Gay Book of Lists* (Boston: Alyson, 1987); "Sodomy Law," *Wikipedia.*

24. Sebastian Buckle, *The Way Out: A History of Homosexuality in Modern Britain* (London: I.B. Taurus, 2015).

25. Ibid.

26. "*Dudgeon v United Kingdom*," *Wikipedia*, en.wikipedia.org/wiki/Dudgeon_v_United_Kingdom.

27. Jethro Mullen, "Alan Turing, Code-Breaker Castrated for Homosexuality, Receives Royal Pardon," CNN, August 19, 2014, www.cnn.com/2013/12/24/world/europe/alan-turing-royal-pardon.

28. "Benedict Cumberbatch in Call to Pardon Convicted Gay Men," BBC News, January 31, 2015, www.bbc.com/news/uk-31070115.

29. Elizabeth Daley, "WATCH: 40 Nations Where Being Gay Is Still a Crime," *The Advocate*, November 30, 2015, www.advocate.com/world/2015/11/30/watch-40-nations-where-being-gay-still-crime.

30. Toby Johnson, "Karl-Heinrich Ulrichs: An Important Historical Figure in Gay Consciousness," www.tobyjohnson.com/KarlHeinrichUlrichs.html; Merrick and Ragan, *Homosexuality in Modern France*.

31. Merrick and Ragan, *Homosexuality in Modern France*.

32. "Timeline of LGBT History," *Wikipedia*, en.wikipedia.org/wiki/Timeline_of_LGBT_history#19th_century.

33. Richard Plant, *The Pink Triangle* (New York: Holt, 1986).

34. Frank Rector, *The Nazi Extermination of Homosexuals* (New York: Stein & Day, 1981).

35. Plant, *The Pink Triangle*; "Pink Triangle," *Wikipedia*, en.wikipedia.org/wiki/Pink_triangle.

36. Plant, *The Pink Triangle*; "Persecution of Homosexuals in Nazi Germany and the Holocaust," *Wikipedia*, en.wikipedia.org/wiki/Persecution_of_homosexuals_in_Nazi_Germany_and_the_Holocaust.

37. "LGBT Rights in Germany," *Wikipedia*, en.wikipedia.org/wiki/LGBT_rights_in_Germany; "Memorial to Homosexuals Persecuted Under Nazism," *Wikipedia*, en.wikipedia.org/wiki/Memorial_to_Homosexuals_Persecuted_Under_Nazism.

38. "Sodomy Law," *Wikipedia*, en.wikipedia.org/wiki/Sodomy_law.

39. Joseph R. Hawkins, "Japan's Journey into Homophobia," *Gay and Lesbian Review Worldwide* 7, no. 1 (2000): 36–38, www.thefreelibrary.com/Japan's+Journey+into+Homophobia.-a077712305.

40. J. Weston Phippen, "Another Loss for India's LGBT Activists," *The Atlantic*, June 29, 2016, www.theatlantic.com/news/archive/2016/06/india-section-377/489293; Denis LeBlanc, "At Least 587 LGBTI Arrested in India in 2014," Erasing 76 Crimes, January 6, 2015, 76crimes.com/2015/01/06/at-least-587-lgbti-arrested-in-india-in-2014.

41. Meredith L. Weiss and Michael J. Bosia, eds., *Global Homophobia: States, Movements and the Politics of Oppression* (University of Illinois Press: Urbana, 2013); "South African Court Ends Sodomy Laws," *New York Times*, May 9, 1998, www.nytimes.com/1998/05/09/world/south-african-court-ends-sodomy-laws.html.

42. Miriam Elder, "Russia Passes Law Banning Gay 'Propaganda,'" *The Guardian*, June 11, 2013, www.theguardian.com/world/2013/jun/11/russia-law-banning-gay-propaganda.

43. Alec Luhn, "LGBT Website Founder Fined Under Russia's Gay Propaganda Laws in Moscow," *The Guardian*, July 29, 2015, www.theguardian.com/world/2015/jul/29/lgbt-yelena-klimova-fined-russia-gay-propaganda-laws.

44. ILGA, "State-Sponsored Homophobia."

45. The European Union Agency for Fundamental Rights, "EU LGBT Survey: European Union Lesbian, Gay, Bisexual and Transgender Survey," 2013, fra.europa.eu/sites/default/files/eu-lgbt-survey-results-at-a-glance_en.pdf.

46. "Sexual Orientation and Military Service," *Wikipedia*, en.wikipedia.org/wiki/Sexual_orientation_and_military_service#Countries_that_allow_openly_gay.2C_lesbian_and_bisexual_people_to_serve.

47. Ibid.

48. Michael K. Lavers, "Randy Berry Marks First Year as LGBT Envoy," *Washington Blade*, April 25, 2016, www.washingtonblade.com/2016/04/25/randy-berry-marks-first-year-as-lgbt-envoy/#sthash.wUmwPlhc.dpuf.

49. Manon Tremblay, ed., *Queer Mobilizations: Social Movement Activism and Canadian Policy* (Vancouver: UBC Press, 2015), www.ubcpress.ca/books/pdf/chapters/2015/QueerMobilizations.pdf.

50. Logan S. Casey and Andrew Reynolds, "This Map Shows the 31 Countries Where Transgender and Gender-Variant Candidates Have Run for Office Since 1977," *Washington Post*, December 16, 2015, www.washingtonpost.com/news/monkey-cage/wp/2015/12/16/this-map-shows-the-31-countries-where-transgender-and-gender-variant-candidates-have-run-for-office-since-1977.

51. ILGA, "1978–2007: A Chronology," ilga.org/about-us/1978-2007-a-chronology.

52. Dan Littauer, "Brazil, Where 44 Percent of World's Anti-LGBT Violence Occurs, Kills Discrimination Bill," *LGBTQ Nation*, December 18, 2013, www.lgbtqnation.com/2013/12/brazil-where-44-of-worlds-anti-lgbt-violence-occurs-kills-discrimination-bill.

53. Norimitsu Onishi, "U.S. Support of Gay Rights in Africa May Have Done More Harm Than Good," *New York Times*, December 20, 2015, www.nytimes.com/2015/12/21/world/africa/us-support-of-gay-rights-in-africa-may-have-done-more-harm-than-good.html.

54. Lavers, "Randy Berry Marks First Year as LGBT Envoy."

55. Neil Grungras, "Stop Neglecting the True State of LGBT Refugees," *The Advocate*, January 12, 2016, www.advocate.com/commentary/2016/1/12/stop-neglecting-true-state-lgbt-refugees.

56. Jeffrey Gettleman, "Uganda Anti-Gay Law Struck Down by Court," *New York Times*, August 1, 2014, www.nytimes.com/2014/08/02/world/africa/uganda-anti-gay-law-struck-down-by-court.html.

57. Jim Burroway, "Slouching Toward Kampala: Uganda's Deadly Embrace of Hate," *Box Turtle Bulletin*, November 29, 2012, www.boxturtlebulletin.com/slouching-toward-kampala7; Nicholas Opiyo, "Uganda's Least Equal Voters: The L.G.B.T.I.," *New York Times*, February 16, 2016, www.nytimes.com/2016/02/17/opinion/ugandas-least-equal-voters-the-lgbti.html.

58. Center for Constitutional Rights, "Sexual Minorities Uganda v. Scott Lively," June 2016, ccrjustice.org/home/what-we-do/our-cases/sexual-minorities-uganda-v-scott-lively; Sarah S. Kilborne, "Hate on Trial: What the Case Against Scott Lively Really Means," *Slate*, December 16, 2014, www.slate.com/blogs/outward/2014/12/16/scott_lively_alien_tort_statute_means_lgbt_ugandans_can_sue_him_in_america.html.

59. Planet Romeo, "The Gay Happiness Index," 2015, www.planetromeo.com/en/lgbt/gay-happiness-index.

60. Ibid.

Marriage and Family

1. Frank Phillips, "Majority in Mass. Poll Oppose Gay Marriage," *Boston Globe*, February 22, 2004, archive.boston.com/news/local/articles/2004/02/22/majority_in_mass_poll_oppose_gay_marriage/?page=full.

2. Jason Pierceson, *Same-Sex Marriage in the United States: The Road to the Supreme Court* (New York: Rowman & Littlefield, 2013).

3. Ibid.

4. Richard Wolf, "Timeline: Same-Sex Marriage Through the Years," *USA Today*, June 26, 2015, www.usatoday.com/story/news/politics/2015/06/24/same-sex-marriage-timeline/29173703.

5. Donald J. Cantor et al., *Same-Sex Marriage: The Legal and Psychological Evolution in America* (Middletown, CT: Wesleyan University Press, 2006); Austin Sarat and Stuart A. Scheingold, eds., *Cause Lawyers and Social Movements* (Palo Alto, CA: Stanford University Press, 2006).

6. Carol Taylor, "Boulder Was Trendsetter for Same-Sex Marriage," *Daily Camera*, May 26, 2013, www.dailycamera.com/ci_23316471/boulder-acknowleged-same-sex-marriage-1975.

7. Ibid. and Carolyn Tyler, "Attorney General Suthers' Statement Regarding Boulder County Clerk and Recorder's Issuance of Invalid Same-Sex Marriage Licenses," Office of the Colorado Attorney General, June 25, 2014, coag.gov/press-room/press-releases/06-25-14.

8. Pierceson, *Same-Sex Marriage in the United States*.

9. Ibid.

10. David W. Dunlap, "Some States Trying to Stop Gay Marriages Before They Start," *New York Times*, March 15, 1995, www.nytimes.com/1995/03/15/us/some-states-trying-to-stop-gay-marriages-before-they-start.html.

11. "Defense of Marriage Act," *Wikipedia*, en.wikipedia.org/wiki/Defense_of_Marriage_Act.

12. Suzanna Caldwell, "A Short History of Same-Sex Marriage in Alaska," *Alaska Dispatch News*, October 17, 2014, www.adn.com/alaska-news/article/short-history-alaskas-same-sex-marriage-ban/2014/10/17.

13. U.S. General Accounting Office, "Defense of Marriage Act: Update to Prior Report," January 23, 2004, www.gao.gov/products/GAO-04-353R.

14. Carey Goldberg, "Vermont Gives Final Approval to Same-Sex Unions," *New York Times*, April 26, 2000, www.nytimes.com/2000/04/26/us/vermont-gives-final-approval-to-same-sex-unions.html.

15. "Nebraska Initiative 416," *Wikipedia*, en.wikipedia.org/wiki/Nebraska_Initiative_416#cite_note-NE_result-1.

16. Pew Research Center, "Gay Marriage Timeline," www.pewforum.org/2008/04/01/gay-marriage-timeline.

17. Ibid.

18. Elisabeth Bumiller, "Same Sex Marriage: The President; Bush Backs Ban in Constitution on Gay Marriage," *New York Times*, February 25, 2004, www.nytimes.com/2004/02/25/us/same-sex-marriage-the-president-bush-backs-ban-in-constitution-on-gay-marriage.html.

19. "History of Same-Sex Marriage in the United States," *Wikipedia*, February 2016, en.wikipedia.org/wiki/History_of_same-sex_marriage_in_the_United_States.

20. Pew Research Center, "Gay Marriage Timeline."

21. Ibid.

22. Robert D. McFadden, "Gay Marriage Is Ruled Legal in Connecticut," *New York Times*, October 10, 2008, www.nytimes.com/2008/10/11/nyregion/11marriage.html.

23. Jesse McKinley and Laurie Goodstein, "Bans in 3 States on Gay Marriage," *New York Times*, November 5, 2008, www.nytimes.com/2008/11/06/us/politics/06marriage.html.

24. "History of Same-Sex Marriage in the United States," *Wikipedia*.

25. Abby Goodnough, "A Setback in Maine for Gay Marriage, but Medical Marijuana Law Expands," *New York Times*, November 4, 2009, www.nytimes.com/2009/11/05/us/politics/05maine.html.

26. Richard Wolf, "Timeline: Same-Sex Marriage Through the Years," *USA Today*, June 26, 2015, www.usatoday.com/story/news/politics/2015/06/24/same-sex-marriage-timeline/29173703.

27. Jesse McKinley and John Schwartz, "Court Rejects Same-Sex Marriage Ban in California," *New York Times*, August 4, 2010, www.nytimes.com/2010/08/05/us/05prop.html.

28. Charlie Savage and Sheryl Gay Stolberg, "In Shift, U.S. Says Marriage Act Blocks Gay Rights," *New York Times*, February 23, 2011, www.nytimes.com/2011/02/24/us/24marriage.html.

29. Nicholas Confessore and Michael Barbaro, "New York Allows Same-Sex Marriage, Becoming Largest State to Pass Law," *New York Times*, June 24, 2011, www.nytimes.com/2011/06/25/nyregion/gay-marriage-approved-by-new-york-senate.html.

30. Adam Nagourney, "Court Strikes Down Ban on Gay Marriage in California," *New York Times*, February 7, 2012, www.nytimes.com/2012/02/08/us/marriage-ban-violates-constitution-court-rules.html.

31. Wolf, "Timeline: Same-Sex Marriage Through the Years."

32. Ashley Fantz, "Washington Voters Pass Same-Sex Marriage, CNN Projects," CNN, November 9, 2012, www.cnn.com/2012/11/09/us/washington-passes-same-sex-marriage; Erick Eckholm, "As Victories Pile Up, Gay Rights Advocates Cheer 'Milestone Year,'" *New York Times*, November 7, 2012, www.nytimes.com/2012/11/08/us/same-sex-marriage-gains-cheer-gay-rights-advocates.html.

33. Adam Liptak, "Justices to Hear Two Challenges on Gay Marriage," *New York Times*, December 7, 2012, www.nytimes.com/2012/12/08/us/supreme-court-agrees-to-hear-two-cases-on-gay-marriage.html.

34. Wolf, "Timeline: Same-Sex Marriage Through the Years."

35. Ibid.

36. Ibid.

37. Ibid.

38. Adam Liptak, "Supreme Court to Decide Marriage Rights for Gay Couples Nationwide," *New York Times*, January 16, 2015, www.nytimes.com/2015/01/17/us/supreme-court-to-decide-whether-gays-nationwide-can-marry.html.

39. ProCon.org, "State-by-State History of Banning and Legalizing Gay Marriage, 1994–2015," gaymarriage.procon.org/view.resource.php?resourceID=004857.

40. Justin McCarthy, "U.S. Support for Gay Marriage Stable After High Court Ruling," Gallup, July 17, 2015, www.gallup.com/poll/184217/support-gay-marriage-stable-high-court-ruling.aspx.

41. Wolf, "Timeline: Same-Sex Marriage Through the Years."

42. Williams Institute, "Weddings by 123,000 Same-Sex Couples in the Last Year Boosted National Economy by Over $1.58 Billion," June 22, 2016, williamsinstitute.law.ucla.edu/press/press-releases/weddings-by-123000-same-sex-couples-in-the-last-year-boosted-national-economy-by-over-1-58-billion.

43. Ibid.

44. Esther D. Rothblum, Kimberly F. Balsam, and Sondra E. Solomon, "The Longest 'Legal' U.S. Same-Sex Couples Reflect on Their Relationships," *Journal of Social Issues* 67, no. 21 (2011): 302–315, doi: 10.1111/j.1540-4560.2011.01699.x.

45. Richard G. Wight, Allen J. LeBlanc, and M.V. Lee Badgett, "Same-Sex Legal Marriage and Psychological Well-Being: Findings from the California Health Interview Survey," *American Journal of Public Health* 103, no. 2 (2013): 339–46, doi: 10.2105/AJPH.2012.301113.

46. Stephen M. Haas and Sarah W. Whitton, "The Significance of Living Together and Importance of Marriage in Same-Sex Couples," *Journal of Homosexuality* 62, no. 9 (2015): 1241–63, doi: 10.1080/0091869.2015.1037137.

47. Karen Heller, "Freedom to Marry Is Going Out of Business. And Everybody's Thrilled," *Washington Post*, July 30, 2015, www.washingtonpost.com/lifestyle/style/freedom-to-marry-is-going-out-of-business-and-everybodys-thrilled/2015/07/30/5ca89b5c-322b-11e5-8f36-18d1d501920d_story.html; Freedom to Marry, "Funding the Campaign," June 2016, www.freedomtomarry.org/lessons-learned/funding-the-campaign.

48. Andrew R. Flores and Scott Barclay, "Backlash, Consensus, Legitimacy, or Polarization: The Effect of Same-Sex Marriage Policy on Mass Attitudes," Williams Institute, January 2016, williamsinstitute.law.ucla.edu/research/marriage-and-couples-rights/effect-of-same-sex-marriage-policy-on-mass-attitudes.

49. Billy Corriher, "A Handful of Elected State Judges Continue to Deny Marriage Equality," Center for American Progress, December 1, 2015, cdn.americanprogress.org/wp-content/uploads/2015/11/30105912/JudgesMarriageDefiance-brief2.pdf.

50. Alan Blinder, "Top Alabama Judge Orders Halt to Same-Sex Marriage Licenses," *New York Times*, January 6, 2016, www.nytimes.com/2016/01/07/us/top-alabama-judge-orders-halt-to-same-sex-marriage-licenses.html.

51. Brian Lyman, Brad Harper, and Andrew Yawn, "Roy Moore's Same-Sex Marriage Order Appears to Have Little Effect," *Montgomery Advertiser*, January 7, 2016, www.montgomeryadvertiser.com/story/news/politics/southunionstreet/2016/01/07/roy-moores-ssm-order-appears-have-little-effect/78419978.

52. ACLU, "Anti-LGBT Religious Exemption Legislation Across the Country," June 2016, www.aclu.org/anti-lgbt-religious-exemption-legislation-across-country?redirect=anti-lgbt-religious-refusals-legislation-across-country#mrealtedref16.

53. Alexis Dinno and Chelsea Whitney, "Same Sex Marriage and the Per-

ceived Assault on Opposite Sex Marriage," *PLoS ONE* 8, no. 6 (2013): 1–8, doi: 10.1371/journal.pone.0065730

54. M.V. Lee Badgett and Christy Mallory, "Patterns of Relationship Recognition for Same-Sex Couples: Divorce and Terminations," Williams Institute, December 2014, williamsinstitute.law.ucla.edu/wp-content/uploads/Badgett-Mallory-Divorce-Terminations-Dec-2014.pdf.

55. Pew Research Center, "Gay Marriage Around the World," www.pewforum.org/2015/06/26/gay-marriage-around-the-world-2013.

56. Gary J. Gates, "LGBT Parenting in the United States," Williams Institute, February 2013, williamsinstitute.law.ucla.edu/wp-content/uploads/LGBT-Parenting.pdf.

57. Ibid.

58. Ibid.

59. Williams Institute, "Metro Areas with Highest Percentages of Same-Sex Couples Raising Children Are in States with Constitutional Bans on Marriage," May 20, 2013, williamsinstitute.law.ucla.edu/press/press-releases/metro-areas-with-highest-percentages-of-same-sex-couples-raising-children-are-in-states-with-constitutional-bans-on-marriage.

60. Amira Hasenbush et al., "The LGBT Divide: A Data Portrait of LGBT People in the Midwestern, Mountain & Southern States," Williams Institute, December 2014, williamsinstitute.law.ucla.edu/wp-content/uploads/LGBT-divide-Dec-2014.pdf.

61. Darrel M. Montero, "America's Progress in Achieving the Legalization of Same-Gender Adoption: Analysis of Public Opinion, 1994 to 2012," *Social Work* 59, no. 4 (2014): 321–8, doi: 10.1093/sw/swu038; Charley Lanyon, "Fresh Intelligence: Same-Sex Adoption Is Legal in All 50 States, and Senators Now Work Less Than 3 Days a Week," *New York*, May 3, 2016, nymag.com/daily/intelligencer/2016/05/fresh-intelligence-same-sex-adoption-legal.html.

62. Ibid.

63. Movement Advancement Project, "Foster and Adoption Laws," March 2016, www.lgbtmap.org/equality-maps/foster_and_adoption_laws.

64. Creative Family Connections, LLC, "Gestational Surrogacy Law Across the United States," June 2016, www.creativefamilyconnections.com/#!surrogacy-law-by-state/f49jq.

65. Joseph G. Kosciw and Elizabeth M. Diaz, "Involved, Invisible, Ignored: The Experiences of Lesbian, Gay, Bisexual and Transgender Parents and Their Children in Our Nation's K–12 Schools," GLSEN, 2008, files.eric.ed.gov/fulltext/ED500474.pdf.

66. Ibid.

67. Gates, "LGBT Parenting in the United States."

68. HRC, "Professional Organizations on LGBT Parenting," March 2016, www.hrc.org/resources/professional-organizations-on-lgbt-parenting.

69. Public Policy Research Portal at Columbia Law School, "What Does the Scholarly Research Say About the Wellbeing of Children with Gay or Lesbian Parents?" whatweknow.law.columbia.edu/topics/lgbt-equality/what-does-the-scholarly-research-say-about-the-wellbeing-of-children-with-gay-or-lesbian-parents.

70. Ibid.

71. Rebecca L. Stotzer, Jody L. Herman, and Amira Hasenbush,

"Transgender Parenting: A Review of Existing Research," Williams Institute, October 2014, williamsinstitute.law.ucla.edu/wp-content/uploads/transgender-parenting-oct-2014.pdf.

Media

1. "Biden Breaks Down Stance on Same-Sex Marriage," *Meet the Press*, May 6, 2012, www.nbcnews.com/video/meet-the-press/47312632#47312632.

2. Kris Franklin, "Homophobia and 'The Matthew Shepard Effect' in *Lawrence v. Texas*," *New York School of Law Review* 48, no. 4 (2004): 657–95, www.nylslawreview.com/wp-content/uploads/sites/16/2014/01/NYLS_Law_Review.Volume-48.Issue-4.Franklin-article.pdf.

3. "Finding a Voice Through Social Media: The LGBT Community," Salzburg Academy on Media and Global Change, 2013, www.salzburg.umd.edu/print/unesco/social-media-and-lgbt-community.

4. *Variety* Staff, "How Entertainment Shapes Public Opinion on Gay Rights: The *Variety* Survey," *Variety*, June 29, 2015, variety.com/2015/biz/news/marriage-equality-variety-opinion-poll-1201529568.

5. Sarah Kate Ellis, "GLAAD President and CEO on How Hollywood Movies Treat Gays: 'A Bleak Picture,'" *Hollywood Reporter*, April 15, 2015, www.hollywoodreporter.com/news/glaad-president-ceo-how-hollywood-788919.

6. Larry P. Gross, *Up from Invisibility: Lesbians, Gay Men, and the Media in America* (New York: Columbia University Press, 2001).

7. Ibid.

8. Ibid.

9. Lynne Yamaguchi Fletcher, *The First Gay Pope and Other Records* (Boston: Alyson, 1992).

10. Jennie Wood, "Timeline: Gays in Pop Culture 1934–2010," *InfoPlease*, www.infoplease.com/entertainment/gays-in-pop-culture-timeline.html.

11. Ibid.

12. Jack Myers, "*Will & Grace*: The TV Series That Changed America," *Huffington Post*, June 30, 2014, www.huffingtonpost.com/jack-myers/will-grace-the-tv-series-that-changed-america_b_5543315.html.

13. Bradley Bond, "GLOing Depictions of Sexual Minorities: The Evolution of Gay- and Lesbian-Oriented Digital Media," *Journal Technoculture: An Online Journal of Technology in Society* 4 (2014): 1–17; "Ellen DeGeneres," *Wikipedia*, en.wikipedia.org/wiki/Ellen_DeGeneres; "The World's Highest-Paid Celebrities," *Forbes*, www.forbes.com/profile/ellen-degeneres; twittercounter.com/TheEllenShow; www.facebook.com/ellentv.

14. Joyce Chen, "Ellen DeGeneres on Coming Out as Gay: 'I Didn't Think I Was Going to Come Out, Period,'" *Us Weekly*, October 23, 2015, www.usmagazine.com/celebrity-news/news/ellen-degeneres-on-coming-out-as-gay-i-didnt-think-i-was-going-to-20152310.

15. Andrew Sullivan, "Anderson Cooper: 'The Fact Is, I'm Gay,'" *The Dish*, July 2, 2012, dish.andrewsullivan.com/2012/07/02/anderson-cooper-the-fact-is-im-gay.

16. Jeff Bercovici, "Anderson Cooper Comes Out as TV's First Openly Gay Prime Time Anchor," *Forbes*, July 2, 2012, www.forbes.com/sites

/jeffbercovici/2012/07/02/anderson-cooper-comes-out-as-tvs-first-openly-gay-anchor/#283123d33719.

17. Nikki Usher, "Anderson Cooper and Jodie Foster: The Glass Closet and Gay Visibility in the Media," *QED: A Journal in GLBTQ Worldmaking* 1, no. 1 (2014): 193–198, muse.jhu.edu/article/537857.

18. Ted Johnson, "Maddow's Unique Style Spikes Ratings," *Variety*, March 8, 2009, variety.com/2009/tv/news/maddow-s-unique-style-spikes-ratings-1118000926.

19. Bill Carter, "Gay CNN Anchor Sees Risk in Book," *New York Times*, May 15, 2011, www.nytimes.com/2011/05/16/business/media/16anchor.html.

20. Ryan Gajewski, "Thomas Roberts Hosts 'NBC Nightly News' as First Openly Gay Network Anchor: Twitter Reacts," *Hollywood Reporter*, July 19, 2015, www.hollywoodreporter.com/news/thomas-roberts-hosts-nbc-nightly-809767.

21. Christopher Pullen, "The Murder of Lawrence King and LGBT Online Stimulations of Narrative Copresence," in Christopher Pullen and Margaret Cooper, eds., *LGBT Identity and Online New Media* (New York: Routledge, 2010).

22. Ibid.

23. Zeke Barlow, "Brandon McInerney Sentenced to 21 Years in Prison for Killing Larry King," *Ventura County Star*, December 19, 2011, www.vcstar.com/news/crime/brandon-mcinerney-sentenced-to-21-years-in-prison-for-killing-larry-king-ep-364098277-352204661.html.

24. "Logo TV," *Wikipedia*, en.wikipedia.org/wiki/Logo_TV.

25. Ibid.; "RuPaul's Drag Race," *Wikipedia*, en.wikipedia.org/wiki/RuPaul's_Drag_Race.

26. GLAAD, "Where We Are on TV: 2015–16," www.glaad.org/files/GLAAD-2015-WWAT.pdf.

27. Ross A. Lincoln, "Emmys: Jeffrey Tambor Wins Best Actor, Comedy for 'Transparent,'" *Deadline*, September 20, 2015, deadline.com/2015/09/jeffrey-tambor-emmys-best-actor-comedy-1201538862.

28. Ibid.

29. Ibid.

30. Ibid.

31. Ibid.

32. "Movies That Primarily Deal with Homosexual Themes or Where the Main Characters Are Gay: 1980–Present," Box Office Mojo, www.boxofficemojo.com/genres/chart/?id=gay.htm.

33. IMDB.com.

34. Curtis M. Wong, "Here Are 10 Openly Gay People Who Won Oscars Before Sam Smith," *Huffington Post*, February 29, 2016, www.huffingtonpost.com/entry/gay-oscar-winners_us_56d4733ee4b0bf0dab32c8bb.

35. Ibid.

36. Ibid.

37. Ibid.

38. Ibid.

39. Ibid.

40. James Nichols, "30 Bisexual Celebrities," *Huffington Post*, October

19, 2013, www.huffingtonpost.com/2013/10/19/30-bisexual-celebrities_n_4023562.html; IMDB.com.

41. Claude J. Summers, *The Queer Encyclopedia of Film & Television* (San Francisco: Cleis Press, 2005).

42. Wong, "Here Are 10 Openly Gay People Who Won Oscars Before Sam Smith."

43. Ibid.

44. "Debra Chasnoff," *Wikipedia*, en.wikipedia.org/wiki/Debra_Chasnoff.

45. Wong, "Here Are 10 Openly Gay People Who Won Oscars Before Sam Smith."

46. Rob Epstein, "Pioneering Gay Oscar Winner Offers Sam Smith a History Lesson," *Hollywood Reporter*, March 3, 2016, www.hollywoodreporter.com/news/sam-smith-gets-history-lesson-872422.

47. Vanessa Thorpe, "Curtain Rises on Gielgud's Gay Scandal," *The Guardian*, February 9, 2008, www.theguardian.com/stage/2008/feb/10/theatre.gayrights; Wong, "Here Are 10 Openly Gay People Who Won Oscars Before Sam Smith."

48. Trish Bendix, "Linda Hunt: The Most Under-Recognized Oscar-Winning Lesbian Actress Alive," *AfterEllen*, October 14, 2015, www.afterellen.com/tv/457407-linda-hunt-recognized-oscar-winning-lesbian-actress-alive.

49. Louis Virtel, "Can You Name All the Openly Gay Oscar-Winning Actors?" January 25, 2016, www.hitfix.com/the-dartboard/can-you-name-all-the-openly-gay-oscar-winning-actors; "Jodie Foster," *Wikipedia*, en.wikipedia.org/wiki/Jodie_Foster#Personal_life.

50. /bent, "Here's the 10 Actors That Won Oscars for Playing LGBT Roles (and Their Speeches)," *IndieWire*, January 8, 2015, www.indiewire.com/2015/01/heres-the-10-actors-that-won-oscars-for-playing-lgbt-roles-and-their-speeches-215728.

51. "List of LGBT-Related Films," *Wikipedia*, en.wikipedia.org/wiki/List_of_lesbian,_gay,_bisexual_or_transgender-related_films.

52. *Advocate* editors, "The Top 175 Essential Films of All Time for LGBT Viewers," *The Advocate*, June 23, 2014, www.advocate.com/arts-entertainment/film/2014/06/23/top-175-essential-films-all-time-lgbt-viewers.

53. GLAAD, "2016 GLAAD Studio Responsibility Index," www.glaad.org/sri/2016.

54. Brian Mustanski, Tom Lyons, and Steve C. Garcia, "Internet Use and Sexual Health of Young Men Who Have Sex with Men: A Mixed-Methods Study," *Archives of Sexual Behavior* 40, no. 2 (2011): 289–300, doi: 10.1007/s10508-009-9596-1.

55. Bradley J. Bond, Veronica Hefner, and Kristin L. Drogos, "Information-Seeking Practices During the Sexual Development of Lesbian, Gay, and Bisexual Individuals: The Influence and Effects of Coming Out in a Mediated Environment," *Sexuality & Culture* 13, no. 1 (2009): 32–50, doi: 10.1007/s12119-008-9041-y.

56. www.youtube.com.

57. Elizabeth Daley, "More Than 6 Million Americans Have Come Out on Facebook," *The Advocate*, October 16, 2015, www.advocate.com/world/2015/10/16/more-6-million-americans-have-come-out-facebook; James

McDonald, "26 Million People Change Profile Pictures with Facebook's Rainbow Pride Filter," *Out*, June 29, 2015, www.out.com/popnography/2015/6/29/26-million-people-change-profile-pictures-facebooks-rainbow-pride-filter.

58. S. Mo Jang and Hoon Lee, "When Pop Music Meets a Political Issue: Examining How 'Born This Way' Influences Attitudes Toward Gays and Gay Rights Policies," *Journal of Broadcasting & Electronic Media* 58, no. 1 (2014): 114–30, doi: 10.1080/08838151.2013.875023.

59. "Past Winners," Grammys.com, www.grammy.com/nominees/search; Randy Lewis, "Sam Smith Takes Top Honors at Grammys," *Los Angeles Times*, February 9, 2015, www.latimes.com/entertainment/music/la-et-ms-grammys-main-20150209-story.html.

60. Matt Yazge et al., *Proudly Setting Trends: The 2015 LGBT Consumer Report*, Nielsen, July 7, 2015, www.nielsen.com/us/en/insights/reports/2015/proudly-setting-trends-the-2015-lgbt-consumer-report.html.

61. "LGBT Rappers," *Wikipedia*, en.wikipedia.org/wiki/Category:LGBT_rappers.

62. "LGBT Books," Amazon.com, www.amazon.com/s/ref=nb_sb_ss_i_1_5?url=search-alias%3Daps&field-keywords=lgbt+books&sprefix=LGBT+%2Caps%2C164.

63. Lambda Literary, "LGBT Bookstores," www.lambdaliterary.org/resources/bookstores/#AZ; Lesbian & Gay Bookstore Index, "Lesbian and Gay Bookshops," www.qrd.org/qrd/www/media/print/bookstores/glbbnets.html.

64. "List of LGBT Periodicals," *Wikipedia*, en.wikipedia.org/wiki/List_of_LGBT_periodicals; Bennett L. Singer and David Deschamps, *Gay & Lesbian Stats* (New York: New Press, 1994).

65. "Tony Award Winners 2015: Full List," *Hollywood Reporter*, June 7, 2015, www.hollywoodreporter.com/news/tony-awards-winners-2015-full-800659.

66. Lambda Literary, "A Brief History of Lambda Literary," www.lambdaliterary.org/lambda-literary-foundation/llf-history; "Lambda Literary Award," *Wikipedia*, en.wikipedia.org/wiki/Lambda_Literary_Award.

67. Malinda Lo, "2014 LGBT YA by the Numbers," December 10, 2014, www.malindalo.com/2014/12/2014-lgbt-ya-by-the-numbers.

68. Daniel Chomsky and Scott Barclay, "The Editor, the Publisher, and His Mother: The Representation of Lesbians and Gays in the *New York Times*," *Journal of Homosexuality* 60, no. 10 (2013): 1389–408, doi: 10.1080/00918369.2013.819196.

69. "GLAAD," *Wikipedia*, en.wikipedia.org/wiki/GLAAD.

70. Debra L. Mason and Cathy Ellen Rosenholtz, "Missing Voices: A Study of Religious Voices in Mainstream Media Reports About LGBT Equality," GLAAD and University of Missouri Center on Religion & the Professions, April 11, 2012, www.glaad.org/files/GLAAD_MissingVoices_factsheet.pdf.

Public Opinion

1. Jonathan Rauch, "A Gay Awakening," *American Review*, August 2013, www.jonathanrauch.com/jrauch_articles/gay-marriage-why-it-happened.

2. Pew Research Center, "Growing Support for Gay Marriage: Changed Minds and Changing Demographics," March 20, 2013, www.people-press.org/2013/03/20/growing-support-for-gay-marriage-changed-minds-and-changing-demographics.

3. Gallup, "Gay and Lesbian Rights: Gallup Historical Trends," www.gallup.com/poll/1651/gay-lesbian-rights.aspx; Pew Research Center, "Section 2: Knowing Gays and Lesbians, Religious Conflicts, Beliefs About Homosexuality," June 8, 2015, www.people-press.org/2015/06/08/section-2-knowing-gays-and-lesbians-religious-conflicts-beliefs-about-homosexuality.

4. Jean M. Twenge, Nathan T. Carter, and W. Keith Campbell, "Time Period, Generational, and Age Differences in Tolerance for Controversial Beliefs and Lifestyles in the United States, 1972–2012," *Social Forces* (2015): 379–399, doi: 10.1093/sf/sov050.

5. Gallup, "Gay and Lesbian Rights: Gallup Historical Trends."

6. Ibid.

7. Andrew R. Flores, "National Trends in Public Opinion on LGBT Rights in the United States," Williams Institute, November 2014, williamsinstitute.law.ucla.edu/wp-content/uploads/POP-natl-trends-nov-2014.pdf.

8. Frank Newport, "Americans Continue to Shift Left on Key Moral Issues," Gallup, May 26, 2015, www.gallup.com/poll/183413/americans-continue-shift-left-key-moral-issues.aspx.

9. Frank Newport, "Americans Favor Rights for Gays, Lesbians to Inherit, Adopt," Gallup, December 17, 2012, www.gallup.com/poll/159272/americans-favor-rights-gays-lesbians-inherit-adopt.aspx.

10. Art Swift, "Most Americans Say Same-Sex Couples Entitled to Adopt," Gallup, May 30, 2014, www.gallup.com/poll/170801/americans-say-sex-couples-entitled-adopt.aspx.

11. Gallup, "Gay and Lesbian Rights."

12. Flores, "National Trends in Public Opinion on LGBT Rights in the United States."

13. Jessica R. Sevecke et al., "Effects of Interaction Experiences and Undergraduate Coursework on Attitudes Toward Gay and Lesbian Issues," *Journal of Homosexuality* 62, no. 6 (2015): 821–40, doi: 10.1080/00918369.2014.999493.

14. Public Religion Research Institute, *American Values Atlas*, 2015, ava.publicreligion.org/#lgbt/2015/States/lgbtdis.

15. "Americans Favor Federal Job Protections Based on Sexual Orientation and Gender Identity," The Harris Poll, October 30, 2014, www.outandequal.org/connect/about/media-announcements/2014-harris-poll.

16. Joel Rudin et al., "Transforming Attitudes About Transgender Employee Rights," *Journal of Management Education* 40, no. 1 (2016): 30–46, doi: 10.1177/1052562915609959.

17. Gallup, "Marriage: Gallup Historical Trends," www.gallup.com/poll/117328/marriage.aspx.

18. Public Religion Research Institute, *American Values Atlas*, 2015.

19. Pew Research Center, "Changing Attitudes on Gay Marriage," May 12, 2016, www.pewforum.org/2016/05/12/changing-attitudes-on-gay-marriage.

20. Ibid.

21. Jens Manuel Krogstad, "What LGBT Americans Think of Same-Sex

Marriage," Pew Research Center, January 27, 2015, www.pewresearch.org/fact-tank/2015/01/27/what-lgbt-americans-think-of-same-sex-marriage.

22. David Masci, "Americans Are Still Divided on Why People Are Gay," Pew Research Center, March 6, 2015, www.pewresearch.org/fact-tank/2015/03/06/americans-are-still-divided-on-why-people-are-gay.

23. Gallup, "Gay and Lesbian Rights: Gallup Historical Trends."

24. Pew Research Center, "A Survey of LGBT Americans: Attitudes, Experiences and Values in Changing Times," June 13, 2013, www.pewsocialtrends.org/2013/06/13/a-survey-of-lgbt-americans.

25. Ibid.

Religion

1. Joe Perez, "Gay Affirmative," *Gay Spirituality*, November 21, 2014, gayspirituality.com.

2. "List of Churches by State," Gaychurch.org, www.gaychurch.org/find_a_church; Association of Statisticians of American Religious Bodies, "U.S. Religion Census 2010: Summary Findings," May 1, 2012, www.rcms2010.org/press_release/ACP%2020120501.pdf.

3. ACLU, "Anti-LGBT Religious Exemption Legislation Across the Country," www.aclu.org/anti-lgbt-religious-exemption-legislation-across-country#rfra16.

4. Ted Cruz, "I'm Proud to Stand with Governor Mike Pence, and I Urge Americans to Do the Same," tedcruz.org, March 30, 2015, www.tedcruz.org/news/cruz-im-proud-to-stand-with-gov-mike-pence-and-i-urge-americans-to-do-the-same.

5. Tim Cook, "Pro-discrimination 'Religious Freedom' Laws Are Dangerous," *Washington Post*, March 29, 2015, www.washingtonpost.com/opinions/pro-discrimination-religious-freedom-laws-are-dangerous-to-america/2015/03/29/bdb4ce9e-d66d-11e4-ba28-f2a685dc7f89_story.html.

6. Frank Newport, "LGBT Population in U.S. Significantly Less Religious," Gallup, August 11, 2014, www.gallup.com/poll/174788/lgbt-population-significantly-less-religious.aspx.

7. Eliel Cruz, "Report: Half of Americans Identify as Christians," *The Advocate*, May 12, 2015, www.advocate.com/politics/religion/2015/05/12/report-half-lgb-americans-identify-christian.

8. Pew Research Center, "America's Changing Religious Landscape," May 12, 2015, www.pewforum.org/2015/05/12/americas-changing-religious-landscape.

9. J. Michael Wilkerson et al., "Performance of the Duke Religion Index and the Spiritual Well-Being Scale in Online Samples of Men Who Have Sex with Men," *Journal of Religion & Health* 52, no. 2 (2013): 610–21, doi: 10.1007/s10943-012-9594-9.

10. Public Religion Research Institute, "A Shifting Landscape: A Decade of Change in American Attitudes About Same-Sex Marriage and LGBT Issues," February 26, 2014, publicreligion.org/site/wp-content/uploads/2014/02/2014.LGBT_REPORT.pdf.

11. Tobin Grant, "Gays & Lesbians in American Religion—Three Charts on the Surprising Data," Religion News Service, March 24, 2015, tobin

grant.religionnews.com/2015/03/24/gays-lesbians-american-religion-three-charts-surprising-data/#sthash.fM1PYLx4.dpuf.

12. Alexandra Sandstrom, "Religious Groups' Policies on Transgender Members Vary Widely," Pew Research Center, December 2, 2015, www.pewresearch.org/fact-tank/2015/12/02/religious-groups-policies-on-transgender-members-vary-widely.

13. Pew Research Center, "The Future of World Religions," April 2, 2015, www.pewforum.org/2015/04/02/religious-projections-2010-2050.

14. Scott Thumma and Dave Travis, *Beyond Megachurch Myths: What We Can Learn from America's Largest Churches* (San Fancicsco: Jossey-Bass, 2007); "List of Churches by State," Gaychurch.org, www.gaychurch.org/find_a_church.

15. "LGBT-Affirming Christian Denominations," *Wikipedia*, en.wikipedia.org/wiki/LGBT-affirming_Christian_denominations.

16. George Weigel, "World Religions by the Numbers," Catholic Education Resource Center, www.catholiceducation.org/en/controversy/common-misconceptions/world-religions-by-the-numbers.html.

17. Donald B. Cozzens, *The Changing Face of the Priesthood* (Collegeville, MN: The Liturgical Press, 2000).

18. Wayne R. Dynes, ed., *Encyclopedia of Homosexuality* (New York: Garland, 1990).

19. Reuters, "Pope Francis Says Church Should Apologize to Gays," *New York Times*, June 26, 2016, www.nytimes.com/2016/06/27/world/europe/pope-francis-gays-christians-apologize.html.

20. J. Gordon Melton, *The Church Speaks on Homosexuality* (Detroit: Gale, 1991).

21. "Global Trend: World's Oldest Protestant Churches Now Ordain Gays and Lesbians," United Church of Christ, May 31, 2002, www.ucc.org/global-trend-worlds-oldest.

22. Episcopal Church, "LGBTQ and the Church," www.episcopalchurch.org/page/lgbt-church.

23. Ibid.

24. Trudy Ring, "Episcopal Church to Allow Same-Sex Marriages," *The Advocate*, July 2, 2015, www.advocate.com/politics/religion/2015/07/02/episcopal-church-allow-same-sex-marriages.

25. Pew Research Center, "The Future of World Religions."

26. Tehmina Kazi, "The Ottoman Empire's Secular History Undermines Sharia Claims," *The Guardian*, October 7, 2011, www.theguardian.com/commentisfree/belief/2011/oct/07/ottoman-empire-secular-history-sharia.

27. "LGBT in Islam," *Wikipedia*, en.wikipedia.org/wiki/LGBT_in_Islam.

28. Donald L. Boisvert and Jay Emerson Johnson, eds., *Queer Religion: Homosexuality in Modern Religious History, Volume 1* (Santa Barbara: Praeger, 2012).

29. PFLAG, "Education & Programs: Resources," www.pflag.org/resource/faith-resources-muslims.

30. Pew Research Center, "The Future of World Religions."

31. "LGBT topics and Hinduism," *Wikipedia*, en.wikipedia.org/wiki/LGBT_topics_and_Hinduism.

32. Ibid.

33. Boisvert and Johnson, *Queer Religion*.

34. Pew Research Center, "The Future of World Religions."

35. Dharmachari Jnanavira, "Homosexuality in the Japanese Buddhist Tradition," *Western Buddhist Review*, vol. 3 (2001), www.westernbuddhistreview.com/vol3/homosexuality.html.

36. Ibid.

37. Gay Buddhist Sangha, "About Us," www.gaybuddhistsangha.org/index.html.

38. Jewish Telegraphic Agency, "Survey: Jews, Buddhists Are Biggest U.S. Supporters of Gay Marriage," April 22, 2015, www.jta.org/2015/04/22/news-opinion/united-states/survey-jews-buddhists-are-biggest-u-s-supporters-of-gay-marriage.

39. Pew Research Center, "The Future of World Religions."

40. Institute for Judaism & Sexual Orientation, "Jewish LGBT Organizations," ijso.huc.edu/SynOrg/JewishLGBT.

41. Ibid. and Amy Stone, "Out and Ordained," *Lilith*, Summer 2011, www.lilith.org/pdfs/LILSu11_FINAL_Outandordained.pdf.

42. Dawn Ennis, "Largest Jewish Group in North America Embraces Transgender Congregants," *The Advocate*, November 6, 2015, www.advocate.com/religion/2015/11/06/watch-reform-jews-embrace-transgender-congregants.

43. The Church of Jesus Christ of Latter-Day Saints, "Facts and Statistics," www.mormonnewsroom.org/facts-and-statistics/country/united-states.

44. "Homosexuality and the Church of Jesus Christ of Latter-Day Saints," *Wikipedia*, en.wikipedia.org/wiki/Homosexuality_and_The_Church_of_Jesus_Christ_of_Latter-day_Saints.

45. Ibid.

46. Jesse McKinley and Kirk Johnson, "Mormons Tipped the Scale in Ban on Gay Marriage," *New York Times*, November 14, 2008, www.nytimes.com/2008/11/15/us/politics/15marriage.html.

47. "California Proposition 8, the 'Eliminates Right of Same-Sex Couples to Marry' Initiative (2008)," *Ballotpedia*, ballotpedia.org/California_Proposition_8,_the_%22Eliminates_Right_of_Same-Sex_Couples_to_Marry%22_Initiative_(2008).

48. Laurie Goodstein, "Mormons Sharpen Stand Against Same-Sex Marriage," *New York Times*, November 6, 2015, www.nytimes.com/2015/11/07/us/mormons-gay-marriage.html.

49. Neal Broverman, "WATCH: Thousands Quit Mormon Church in Wake of Antigay Policy," *The Advocate*, November 15, 2015, www.advocate.com/religion/2015/11/15/watch-thousands-quit-mormon-church-wake-antigay-policy.

50. Mark Joseph Stern, "The Tragic Results of the Mormon Church's New Policy Against Gay Members," *Slate*, February 8, 2016, www.slate.com/blogs/outward/2016/02/08/mama_dragons_respond_to_gay_mormon_youth_suicide.html.

51. Tobin Grant, "Ranking Religions on Acceptance of Homosexuality and Reactions to SCOTUS Ruling," June 30, 2015, *Religious News Service*, tobingrant.religionnews.com/2015/06/30/ranking-churches-on-accept

ance-of-homosexuality-plus-their-reactions-to-scotus-ruling/#sthash.Xk8ANXkn.dpuf.

52. Wayne R. Dynes and Stephen Donaldson, *Homosexuality and Religion and Philosophy* (New York: Garland, 1992).

53. Melton, *The Church Speaks on Homosexuality.*

54. "First Church of One Brotherhood Collection, 1956–1976," Online Archives of California, www.oac.cdlib.org/findaid/ark:/13030/c8251gm3/entire_text; David Hughes, "Chuck Rowland: Biographical Profile," Out History, qualityofmercy.com/hull/rowland_outhistory.html.

55. Michael Lemberger, "Gay Synagogues' Uncertain Future," *Tablet*, March 11, 2013, www.tabletmag.com/jewish-life-and-religion/126512/gay-synagogues-uncertain-future.

56. Ibid.

57. "History of MCC," MCC, mccchurch.org/overview/history-of-mcc.

58. "Global Presence," MCC, mccchurch.org/overview/global-presence.

59. Warren J. Blumenfeld and Diane Raymond, *Looking at Gay and Lesbian Life* (Boston: Beacon, 1988).

60. Matthew Vines, "The Gay Debate: The Bible and Homosexuality," www.matthewvines.com/transcript.

61. "13 Bible Passages Homophobes Disregard," *The Advocate*, January 20, 2016, www.advocate.com/religion/2016/1/20/13-bible-passages-homophobes-disregard.

62. Kate Zavadaski, "Christian Colleges Get License to Discriminate from Obama Administration," *Daily Beast*, December 22, 2015, www.thedailybeast.com/articles/2015/12/22/christian-colleges-get-license-to-discriminate-from-obama-administration.html.

63. "Religious Freedom Restoration Act (Indiana)," *Wikipedia*, en.wikipedia.org/wiki/Religious_Freedom_Restoration_Act_%28Indiana%29.

64. Ibid. and Kerry Eleveld, "#BoycottIndiana Trends #1 on Twitter," *Daily Kos*, www.dailykos.com/story/2015/3/27/1373712/--BoycottIndiana-trends-1-on-Twitter.

65. Monica Davey, Campbell Robertson, and Richard Pérez-Peña, "Indiana and Arkansas Revise Rights Bills, Seeking to Remove Divisive Parts," *New York Times*, April 2, 2015, www.nytimes.com/2015/04/03/us/indiana-arkansas-religious-freedom-bill.html.

66. Emma Green, "Can States Protect LGBT Rights Without Compromising Religious Freedom?" *The Atlantic*, January 6, 2016, www.theatlantic.com/politics/archive/2016/01/lgbt-discrimination-protection-states-religion/422730.

67. Trudy Ring, "Georgia Lawmakers Make Antigay Bill Worse, Send to Governor," *The Advocate*, March 16, 2016, www.advocate.com/politics/2016/3/16/georgia-lawmakers-make-antigay-bill-worse-send-governor; "Religious Freedom Bill," *Wikipedia*, en.wikipedia.org/wiki/Religious_freedom_bill#cite_note-3.

68. Sunnivie Brydum, "Miss. Gov. Signs Sweeping Anti-LGBT 'Religious Liberty' Law," *The Advocate*, April 5, 2016, www.advocate.com/religion/2016/4/05/mississippi-governor-signs-sweeping-anti-lgbt-religious-liberty-law; Emma Margolin, "Federal Judge Strikes Down Mississippi 'Religious

Freedom' Law," NBC News, July 1, 2016, www.nbcnews.com/news/us-news/federal-judge-strikes-down-mississippi-religious-freedom-law-n602391.

Sex

1. Hara Estroff Marano, "Gay Love, Straight Sense: 5 Lessons Everyone Can Learn from Same-Sex Couples," *Psychology Today*, March 9, 2015, www.psychologytoday.com/articles/201503/gay-love-straight-sense.

2. Michael S. Kimmel, *The Gender of Desire: Essays on Male Sexuality* (Albany: State University of New York Press, 2005).

3. Justin Hernandez, "Survey Reveals How Gay Singles Look for Love (and Hookups)," *The Advocate*, February 20, 2014, www.advocate.com/health/love-and-sex/2014/02/20/survey-reveals-how-gay-singles-look-love-and-hookups.

4. Aaron Smith and Monica Anderson, "5 Facts About Online Dating," Pew Research Center, February 29, 2016, www.pewresearch.org/fact-tank/2016/02/29/5-facts-about-online-dating.

5. Victoria Ho, "Grindr Sells 60% Stake to Chinese Investor, Faces Growing Competition," Mashable, January 12, 2016, mashable.com/2016/01/12/grindr-china-blued/#5JiiN5ev_mqo.

6. Matt Hamilton, "Gay Bathhouses Nationwide Face Uncertain Future," *USA Today*, August 23, 2014, www.usatoday.com/story/money/business/2014/08/23/gay-bathhouses-nationwide-face-uncertain-future/14491371.

7. "Ultimate Lesbian Sex Survey Archives," Autostraddle, 2015, www.autostraddle.com/tag/ultimate-lesbian-sex-survey.

8. Ibid.

9. Joshua G. Rosenberger et al., "Sexual Behaviors and Situational Characteristics of Most Recent Male-Partnered Sexual Event Among Gay and Bisexually Identified Men in the United States," *The Journal of Sexual Medicine* 8, no. 11 (2011): 3040–50, doi: 10.1111/j.1743-6109.2011.02438.x.

10. Christian Grov et al., "Rules About Casual Sex Partners, Relationship Satisfaction, and HIV Risk in Partnered Gay and Bisexual Men," *Journal of Sex & Marital Therapy* 40, no. 2 (2014): 105–22, doi: 10.1080/0092623X.2012.691948.

11. Joshua G. Rosenberger et al., "Sexual Behaviors, Sexual Health Practices, and Community Engagement Among Gay and Bisexually Identified Men Living in Rural Areas of the United States," *Journal of Homosexuality* 61, no. 8 (2014): 1192–1207, doi: 10.1080/00918369.2014.872525.

12. Douglas Bruce et al., "Age-Concordant and Age-Discordant Sexual Behavior Among Gay and Bisexual Male Adolescents," *Archives of Sexual Behavior* 41, no. 2 (April 2012): 441–48, doi: 10.1007/s10508-011-9730-8.

13. Casey E. Copen, Anjani Chandra, and Isaedmarie Febo-Vazquez, "Sexual Behavior, Sexual Attraction, and Sexual Orientation Among Adults Aged 18–44 in the United States: Data from the 2011–2013 National Survey of Family Growth," *National Health Statistics Report*, no. 88 (January 7, 2016), www.cdc.gov/nchs/data/nhsr/nhsr088.pdf.

14. Cathy J. Reback and Sherry Larkins, "Maintaining a Heterosexual Identity: Sexual Meanings Among a Sample of Heterosexually Identified

Men Who Have Sex with Men," *Archives of Sexual Behavior* 39, no. 3 (2010): 766–73, doi: 10.1007/s10508-008-9437-7.

15. Diana S. Fleischman, Daniel M.T. Fessler, and Argine Evelyn Cholakians, "Testing the Affiliation Hypothesis of Homoerotic Motivation in Humans: The Effects of Progesterone and Priming," *Archives of Sexual Behavior* 44, no. 5 (2015): 1395–1404, doi: 10.1007/s10508-014-0436-6.

16. Justin R. Garcia et al., "Variation in Orgasm Occurrence by Sexual Orientation in a Sample of U.S. Singles," *Journal of Sexual Medicine* 11, no. 11 (2014): 2645–52, doi: 10.1111/jsm.12669.

17. Riese, "87% of Queer Women Are into Porn or Erotica, But Not All of It Is Lesbionic," Autostraddle, June 18, 2015, www.autostraddle.com/87-of-queer-women-are-into-porn-smut-andor-erotica-285552.

18. Tim Murphy, "The Porn Problem: Why Are So Many Adult Film Actors Dying?" *Out*, May 9, 2013, www.out.com/news-opinion/2013/05/09/porn-problem-star-death-arpad-miklos.

19. Ibid.

20. Dylan J. Stein et al., "Viewing Pornography Depicting Unprotected Anal Intercourse: Are There Implications for HIV Prevention Among Men Who Have Sex with Men?" *Archives of Sexual Behavior* 41, no. 2 (2012): 411–19, www.ncbi.nlm.nih.gov/pmc/articles/PMC3310969.

21. Martin J. Downing Jr. et al., "Sexually Explicit Media on the Internet: A Content Analysis of Sexual Behaviors, Risk, and Media Characteristics in Gay Male Adult Videos," *Archives of Sexual Behavior* 43, no. 4 (2014): 811–21, doi: 10.1007/s10508-013-0121-1.

22. Emily Crockett, "Transgender Sex Workers Are Mistreated by the Institutions That Are Supposed to Help Them," *Vox*, December 27, 2015, www.vox.com/2015/12/27/10669996/transgender-sex-workers-report; Erin Fitzgerald et al., "Meaningful Work: Transgender Experiences in the Sex Trade," Best Practices Policy Project, Red Umbrella Project, and National Center for Transgender Equality, December 2015, www.bestpracticespolicy.org/wp-content/uploads/2015/12/Meaningful-Work-Full-Report.pdf.

23. Meredith Dank, Lilly Yu, and Jennifer Yahner, "Access to Safety: Health Outcomes, Substance Use and Abuse, and Service Provision for LGBTQ Youth, YMSM, and YWSW Who Engage in Survival Sex," Urban Institute, February 18, 2016, www.urban.org/research/publication/access-safety-health-outcomes-substance-use-and-abuse-and-service-provision-lgbtq-youth-ymsm-and-ywsw-who-engage-survival-sex/view/full_report.

24. John Scott, Denton Callander, and Victor Minichiello, "Clients of Male Sex Workers" in Victor Minichiello and John Scott, eds., *Male Sex Work and Society* (New York: Harrington Park Press, 2014).

25. Trevon D. Logan, "Personal Characteristics, Sexual Behaviors, and Male Sex Work: A Quantitative Approach," *American Sociological Review* 75, no. 5 (October 2010): 679–704, doi: 10.1177/0003122410379581.

26. Department of Justice, U.S. Attorney's Office, Eastern District of New York, "Largest Online Male Escort Service Raided," August 25, 2015, www.justice.gov/usao-edny/pr/largest-online-male-escort-service-raided; Nathan Tempey, "Why Is Homeland Security Going After Male Escort Website Rentboy After 18 Years?" *Gothamist*, August 25, 2015, gothamist.com/2015/08/25/feds_bust_rentboy.php.

27. ProCon, "100 Countries and Their Prostitution Policies," updated May 18, 2016, prostitution.procon.org/view.resource.php?resourceID=000772.

28. Catherine Murphy, "Sex Workers' Rights Are Human Rights," Amnesty International, August 14, 2015, www.amnesty.org/en/latest/news/2015/08/sex-workers-rights-are-human-rights.

29. Ibid.

30. "NRS 244.345: Dancing halls, escort services, entertainment by referral services and gambling games or devices; limitation on licensing of houses of prostitution," *Nevada Revised Statutes*, 2011, www.leg.state.nv.us/nrs/NRS-244.html#NRS244Sec345.

31. "Men Back on Menu at a Brothel in Nevada," Associated Press, August 6, 2012, archive.azcentral.com/offbeat/articles/20120806nevada-men-back-menu-brothel.html; "Kit Kat Guest Ranch," *Wikipedia*, en.wikipedia.org/wiki/Kit_Kat_Guest_Ranch; author telephone interview with proprietor of Kit Kat Guest Ranch, June 22, 2016.

32. "Adam4Adam," *Wikipedia*, en.wikipedia.org/wiki/Adam4Adam; alexa.com; adam4adam.com.w3snoop.com.

33. Benedict Brook, "Four out of Five Gay Men Now Find Their Long Term Partners Online," *Star Observer*, April 9, 2015, www.starobserver.com.au/news/local-news/four-out-of-five-gay-men-now-find-their-long-term-partners-online/134922.

34. Daniel Farr, "A Very Personal World: Advertisement and Identity of Trans-persons on Craigslist," in Christopher Pullen and Margaret Cooper, eds., *LGBT Identity and Online New Media* (New York: Routledge, 2010).

35. Mike Isaac, "Grindr Sells Stake to Chinese Company," *New York Times*, January 11, 2016, www.nytimes.com/2016/01/12/technology/grindr-sells-stake-to-chinese-company.html; "The Grinder Fact Sheet," grindr.com.

36. Matthew Tharrett, "18 Percent of Grindr Users Are Still in the Closet, Six Percent Will Never Come Out," *Queerty*, June 27, 2014, www.queerty.com/18-percent-of-grindr-users-are-still-in-the-closet-six-percent-will-never-come-out-20140627.

37. Renato Barucco and Luis Freddy Molano, "Zero Feet Away: Perspective on HIV/AIDS and Unprotected Sex in Men Who Have Sex with Men Utilizing Location-Based Mobile Apps," *Community Healthcare Network Report*, January 2013, www.chnnyc.org/wp-content/files/Final-Grindr-PR-FINAL-1-232.pdf.

38. Ibid.

39. Shashank Bengali and Jonathan Kaiman, "In Countries Where Gay Sex Is Taboo, Grindr and Other Apps Open a (Sometimes Perilous) Window," *Los Angeles Times*, January 16, 2016, www.latimes.com/world/asia/la-fg-asia-grindr-20160116-story.html.

40. "Launch of HER App Gives Lesbians Wide Choice of Dating Apps to Use," *DigitPedia*, March 19, 2015, www.digitpedia.com/lesbian-dating-apps/14144.

41. Ibid.; Shalene Gupta, "A Dating App for Lesbians, by a Lesbian," *Fortune*, February 26, 2015, fortune.com/2015/02/26/dating-app-lesbians.

42. Stephanie Lulay, "Scissr Lesbian Dating App Like Grindr but 'Classier,' Chicago Creator Says," *DNAinfo*, December 6, 2014, www.dnainfo.com

/chicago/20141216/west-loop/chicago-made-lesbian-dating-app-scissr-debuts-soon.

43. Alisa Stevens, "Sex in Prison: Experiences of Former Prisoners," Howard League for Penal Reform, 2015, socialwelfare.bl.uk/subject-areas/services-client-groups/adult-offenders/howardleagueforpenalreform/174664Sex_in_prison_web.pdf.

44. Joshua A. Tabak and Vivian Zayas, "The Roles of Featural and Configural Face Processing in Snap Judgments of Sexual Orientation," *PLoS ONE*, May 16, 2012, journals.plos.org/plosone/article?id=10.1371/journal.pone.0036671; Joshua A. Tabak and Vivian Zayas, "The Science of 'Gaydar,'" *New York Times*, June 1, 2012, www.nytimes.com/2012/06/03/opinion/sunday/the-science-of-gaydar.html.

45. William T. L. Cox et al., "Inferences About Sexual Orientation: The Roles of Stereotypes, Faces, and the Gaydar Myth," *Journal of Sex Research* 53, no 2. (2016): 157–71, doi: 10.1080/00224499.2015.1015714; Devin Lowe, "The Science of Stereotyping: Challenging the Validity of 'Gaydar,'" September 3, 2015, University of Wisconsin–Madison press release, news.wisc.edu/the-science-of-stereotyping-challenging-the-validity-of-gaydar.

Sports and Leisure Activities

1. Mark Lee, "Are Sports the Final Frontier for Gay Acceptance?" *Washington Blade*, August 20, 2014, www.washingtonblade.com/2014/08/20/sports-final-frontier-gay-acceptance.

2. Ibid.

3. Emily Zak, "Scoring Acceptance: Eliminating Homophobia in Sports," April 4, 2016, Heart Beings, www.heartbeings.com/scoring-acceptance-eliminating-homophobia-sports.

4. John Carvalho, "Bill Tilden: The Flawed Life of a Gay Tennis Icon," Outsports, July 24, 2014, www.outsports.com/2014/6/24/5836830/bill-tilden-gay-tennis-wimbledon-history; "Bill Tilden," *Wikipedia*, en.wikipedia.org/wiki/Bill_Tilden.

5. Mike Wise, "Dave Kopay Knows What Questions Should Be Asked by NFL," *Washington Post*, March 2, 2103, www.washingtonpost.com/sports/redskins/dave-kopay-knows-what-questions-should-be-asked-by-nfl/2013/03/02/2a12ebd2-82c1-11e2-b99e-6baf4ebe42df_story.html; "Dave Kopay," *Wikipedia*, en.wikipedia.org/wiki/David_Kopay.

6. Robert Aldrich and Garry Wotherspoon, eds., *Who's Who in Contemporary Gay and Lesbian History, Vol. 2* (London: Routledge, 2001).

7. "John Curry," *Wikipedia*, en.wikipedia.org/wiki/John_Curry; Pat Griffin, "LGBT Sports History Timeline," GLSEN, sports.glsen.org/wp-content/uploads/2013/10/Nike-LGBT-Sports-Timeline-Final3.pdf.

8. "Renée Richards," *Wikipedia*, en.wikipedia.org/wiki/Renée_Richards.

9. "Billie Jean King," *Wikipedia*, en.wikipedia.org/wiki/Billie_Jean_King.

10. "Tennis," MartinaNavratilova.com, www.martinanavratilova.com/tennis; "Martina Navratilova," *Wikipedia*, en.wikipedia.org/wiki/Martina_Navratilova.

11. Isabella Moschen, "A Timeline of Incremental Progress," *New York*

Times, September 22, 2012, bruni.blogs.nytimes.com/2012/09/22/a-timeline-of-incremental-progress.

12. Pat Griffin, "LGBT Sports History Timeline."

13. "Justin Fashanu," *Wikipedia*, en.wikipedia.org/wiki/Justin_Fashanu; "Brief History of Gay Athletes," ESPN, December 18, 1998, espn.go.com/otl/world/timeline.html.

14. Cyd Zeigler, "Moment #96: Savoy Howe Becomes First Out Lesbian in Women's Boxing," Outsports, July 8, 2011, www.outsports.com/2011/7/8/4051496/moment-96-savoy-howe-becomes-first-out-lesbian-in-womens-boxing.

15. Moschen, "A Timeline of Incremental Progress"; "Greg Louganis," *Wikipedia*, en.wikipedia.org/wiki/Greg_Louganis.

16. Richard Sandomir, "After Petition, Greg Louganis Gets His Wheaties Box," *New York Times*, April 4, 2016, www.nytimes.com/2016/04/05/sports/greg-louganis-wheaties-box-petition-general-mills.html.

17. Ibid.

18. Patrick Skene, "The Courageous Journey of Ian Roberts, Rugby League's First Openly Gay Player," *The Guardian*, August 17, 2015, www.theguardian.com/sport/blog/2015/aug/18/the-courageous-journey-of-ian-roberts-rugby-leagues-first-openly-gay-player.

19. Lou Chibbaro Jr., "A Timeline of Progress in U.S. Sports," *Washington Blade*, August 30, 2013, www.washingtonblade.com/2013/08/30/a-timeline-of-progress-in-us-sports-lgbt-sports-issue.

20. "Muska: More Honesty Needed," ESPN, December 17, 1998, espn.go.com/otl/world/muska.html.

21. "Outsports," *Wikipedia*, en.wikipedia.org/wiki/Outsports.

22. Robert Lipsyte, "Icon Recast: Support for a Gay Athlete," *New York Times*, April 30, 2000, www.nytimes.com/2000/04/30/sports/icon-recast-support-for-a-gay-athlete.html.

23. Moschen, "A Timeline of Incremental Progress."

24. Josh Martin, "Jason Collins Comes Out as Gay: A Timeline of Athletes and Homosexuality," *Bleacher Report*, May 1, 2013, bleacherreport.com/articles/1623032-jason-collins-comes-out-as-gay-a-timeline-of-athletes-and-homosexuality.

25. Timothy Bella, "Timeline: Michael Sam and 40 Years of LGBT Rights in Sports," Al Jazeera America, February 11, 2014, america.aljazeera.com/watch/shows/america-tonight/america-tonight-blog/2014/2/11/timeline-michaelsamand40yearsoflgbtaccomplishmentsinsports.html.

26. Moschen, "A Timeline of Incremental Progress."

27. Katie Thomas, "Transgender Man Is on Women's Team," *New York Times,* November 1, 2010, www.nytimes.com/2010/11/02/sports/ncaabasketball/02gender.html.

28. Danica Coto, "Puerto Rican Boxer Orlando Cruz Announces He's Gay," Associated Press, October 4, 2012, www.washingtontimes.com/news/2012/oct/4/puerto-rican-boxer-orlando-cruz-announces-hes-gay.

29. Jeff Z. Klein and Judy Battista, "Major Sports Leagues Prepare for the 'I'm Gay' Disclosure," *New York Times*, April 11, 2013, www.nytimes.com/2013/04/12/sports/hockey/nhl-announces-initiative-in-support-of-gay-athletes.html.

30. Alex Leichenger, "What's Next in the Fight for LGBT Equality in Sports?" *ThinkProgress*, May 1, 2014, thinkprogress.org/sports/2014/05/01/3424736/next-steps-for-lgbt-acceptance-in-sports; "Jason Collins," *Wikipedia*, en.wikipedia.org/wiki/Jason_Collins.

31. Lindsay Gibbs, "Michael Sam Says Coming Out as Gay Played a 'Huge Part' in NFL Teams Not Signing Him," *ThinkProgress*, May 6, 2016, thinkprogress.org/sports/2016/05/06/3776234/michael-sam-nfl-coming-out.

32. "Gay Games," *Wikipedia*, en.wikipedia.org/wiki/Gay_Games.

33. "Gay Games," *Wikipedia*, en.wikipedia.org/wiki/Gay_Games#2014_Gay_Games_Cleveland_and_Akron.

34. "List of LGBT Events," *Wikipedia*, en.wikipedia.org/wiki/List_of_LGBT_events.

35. International Gay Rodeo Association, "Rodeo Event Calendar," www.igra.com/CalendarRodeoPublic.htm.

36. "List of Largest LGBT Events," *Wikipedia*, en.wikipedia.org/wiki/List_of_largest_LGBT_events; Seth Milstein, "How Many People Marched in NYC Pride 2016? This Year's Celebration Saw a Record Turnout," *Bustle*, June 27, 2016, www.bustle.com/articles/169230-how-many-people-marched-in-nyc-pride-2016-this-years-celebration-saw-a-record-turnout.

37. Kenneth Kiesnoski, "Gays Attracting Attention of Mainstream Travel Industry," *Lake Tahoe News*, June 2, 2012, www.laketahoenews.net/2012/06/gays-attracting-attention-of-mainstream-travel-industry.

38. Ibid.

39. Community Marketing & Insights, "CMI's 19th LGBT Tourism & Hospitality Survey," December 2014, www.communitymarketinginc.com/documents/temp/CMI_LGBTTravelStudy2014.pdf.

40. Ibid.

41. Ibid.

42. Ibid.

43. The White House, "President Obama Designates Stonewall National Monument," June 24, 2016, www.whitehouse.gov/the-press-office/2016/06/24/president-obama-designates-stonewall-national-monument.

44. Center Link: The Community of LGBT Centers and Movement Advancement Project, "2014 LGBT Community Center Survey Report: Assessing the Capacity and Programs of Lesbian, Gay, Bisexual, and Transgender Community Centers," June 2014, www.lgbtcenters.org/Data/Sites/1/SharedFiles/documents/news/cc2014finalreport-opt.pdf; "Los Angeles LGBT Center," *Wikipedia*, en.wikipedia.org/wiki/Los_Angeles_LGBT_Center.

45. Center Link: The Community of LGBT Centers and Movement Advancement Project, "2014 LGBT Community Center Survey Report."

46. Logo, "Logo Research: Gay Men in America: Community at a Crossroads," September 23, 2015, thepub.viacom.com/sites/logopress/Pages/Logo-Research-Gay-Men-in-America-Community-at-a-Crossroads.aspx.

Transgender

1. Julia Serano, *Whipping Girl: A Transsexual Woman on Sexism and the Scapegoating of Femininity* (Berkeley, CA: Seal Press, 2007).

2. Jaime M. Grant, Ph.D. et al., "Injustice at Every Turn: A Report of the National Transgender Discrimination Survey," The National Center for Transgender Equality and the National Gay and Lesbian Task Force, 2011, www.transequality.org/sites/default/files/docs/resources/NTDS_Report.pdf.

3. Lucy Westcott, "Mississippi Governor Phil Bryant Signs Anti-LGBT Bill Into Law," *Newsweek*, April 5, 2016, www.newsweek.com/mississippi-anti-lgbt-bill-law-444324.

4. Nicholas M. Teich, *Transgender 101: A Simple Guide to a Complex Issue* (New York: Columbia University Press, 2012).

5. Laura Erickson-Schroth, ed., *Trans Bodies, Trans Selves: A Resource for the Transgender Community* (New York: Oxford University Press, 2014).

6. Andrew R. Flores et al., "How Many Adults Identify as Transgender in the United States?," Williams Institute, June 2016, williamsinstitute.law.ucla.edu/wp-content/uploads/How-Many-Adults-Identify-as-Transgender-in-the-United-States.pdf.

7. Teich, *Transgender 101*; Trystan Cotton, "Surgery," *Transgender Studies Quarterly* 1, no. 1–2 (2014): 205–207, doi: 0.1215/23289252-2400028; Zachary Pullin (Chippewa Cree), "Two Spirit: The Story of a Movement Unfolds," *Native Peoples*, May–June 2014, www.nativepeoples.com/Native-Peoples/May-June-2014/Two-Spirit-The-Story-of-a-Movement-Unfolds.

8. Abby Ohlheiser, "Meet the White House's First Transgender Staffer," *Washington Post*, August 18, 2015, www.washingtonpost.com/news/the-fix/wp/2015/08/18/the-white-house-has-appointed-its-first-transgender-staffer.

9. Will Oremus, "Here Are All the Different Genders You Can Be on Facebook," *Slate*, February 13, 2014, www.slate.com/blogs/future_tense/2014/02/13/facebook_custom_gender_options_here_are_all_56_custom_options.html.

10. Linda Poon, "'Ze' or 'They'? A Guide to Using Gender-Neutral Pronouns," *CityLab*, September 28, 2015, www.citylab.com/navigator/2015/09/ze-or-they-a-guide-to-using-gender-neutral-pronouns/407167; Dennis Baron, "The Words That Failed: A Chronology of Early Nonbinary Pronouns," www.english.illinois.edu/-people-/faculty/debaron/essays/epicene.htm.

11. National LGBTQ Task Force, "Wonky Wednesday: Trans People & Sexual Orientation," June 5, 2013, thetaskforceblog.org/2013/06/05/wonky-wednesday-trans-people-sexual-orientation.

12. Grant et al., "Injustice at Every Turn."

13. Ibid.

14. Dave Philipps, "North Carolina Bans Local Anti-Discrimination Policies," *New York Times*, March 23, 2016, www.nytimes.com/2016/03/24/us/north-carolina-to-limit-bathroom-use-by-birth-gender.html.

15. HRC Staff, "#AM_Equality Tip Sheet: April 21, 2016," *HRC Blog*, April 21, 2016, www.hrc.org/blog/am-equality-tip-sheet-april-21-2016.

16. Noah Michelson, "Dolly Parton Tramples Trans Bathroom Bigotry in Just 14 Seconds," *Huffington Post*, June 7, 2016, www.huffingtonpost.com/entry/dolly-parton-transgender-bathrooms_us_5756c4ebe4b07823f9512e9d.

17. Westcott, "Mississippi Governor Phil Bryant Signs Anti-LGBT Bill into Law."

18. "Mississippi's HB 1523, Set to Go into Effect July 1, Permits

Discrimination Against the State's LGBT Population of More Than 60,000," Williams Institute, June 23, 2016, williamsinstitute.law.ucla.edu/press/press-releases/mississippis-hb-1523-set-to-go-into-effect-july-1-permits-discrimination-against-the-states-lgbt-population-of-more-than-60000.

19. Mark Joseph Stern, "Mississippi's Anti-LGBTQ Law Is About to Go Down in Flames," *Slate*, June 17, 2016, www.slate.com/blogs/outward/2016/06/17/mississippi_hb_1523_law_is_an_establishment_clause_violation.html; Royce Swayze and Sarah Fowler, "Judge: HB 1523 Violates Religious Neutrality, Equal Protection," *The Clarion-Ledger*, July 1, 2016, www.clarionledger.com/story/news/2016/07/01/house-bill-1523-struck-down/86587988.

20. Sunnivie Brydum, "Miss. Gov. Signs Sweeping Anti-LGBT 'Religious Liberty' Law," *The Advocate*, April 5, 2016, www.advocate.com/religion/2016/4/05/mississippi-governor-signs-sweeping-anti-lgbt-religious-liberty-law.

21. Jennifer Bendery and Michelangelo Signorile, "Everything You Need to Know About the Wave of 100+ Anti-LGBT Bills Pending in States," *Huffington Post*, April 16, 2016, www.huffingtonpost.com/entry/lgbt-state-bills-discrimination_us_570ff4f2e4b0060ccda2a7a9.

22. Alison Gill and Brynn Tannehill, "A User's Guide to This Year's Transphobic Legislation," *The Advocate*, February 2, 2016, www.advocate.com/transgender/2016/2/02/users-guide-years-transphobic-legislation.

23. Tiq Milan, "First Came the Trans Tipping Point—Now We've Got the Backlash," *The Guardian*, April 21, 2016, www.theguardian.com/commentisfree/2016/apr/21/transgender-rights-backlash-anti-lgbt-legislation.

24. Grant et al., "Injustice at Every Turn."

25. ACLU, "Know Your Rights: Transgender People and the Law," www.aclu.org/know-your-rights/transgender-people-and-law.

26. Sari L. Reisner et al., "Legal Protections in Public Accommodations Settings: A Critical Public Health Issue for Transgender and Gender-Nonconforming People," *The Milbank Quarterly* 93, no. 3 (2015): 484–515, doi: 10.1111/1468-0009.12127.

27. Jennifer Polish, "The Language of Asylum Law: Obstacles for Transgender Asylum Seekers," *Law Street*, July 31, 2015, lawstreetmedia.com/issues/law-and-politics/language-asylum-law-obstacles-transgender-asylum-seekers; David Stout, "Court Rules Cross-Dresser Can Stay in the U.S. on Asylum Claim," *New York Times*, August 26, 2000, www.nytimes.com/2000/08/26/us/court-rules-cross-dresser-can-stay-in-the-us-on-asylum-claim.html.

28. U.S. Department of Justice, "The Matthew Shepard and James Byrd, Jr., Hate Crimes Prrevention Act of 2009," www.justice.gov/crt/matthew-shepard-and-james-byrd-jr-hate-crimes-prevention-act-2009-0.

29. Teich, *Transgender 101*.

30. Erickson-Schroth, ed., *Trans Bodies, Trans Selves*.

31. Matt Schiavenza, "LGBT Activists Are Still Fighting," *The Atlantic*, June 28, 2015, www.theatlantic.com/national/archive/2015/06/ice-transgender-lgbt-immigrants/397046.

32. Chris Johnson, "ICE Issues Guidance for Trans Immigrants in Deten-

tion," *Washington Blade*, June 29, 2015, www.washingtonblade.com/2015/06/29/dhs-issues-guidance-for-trans-immigrants-in-detention.

33. University of California, San Francisco, "First U.S. Study of Transgender Youth Funded by NIH," August 17, 2015, www.ucsf.edu/news/2015/08/131301/first-us-study-transgender-youth-funded-nih.

34. Jesse Green, "S/He," *New York*, May 27, 2012, nymag.com/news/features/transgender-children-2012-6.

35. National LGBTQ Task Force, "HUD Issues New Proposed Rule on Non-Discrimination Protections for Transgender and Non-Conforming People," November 20, 2015, www.thetaskforce.org/hud-issues-new-proposed-rule-on-non-discrimination-protections-for-transgender-and-gender-non-conforming-people.

36. Kathryn J. Woo, "$115K Settlement in Phoenix Transgender Worker Discrimination Case," *Arizona Republic*, January 21, 2016, www.azcentral.com/story/news/local/phoenix/2016/01/21/115k-settlement-phoenix-transgender-worker-discrimination-case/79120452.

37. Michelle Andrews, "HHS Takes Steps Toward Protecting Transgender People Under Health-Care Law," *Washington Post*, September 3, 2012, www.washingtonpost.com/national/health-science/hhs-takes-steps-toward-protecting-transgender-people-under-health-care-law/2012/08/31/83fef586-6a2c-11e1-acc6-32fefc7ccd67_story.html.

38. Cleis Abeni, "HHS Rules Trans Woman Entitled to Surgery Under Medicare," *The Advocate*, January 31, 2016, www.advocate.com/transgender/2016/1/31/hhs-rules-trans-woman-entitled-surgery-under-medicare.

39. ACLU, "Know Your Rights: Transgender People and the Law," www.aclu.org/sites/default/files/field_pdf_file/lgbttransbrochurelaw2015electronic.pdf; Vanessa Vitiello Urquhart, "Planned Parenthood Is Helping Transgender Patients Access Hormone Therapy," *Slate*, January 29, 2016, www.slate.com/blogs/outward/2016/01/29/how_planned_parenthood_helps_transgender_patients_get_hormone_therapy.html.

40. Henk Asscheman et al., "A Long-Term Follow-Up Study of Mortality in Transsexuals Receiving Treatment with Cross-Sex Hormones," *European Journal of Endocrinology* 164, no. 4 (2011): 635–42, doi: 10.1530/EJE-10-1038.

41. Boston University Medical Center, "Transgender Medical Research, Provider Education Lacking," *Science Daily*, December 11, 2013, www.sciencedaily.com/releases/2013/12/131211132720.htm.

42. Association of American Medical Colleges, "AAMC Releases Medical Education Guidelines to Improve Health Care for People Who Are LGBT, Gender Nonconforming, or Born with Differences of Sex Development," November 18, 2014, www.aamc.org/newsroom/newsreleases/414490/11182014.html.

43. Dylan Duncan Thomas and Joshua D. Safer, "A Simple Intervention Raised Resident-Physician Willingness to Assist Transgender Patients Seeking Hormone Therapy," *Endocrine Practice* 21, no. 10 (2015): 1134–42, doi: 10.4158/EP15777.OR.

44. Stanford University, "Two Transsexuals Reflect on University's Pioneering Gender Dysphoria Program," May 3, 2000, news.stanford.edu/news/2000/may3/sexchange-53.html.

45. Teich, *Transgender 101*; Cotton, "Surgery."

46. Teich, *Transgender 101*.

47. Green, "S/He."

48. Anne Vitale, "Rethinking the Gender Identity Disorder Terminology in the Diagnostic and Statistical Manual of Mental Disorders IV," *Trans-Health*, May 28, 2005, www.trans-health.com/2005/rethinking-gid-terminology-dsm.

49. Teich, *Transgender 101*.

50. "Lili Elbe," *Wikipedia*, en.wikipedia.org/wiki/Lili_Elbe.

51. Kenny Thapoung, "The Transgender Community by the Numbers," *Marie Claire*, July 28, 2015, www.marieclaire.com/culture/g3065/transgender-facts-figures.

52. Susan Scutti, "Becoming Transsexual: Getting the Facts on Sex Reassignment Surgery," *Medical Daily*, November 6, 2014, www.medicaldaily.com/becoming-transsexual-getting-facts-sex-reassignment-surgery-309584.

53. Thapoung, "The Transgender Community by the Numbers."

54. HRC, "Creating Equal Access to Quality Heathcare for Transgender Patients," 2015, www.hrc.org/resources/finding-insurance-for-transgender-related-healthcare.

55. "Caitlyn Jenner," *Wikipedia*, en.wikipedia.org/wiki/Caitlyn_Jenner; Tim Maleeny, "The Real Reason Caitlyn Jenner's Show Is Losing Its Audience," *Fortune*, August 24, 2015, fortune.com/2015/08/24/caitlyn-jenner-ratings.

56. "Transgender Celebs You Need to Know," CBS News, 2015, www.cbsnews.com/pictures/transgender-celebrities-you-need-to-know.

57. "Chelsea Manning," *Wikipedia*, en.wikipedia.org/wiki/Chelsea_Manning.

58. Jamie C. Capuzza, "What's in a Name? Transgender Identity, Metareporting, and the Misgendering of Chelsea Manning," in Leland G. Spencer and Jamie C. Capuzza, eds., *Transgender Communication Studies: Histories, Trends and Trajectories* (Lanham, Maryland: Lexington Books, 2015).

59. Tom Vanden Brook, "Military Approves Hormone Therapy for Chelsea Manning," *USA Today*, February 13, 2015, www.usatoday.com/story/news/nation/2015/02/12/chelsea-manning-hormone-therapy/23311813.

60. National Center for Transgender Equality, "A Blueprint for Equality: Reducing Incarceration and Ending Abuse in Prisons (2015)," www.transequality.org/issues/resources/a-blueprint-for-equality-reducing-incarceration-and-ending-abuse-in-prisons-2015; Bureau of Justice Statistics, "Correctional Populations in the United States, 2014," December 29, 2015, www.bjs.gov/index.cfm?ty=pbdetail&iid=5519.

61. National Center for Transgender Equality, "Federal Survey: 40% of Transgender Prisoners Are Sexually Abused Each Year," transgenderequality.wordpress.com/2014/12/18/federal-survey-40-of-transgender-prisoners-are-sexually-abused-each-year.

62. National Center for Transgender Equality, "LGBT People and the Prison Rape Elimination Act," July 1, 2012, www.transequality.org/issues/resources/lgbt-people-and-prison-rape-elimination-act.

63. Cleis Abeni, "Trans Woman Ashley Diamond Reaches Settlement with Ga. Dept. of Corrections," *The Advocate*, February 12, 2016, www

.advocate.com/transgender/2016/2/12/watch-trans-woman-ashley-diamond-reaches-settlement-georgia-department; U.S. Department of Justice, "Justice Department Files Brief to Address Health Care for Prisoners Suffering from Gender Dysphoria," April 3, 2015, www.justice.gov/opa/pr/justice-department-files-brief-address-health-care-prisoners-suffering-gender-dysphoria.

64. Gaëlle Faure, "In France, Transsexuals Celebrate a Small Victory," *Time*, March 1, 2010, content.time.com/time/world/article/0,8599,1968767,00.html.

65. Susan Rinkunas, "The Trans Athlete Behind the Olympic Committee's New Gender Policy," *New York*, January 28, 2016, nymag.com/thecut/2016/01/chris-mosier-transgender-athletes-olympics.html.

66. "LGBT in Islam," *Wikipedia*, en.wikipedia.org/wiki/LGBT_in_Islam.

67. UNAIDS, "The Gap Report," www.unaids.org/en/resources/campaigns/2014/2014gapreport.

68. Henry von Doussa, Jennifer Power, and Damien Riggs, "Imagining Parenthood: The Possibilities and Experiences of Parenthood Among Transgender People," *Culture, Health & Sexuality: An International Journal for Research, Intervention and Care* 17, no. 9 (2015): 1119–31, doi: 10.1080/13691058.2015.1042919.

69. World Medical Association, "WMA Statement on Transgender People," October 2015, www.wma.net/en/30publications/10policies/t13.

70. "About TDOR," International Transgender Day of Remembrance, tdor.info/about-2; Sunnivie Brydum, "Transgender Day of Remembrance 2015: Those We've Lost," *The Advocate*, November 20, 2015, www.advocate.com/transgender/2015/11/20/transgender-day-remembrance-2015-those-weve-lost.

Violence

1. Seth Adam, "GLAAD Responds to Reports Speculating About Orlando Gunman's Sexual Orientation," GLAAD, June 14, 2016, www.glaad.org/blog/glaad-responds-reports-speculating-about-orlando-gunmans-sexual-orientation.

2. Byrne Fone, *Homophobia: A History* (New York: Henry Holt and Co., 2000).

3. Lila Shapiro, "Record Number of Reported LGBT Homicides So Far in 2015," *Huffington Post*, April 2, 2015, www.huffingtonpost.com/2015/04/02/lgbt-homicides_n_6993484.html.

4. Gregory M. Herek, "Hate Crimes and Stigma-Related Experiences Among Sexual Minority Adults in the United States: Prevalence Estimates from a National Probability Sample," *Journal of Interpersonal Violence* 24, no. 1 (2009): 54–74, psc.dss.ucdavis.edu/rainbow/html/Herek_2009_JIV_preprint.pdf.

5. "Florida Shootings: Live Updates," *New York Times*, June 13, 2016, www.nytimes.com/live/orlando-nightclub-shooting-live-updates/medical-center-updates-tally; Lizette Alvarez and Nick Madigan, "In the Dead in Orlando, Puerto Ricans Hear a Roll Call of Their Kin," *New York Times*,

June 14, 2016, www.nytimes.com/2016/06/15/us/in-orlando-victims-puerto-ricans-hear-a-roll-call-of-their-kin.html.

6. Braden Goyette, "Omar Mateen Got 'Very Angry' Seeing Two Men Kissing, Father Tells NBC," *Los Angeles Times*, June 12, 2016, www.latimes.com/nation/la-na-orlando-nightclub-shooting-live-omar-mateen-got-very-angry-seeing-two-1465749495-htmlstory.html.

7. Melanie Garunay, "President Obama on the Tragic Shooting in Orlando," The White House, June 16, 2016, www.whitehouse.gov/blog/2016/06/12/president-obama-tragic-shooting-orlando.

8. Liam Stack, "Before Orlando Shooting, an Anti-Gay Massacre in New Orleans Was Largely Forgotten," *New York Times*, June 14, 2016, www.nytimes.com/2016/06/15/us/upstairs-lounge-new-orleans-fire-orlando-gay-bar.html.

9. Mitch Kellaway and Sunnivie Brydum, "The 21 Trans Women Killed in 2015," *The Advocate*, January 12, 2016, www.advocate.com/transgender/2015/07/27/these-are-trans-women-killed-so-far-us-2015.

10. National Coalition of Anti-Violence Programs, "Lesbian, Gay, Bisexual, Transgender, Queer, and HIV-Affected Hate Violence in 2014," www.avp.org/storage/documents/Reports/2014_HV_Report-Final.pdf.

11. Leah Nelson, "Grammy Award Given to Jamaican Singer of Anti-Gay 'Murder Music,'" Southern Poverty Law Center, February 17, 2011, www.splcenter.org/hatewatch/2011/02/17/grammy-award-given-jamaican-singer-anti-gay-'murder-music'.

12. Buju Banton, "Boom Bye Bye," YouTube.com, June 2016, www.youtube.com/watch?v=aIUZlzd37sI.

13. Nelson, "Grammy Award Given to Jamaican Singer of Anti-Gay 'Murder Music.'"

14. "Pacquiao Among Most Influential Athletes: *Forbes*," ABS-CBN News, April 25, 2012, news.abs-cbn.com/sports/04/25/12/pacquiao-among-most-influential-athletes-forbes.

15. Sean Mandell, "Manny Pacquiao Defends 'Gays Should Be Put to Death' Comment: 'I'm Just Stating the Truth,'" *Towleroad*, January 19, 2016, www.towleroad.com/2016/02/303185.

16. "Manny Pacquiao's Senate Victory Brings Him Closer to Presidency," ESPN, May 19, 2016, espn.go.com/boxing/story/_/id/15604309/boxing-great-manny-pacquiao-wins-senate-seat-philippines.

17. *The Rachel Maddow Show*, MSNBC, November, 25, 2015, www.msnbc.com/rachel-maddow/watch/cruz-ducks-questions-about-religious-radicals-574539331709.

18. CoCo James, Chad Morrow, and Spencer Blake, "Antigay Behaviors Among Young Adults: Prevalence, Patterns, and Motivators in a Noncriminal Population (Replicated)," *Journal of the Utah Academy of Sciences, Arts & Letters* 88 (2011): 546–60.

19. Jeanna Bryner, "Homophobes Might Be Hidden Homosexuals," *Scientific American*, April 10, 2012, www.scientificamerican.com/article/homophobes-might-be-hidden-homosexuals.

20. Wilson Vincent, Dominic J. Parrott, and John L. Peterson, "Combined Effects of Masculine Gender-Role Stress and Sexual Prejudice on Anger and

Aggression Toward Gay Men," *Journal of Applied Psychology* 41, no. 5 (2011): 1237–57, doi: 10.1111/j.1559-1816.2011.00755.x.

21. FBI, "About Hate Crime Statistics," www.fbi.gov/about-us/cjis/ucr/hate-crime/2010/resources/hate-crime-2010-about-hate-crime.

22. FBI, "2014 Hate Crime Statistics: Victims," www.fbi.gov/about-us/cjis/ucr/hate-crime/2014/topic-pages/victims_final.

23. FBI, "Hate Crime Statistics 1996," www.fbi.gov/about-us/cjis/ucr/hate-crime/1996/hatecrime96.pdf.

24. Mark Potok, "Anti-Gay Hate Crimes: Doing the Math," Southern Poverty Law Center, February 27, 2011, www.splcenter.org/fighting-hate/intelligence-report/2011/anti-gay-hate-crimes-doing-math.

25. Anti-Defamation League, "Matthew Shepard and James Byrd, Jr. Hate Crimes Prevention Act Fifth Anniversary," 2014, www.adl.org/assets/pdf/education-outreach/hate-crimes-prevention-act-fifth-anniversary.pdf; Cecilia Muñoz, "Commemorating the Fifth Anniversary of the Shepard-Byrd Hate Crimes Act," *White House Blog*, November 6, 2014, www.whitehouse.gov/blog/2014/11/06/commemorating-fifth-anniversary-shepard-byrd-hate-crimes-act.

26. Ibid.

27. Muñoz, "Commemorating the Fifth Anniversary of the Shepard-Byrd Hate Crimes Act."

28. Movement Advancement Project, "Hate Crime Laws," June 30, 2016, www.lgbtmap.org/equality-maps/hate_crime_laws.

29. Laura Hancock, "Laramie City Council Passes State's First LGBT Anti-Discrimination Ordinance," *Casper Star-Tribune*, May 13, 2015, trib.com/news/state-and-regional/govt-and-politics/laramie-city-council-passes-state-s-first-lgbt-anti-discrimination/article_a0be9412-2f9e-56f9-8b40-2f48965782a7.html.

30. Christy Mallory, Amira Hasenbush, and Brad Sears, "Discrimination and Harassment by Law Enforcement Officers in the LGBT Community," Williams Institute, March 2015, williamsinstitute.law.ucla.edu/wp-content/uploads/LGBT-Discrimination-and-Harassment-in-Law-Enforcement-March-2015.pdf.

31. Brian Tesch et al., "Same-Sex Domestic Violence: Why Victims Are More at Risk," *International Journal of Police Science & Management* 12, no. 4 (Winter 2010): 526–35, doi: 10.1350/ijps.2010.12.4.204.

32. Deborah Sontag, "Push to End Prison Rapes Loses Earlier Momentum," *New York Times*, May 12, 2015, www.nytimes.com/2015/05/13/us/push-to-end-prison-rapes-loses-earlier-momentum.html; Allen J. Beck, Ph.D. et al., "Sexual Victimization in Prisons and Jails Reported by Inmates, 2011–12," Bureau of Justice Statistics, May 2013, www.bjs.gov/content/pub/pdf/svpjri1112.pdf. (Note that data for transgender inmates are combined estimates from three surveys since 2007 and have a 95 percent confidence level; in addition, the report states that "prison and jail inmates have been combined to obtain a sufficient number of non-heterosexual inmates.")

33. Ibid.

34. Taylor N.T. Brown and Jody L. Herman, "Intimate Partner Violence and Sexual Abuse Among LGBT People: A Review of Existing Research," Williams Institute, November 2015, williamsinstitute.law.ucla

.edu/wp-content/uploads/Intimate-Partner-Violence-and-Sexual-Abuse-among-LGBT-People.pdf.

35. Ibid.

36. Ibid.

37. Chai Jindasurat et al., "Lesbian, Gay, Bisexual, Transgender, Queer, and HIV-Affected Intimate Partner Violence in 2014," National Coalition of Anti-Violence Programs, October 2015, www.avp.org/storage/documents/2014_IPV_Report_Final_w-Bookmarks_10_28.pdf.

Workplace

1. Brendan Walsh, "I Had to Deal with Inner Turmoil Almost Daily," *Management Today*, July 10, 2014, www.managementtoday.co.uk/books/1301149/i-deal-inner-turmoil-almost-daily-secret-cost-hiding-sexuality.

2. Timothy Donald Cook, "Tim Cook Speaks Up," *Bloomberg Businessweek*, October 30, 2014, www.bloomberg.com/news/articles/2014-10-30/tim-cook-speaks-up.

3. Ed O'Keefe, "ENDA, Explained," *Washington Post*, November 4, 2013, www.washingtonpost.com/news/the-fix/wp/2013/11/04/what-is-the-employment-non-discrimination-act-enda.

4. ACLU, "Non-Discrimination Laws: State by State Information—Map," accessed June 2016, www.aclu.org/map/non-discrimination-laws-state-state-information-map.

5. ACLU, "*Dawson v. H & H Electric, Inc.*," September 29, 2014, www.aclu.org/cases/lesbian-and-gay-rights/dawson-v-h-h-electric-inc.

6. Josh Howard, "April 27, 1953: For LGBT Americans, a Day That Lives in Infamy," *Huffington Post*, February 2, 2016, www.huffingtonpost.com/josh-howard/april-27-1953-lavender-scare_b_1459335.html.

7. "An Interview with David K. Johnson," University of Chicago Press, 2004, www.press.uchicago.edu/Misc/Chicago/404811in.html.

8. John D'Emilio, *Sexual Politics, Sexual Communities: The Making of a Homosexual Minority in the United States, 1940–1970* (Chicago: University of Chicago Press, 1983).

9. John C. Gonsiorek and James D. Weinrich, eds., *Homosexuality: Research Implications for Public Policy* (Newbury Park, CA: Sage, 1991).

10. Warren Christopher, "Memorandum to All Department Employees," April 22, 1994, U.S. Department of State, www.fedglobe.org/issues/dospolicy.htm.

11. "Executive Order 13087," *Wikipedia*, en.wikipedia.org/wiki/Executive_Order_13087; The White House, "Statement by the President," May 28, 1998, clinton6.nara.gov/1998/05/1998-05-28-statement-on-amendment-to-eeo-executive-order.html.

12. ACLU, "Administration Adds Gender Identity to Equal Employment Opportunity Policies," January 5, 2010, www.aclu.org/news/administration-adds-gender-identity-equal-employment-opportunity-policies.

13. The White House, "Executive Order—Further Amendments to Executive Order 11478, Equal Employment Opportunity in the Federal Government, and Executive Order 11246, Equal Employment Opportunity," July 21,

2014, www.whitehouse.gov/the-press-office/2014/07/21/executive-order-further-amendments-executive-order-11478-equal-employmen.

14. Dana Beyer and Jillian T. Weiss with Riki Wilchins, "New Title VII and EEOC Rulings Protect Transgender Employees," Transgender Law Center, transgenderlawcenter.org/wp-content/uploads/2014/01/TitleVII-Report-Final012414.pdf.

15. Dale Carpenter, "Anti-Gay Discrimination Is Sex Discrimination, Says the EEOC," *Washington Post*, July 16, 2015, www.washingtonpost.com/news/volokh-conspiracy/wp/2015/07/16/anti-gay-discrimination-is-sex-discrimination-says-the-eeoc.

16. Jerome Hunt, "A State-by-State Examination of Nondiscrimination Laws and Policies," Center for American Progress, June 2012, www.americanprogress.org/wp-content/uploads/issues/2012/06/pdf/state_nondiscrimination.pdf.

17. Williams Institute, "Employment Discrimination Against LGBT Workers," williamsinstitute.law.ucla.edu/headlines/research-on-lgbt-workplace-protections.

18. András Tilcsik, "Pride and Prejudice: Employment Discrimination Against Openly Gay Men in the United States," *American Journal of Sociology* 117, no. 2 (2011): 586–626, doi: 10.1086/661653.

19. Movement Advancement Project, HRC, and Center for American Progress, "A Broken Bargain: Discrimination, Fewer Benefits and More Taxes for LGBT Workers," June 2013, www.lgbtmap.org/file/a-broken-bargain-full-report.pdf.

20. U.S. Department of Labor, "Final Rule to Protect Workers from Discrimination Based on Sexual Orientation and Gender Identity Announced by US Labor Department," December 3, 2014, www.dol.gov/newsroom/releases/ofccp/ofccp20141942.

21. Tanya Ballard Brown, "Did You Know It's Legal in Most States to Discriminate Against LGBT People?" National Public Radio, April 28, 2015, www.npr.org/sections/itsallpolitics/2015/04/28/402774189/activists-urge-states-to-protect-the-civil-rights-of-lgbt-people.

22. "Employment Non-Discrimination Act," *Wikipedia*, en.wikipedia.org/wiki/Employment_Non-Discrimination_Act.

23. Lambda Legal et al., "Joint Statement on Withdrawal of Support for ENDA and Call for Equal Workplace Protections for LGBT People," July 8, 2014, www.lambdalegal.org/blog/20140708_joint-statement-withdrawal-support-enda.

24. Lambda Legal, "Equality Act: Frequently Asked Questions," July 23, 2015, www.lambdalegal.org/publications/20150723_equality-act-faq.

25. Chris Johnson, "House Panel Blocks Vote on Equality Act," *Washington Blade*, October 28, 2015, www.washingtonblade.com/2015/10/28/house-panel-blocks-vote-on-equality-act/#sthash.p4g1fL5s.dpuf.

26. Andy Towle, "Illinois Congressman Bob Dold Is First Republican to Sponsor Equality Act," *Towleroad*, January 15, 2016, www.towleroad.com/2016/01/bob-dold.

27. HRC Foundation, "Corporate Equality Index 2016: Rating American Workplaces on Lesbian, Gay, Bisexual and Transgender Equality," hrc-assets

.s3-website-us-east-1.amazonaws.com//files/assets/resources/CEI-2016-FullReport.pdf.

28. Ibid.

29. "The DiversityInc Top 10 Companies for LGBT Employees," 2015, www.diversityinc.com/top-10-companies-lgbt-employees.

30. Brad Sears and Christy Mallory, "How LGBT-Related Workplace Policies Can Have a Positive Impact on the Corporate Bottom Line," Williams Institute, October 2015, escholarship.org/uc/item/2fh9x0zv.

31. Andrea Peterson, "Apple's Tim Cook Just Publicly Announced He's Gay. That's Extremely Rare Among Business Leaders," *Washington Post*, October 30, 2014, www.washingtonpost.com/news/the-switch/wp/2014/10/30/apples-tim-cook-just-publicly-announced-hes-gay-thats-extremely-rare-among-business-leaders; "2015 Leading 100 LGBT Executives," *Financial Times*, October 20, 2015, www.out-standing.org/nominations/2015-role-models/2015-leading-100-lgbt-executives.

32. Alan Cowell, "BP Chief Resigns amid Battle with Tabloid," *New York Times*, May 1, 2007, www.nytimes.com/2007/05/01/business/worldbusiness/01cnd-oil.html.

33. Diane Brady, "Q&A: Former BP CEO John Browne on Getting Out of the Closet," *Bloomberg Businessweek*, June 10, 2014, www.bloomberg.com/news/articles/2014-06-10/q-and-a-former-bp-ceo-john-browne-on-getting-out-of-the-closet#media-1.

34. HRC Foundation, "The Cost of the Closet and the Rewards of Inclusion," May 2014, www.hrc.org/resources/the-cost-of-the-closet-and-the-rewards-of-inclusion.

35. Miriam Frank, *Out in the Union: A Labor History of Queer America* (Philadelphia: Temple University Press, 2014).

36. Katharine K. Sangha, "LGBT Protection in the Workplace—A Survey of State and Local Laws," *Employment Relations Today* 42, no. 2 (2015): 57–68, doi: 10.1002/ert.21500.

37. Movement Advancement Project, "Employment Non-Discrimination Laws," 2016, www.lgbtmap.org/equality-maps/non_discrimination_laws; "LGBT Rights in New Hampshire," *Wikipedia*, en.wikipedia.org/wiki/LGBT_rights_in_New_Hampshire.

38. Christy Mallory and Brad Sears, "Discrimination Against State and Local Government LGBT Employees: An Analysis of Administrative Complaints," Williams Institute, July 2014, williamsinstitute.law.ucla.edu/wp-content/uploads/LGBTQPJ-MALLORYSEARS-2014.pdf.

39. Gretchen Millich, "East Lansing Marks 40th Anniversary of Gay Rights Ordinance," WKAR Public Radio, March 6, 2012, wkar.org/post/east-lansing-marks-40th-anniversary-gay-rights-ordinance.

40. HRC, "Cities and Counties with Non-Discrimination Ordinances That Include Gender Identity," www.hrc.org/resources/cities-and-counties-with-non-discrimination-ordinances-that-include-gender.

41. Karen Leppel, "The Incidence of Self-Employment by Sexual Orientation," *Small Business Economics* 46, no. 3 (2016): 347–63, doi: 10.1007/s11187-016-9699-8.

42. Nicholas Ferroni, "Why America Owes Its Existence and Military to a Gay Man," *Huffington Post*, June 19, 2012, www.huffingtonpost

.com/nicholas-ferroni/american-military-history_b_1606530.html; "Friedrich Wilhelm von Steuben," *Wikipedia*, en.wikipedia.org/wiki/Friedrich_Wilhelm_von_Steuben.

43. Randy Shilts, *Conduct Unbecoming* (New York: St. Martin's, 1993).

44. Ibid.

45. Ibid.

46. Allan Bérubé, *Coming Out Under Fire: The History of Gay Men and Women in World War Two* (New York: Plume, 1990).

47. "Leonard Matlovich," *Wikipedia*, en.wikipedia.org/wiki/Leonard_Matlovich.

48. *New York Daily News*, "The Largest Flag in the World Is Used in New York City In 1994," www.nydailynews.com/news/history-lgbt-rainbow-flag-gallery-1.2271577?pmSlide=1.2271563; "Rainbow Flag," *Wikipedia*, en.wikipedia.org/wiki/Rainbow_flag_(LGBT_movement).

49. Urvashi Vaid, *Virtual Equality: The Mainstreaming of Gay and Lesbian Liberation* (Anchor Books: New York, 1995); Craig A. Rimmerman, ed., *Gay Rights, Military Wrongs: Political Perspectives on Lesbians and Gays in the Military* (New York: Routledge, 1996).

50. "Don't Ask, Don't Tell," *Wikipedia*, en.wikipedia.org/wiki/Don%27t_ask,_don%27t_tell.

51. Ibid.

52. Ed O'Keefe and Jon Cohen, "Most Back Repealing 'Don't Ask, Don't Tell,' Poll Says," *Washington Post*, December 15, 2010, voices.washingtonpost.com/federal-eye/2010/12/most_back_repealing_dont_ask_d.html.

53. "Don't Ask, Don't Tell," *Wikipedia*; Elisabeth Bumiller, "Obama Ends 'Don't Ask, Don't Tell' Policy," *New York Times*, July 22, 2011, www.nytimes.com/2011/07/23/us/23military.html.

54. "Don't Ask, Don't Tell," *Wikipedia*.

55. GAO, "Financial Analysis of Don't Ask, Don't Tell: How Much Does the Gay Ban Cost?," February 2006, www.palmcenter.org/files/active/0/2006-FebBlueRibbonFinalRpt.pdf.

56. Dave Philipps, "Ousted as Gay, Aging Veterans Are Battling Again for Honorable Discharges," *New York Times*, September 6, 2015, www.nytimes.com/2015/09/07/us/gay-veterans-push-for-honorable-discharges-they-were-denied.html.

57. Sunnivie Brydum, "One Vote Left to Confirm Military's First Openly Gay Secretary," *The Advocate*, March 10, 2016, www.advocate.com/military/2016/3/10/one-vote-left-confirm-militarys-first-openly-gay-secretary; Michael S. Schmidt and Charlie Savage, "Eric Fanning Confirmed as Secretary of the Army," *New York Times*, May 17, 2016, www.nytimes.com/2016/05/18/us/eric-fanning-army-secretary.html.

58. Jack Harrison-Quintana and Jody L. Herman, "Still Serving in Silence: Transgender Service Members and Veterans in the National Transgender Discrimination Survey," Williams Institute, August 2013, williamsinstitute.law.ucla.edu/wp-content/uploads/Harrison-Quintana-Herman-LGBTQ-Policy-Journal-2013.pdf.

59. Matthew Rosenberg, "Transgender People Will Be Allowed to Serve Openly in Military," *New York Times*, June 30, 2016, www.nytimes.com/2016/07/01/us/transgender-military.html.

60. Tom Vanden Brook, "Military Approves Hormone Therapy for Chelsea Manning," *USA Today*, February 13, 2015, www.usatoday.com/story/news/nation/2015/02/12/chelsea-manning-hormone-therapy/23311813.

Youth and Education

1. Peter DeWitt, "3 Reasons Why Many Schools Won't Offer LGBT Curriculum," *Education Week*, July 10, 2015, blogs.edweek.org/edweek/finding_common_ground/2015/07/3_reasons_why_many_schools_wont_offer_LGBT_curriculum.html.

2. HRC, "Growing Up LGBT in America," 2012, www.hrc.org/files/assets/resources/Growing-Up-LGBT-in-America_Report.pdf.

3. "The Age of 'Coming Out' Is Now Dramatically Younger," *EurekAlert*, October 10, 2011, www.eurekalert.org/pub_releases/2011-10/afot-tao101011.php.

4. Erik Eckholm, "Boy Scouts End Ban on Gay Leaders, Over Protests by Mormon Church," *New York Times*, July 27, 2015, www.nytimes.com/2015/07/28/us/boy-scouts-end-nationwide-ban-on-gay-leaders.html.

5. Steven Winkeler, "Evansville LGBT Pride Prom Sees Record Attendance," 14-WFIE News, April 12, 2015, www.14news.com/story/28782444/evansville-lgbt-pride-prom-sees-record-attendance.

6. David Carter, "It's Time to Write LGBT History into the Textbooks," *Time*, June 28, 2014, time.com/2935029/stonewall-riots-lgbt-school-curricula.

7. Joseph G. Kosciw et al., "The 2013 National School Climate Survey: The Experiences of Lesbian, Gay, Bisexual and Transgender Youth in Our Nation's Schools," GLSEN, 2014, www.glsen.org/article/2013-national-school-climate-survey.

8. HRC, "Growing Up LGBT in America."

9. "Bullying Definition," StopBullying.gov, www.stopbullying.gov/what-is-bullying/definition.

10. HRC, "Growing Up LGBT in America."

11. Ibid.

12. Ibid.

13. Ibid.

14. Kosciw et al., "The 2013 National School Climate Survey."

15. CDC, "LGBT Youth," 2014, www.cdc.gov/lgbthealth/youth.htm.

16. Kosciw et al., "The 2013 National School Climate Survey."

17. GSA Network, "Frequently Asked Questions About GSA Network," 2016, gsanetwork.org/about-us/faq.

18. GLSEN, "Gay-Straight Alliances: Creating Safer Schools for LGBT Students and Their Allies," 2007, www.glsen.org/sites/default/files/Gay-Straight%20Alliances.pdf.

19. Ibid.

20. California Department of Education, "Frequently Asked Questions: Senate Bill 48," www.cde.ca.gov/ci/cr/cf/senatebill48faq.asp; Neal Broverman, "Calif. Legislature Passes Gay Education Bill," *The Advocate*, July 5, 2011,

www.advocate.com/news/daily-news/2011/07/05/calif-legislature-passes-gay-education-bill.

21. Ibid.

22. Ibid.

23. Carter, "It's Time to Write LGBT History into the Textbooks."

24. GLSEN, "'No Promo Homo' Laws," www.glsen.org/learn/policy/issues/nopromohomo.

25. Hannah Slater, "LGBT-Inclusive Sex Education Means Healthier Youth and Safer Schools," Center for American Progress, June 21, 2013, www.americanprogress.org/issues/lgbt/news/2013/06/21/67411/lgbt-inclusive-sex-education-means-healthier-youth-and-safer-schools.

26. GLSEN, "GLSEN Research Brief Examines LGBT Student Athletes . . . ," February 20, 2013, www.glsen.org/press/glsen-research-brief-examines-lgbt-student-athletes.

27. Ryan M. Kull, Joseph G. Kosciw, and Emily A. Greytak, "From Statehouse to Schoolhouse: Anti-Bullying Policy Efforts in U.S. States and School Districts," GLSEN, 2015, www.glsen.org/article/state-and-school-district-anti-bullying-policies.

28. Ibid.

29. Elizabeth Saewyc et al., "School-Based Strategies to Reduce Suicidal Ideation, Suicide Attempts, and Discrimination Among Sexual Minority and Heterosexual Adolescents in Western Canada," *International Journal of Child, Youth and Family Studies* 5, no. 1 (2014): 89–112, journals.uvic.ca/index.php/ijcyfs/article/view/12856.

30. Kosciw et al., "The 2013 National School Climate Survey."

31. "State Maps: Enumerated Anti-Bullying Laws by State and Nondiscrimination Laws Protecting Students by State," GLSEN, 2016, www.glsen.org/article/state-maps.

32. Mark Berman and Moriah Balingit, "Eleven States Sue Obama Administration over Bathroom Guidance for Transgender Students," *Washington Post*, May 25, 2016, www.washingtonpost.com/news/post-nation/wp/2016/05/25/texas-governor-says-state-will-sue-obama-administration-over-bathroom-directive.

33. Elizabeth M. Diaz and Joseph G. Kosciw, "Shared Differences: The Experiences of Lesbian, Gay, Bisexual, and Transgender Students of Color in Our Nation's Schools," GLSEN, 2009, www.glsen.org/learn/research/national/report-shared-differences.

34. Ibid.

35. Robin Kane et al., "Supporting and Caring for Our Latino Youth," HRC and League of United Latin American Citizens, 2012, hrc-assets.s3-website-us-east-1.amazonaws.com//files/assets/resources/LatinoYouthReport-FINAL.pdf.

36. Ibid.

37. Ibid.

38. Ibid.

39. Ibid.

40. Jase Peeples, "Study: LGBT Teachers Less Likely to Challenge Anti-gay Bullying," *The Advocate*, July 30, 2013, www.advocate.com/latest-news/2013/07/30/study-lgbt-teachers-less-likely-challenge-antigay-bullying.

41. Neal A. Palmer, Joseph G. Kosciw, and Mark J. Bartkiewicz, "Strengths and Silences: The Experiences of Lesbian, Gay, Bisexual and Transgender Students in Rural and Small Town Schools," GLSEN, 2015, www.glsen.org/ruralreport.

42. Ibid.

43. Ibid.

44. "List of Colleges with an LGBT Center," College Equality Index, June 2016, www.collegeequalityindex.org/list-colleges-lgbt-center.

45. Cleis Abeni, "Trans Billionaire Funds World's First Endowed Chair in Trans Studies," *The Advocate*, January 22, 2016, www.advocate.com/transgender/2016/1/22/trans-billionaire-funds-worlds-first-endowed-chair-trans-studies.

46. Point Foundation, "LGBTQ Scholarship Provider Ready for New Applicants," October 14, 2015, pointfoundation.org/wp-content/uploads/2015/10/Point-Scholarship-Applications-2015.pdf.

47. Andy Birkey, "Dozens of Christian Schools Win Title IX Waivers to Ban LGBT Students," *The Column*, December 1, 2015, thecolu.mn/21270/dozens-christian-schools-win-title-ix-waivers-ban-lgbt-students.

48. Lambda Legal and Child Welfare League of America, "LGBT Youth Risk Data," 2012, www.lambdalegal.org/sites/default/files/gdtb_2013_20_youth_risk_data.pdf.

49. Ibid.

50. Ibid.

51. Laura E. Dorso and Gary J. Gates, "Serving Our Youth: Findings from a National Survey of Service Providers Working with Lesbian, Gay, Bisexual and Transgender Youth Who Are Homeless or at Risk of Becoming Homeless," Williams Institute, 2012, williamsinstitute.law.ucla.edu/wp-content/uploads/Durso-Gates-LGBT-Homeless-Youth-Survey-July-2012.pdf.

52. John Wright, "One of Nation's Few Homeless Shelters for LGBT Youth Opens Doors in San Antonio, Texas," *Towleroad*, March 3, 2015, www.towleroad.com/2015/03/one-of-nations-few-lgbtq-youth-homeless-shelters-opens-its-doors-in-san-antonio; Lena Tillett, "LGBT Youth Shelter to Open in Omaha," WOWT.com, February 28, 2016, www.wowt.com/home/headlines/LGBT-Youth-Shelter-to-Open-in-Omaha-370429681.html.

53. CDC, "Health Risks Among Sexual Minority Youth," August 11, 2016, www.cdc.gov/healthyyouth/disparities/smy.htm.

54. Denize Springer, "Family Support Key to LGB Health, Study Shows," San Francisco State University, January 14, 2009, www.sfsu.edu/news/2009/spring/2.html.

55. Arnold H. Grossman and Anthony R. D'Augelli, "Transgender Youth and Life-Threatening Behaviors," *Suicide and Life-Threatening Behavior* 37, no. 5 (2007): 527–37, www.researchgate.net/publication/5879288_Transgender_Youth_and_Life-Threatening_Behaviors; Trevor Project, "Facts About Suicide," www.thetrevorproject.org/pages/facts-about-suicide.

56. Neal A. Palmer et al., "Out Online: The Experiences of Lesbian, Gay, Bisexual and Transgender Youth on the Internet," GLSEN, Center for Innovative Public Health Research, and Crimes Against Children Research Center, 2013, www.glsen.org/sites/default/files/Out%20Online%20FINAL.pdf.

57. HRC, "Growing Up LGBT in America."

58. It Gets Better Project, "What Is the It Gets Better Project?," www.itgetsbetter.org/pages/about-it-gets-better-project.

59. HRC, "Growing Up LGBT in America."

Italicized "f" indicates a figure; italicized "t" indicates a table.

Celebrating 25 Years of Independent Publishing

Thank you for reading this book published by The New Press. The New Press is a nonprofit, public interest publisher celebrating its twenty-fifth anniversary in 2017. New Press books and authors play a crucial role in sparking conversations about the key political and social issues of our day.

We hope you enjoyed this book and that you will stay in touch with The New Press. Here are a few ways to stay up to date with our books, events, and the issues we cover:

- Sign up at www.thenewpress.com/subscribe to receive updates on New Press authors and issues and to be notified about local events
- Like us on Facebook: www.facebook.com/newpressbooks
- Follow us on Twitter: www.twitter.com/thenewpress

Please consider buying New Press books for yourself; for friends and family; or to donate to schools, libraries, community centers, prison libraries, and other organizations involved with the issues our authors write about.

The New Press is a 501(c)(3) nonprofit organization. You can also support our work with a tax-deductible gift by visiting www.thenewpress.com/donate.